The Third Sector in Europe

Edited by

Adalbert Evers

Professor for Comparative Health and Social Policy
Justus-Liebig-Universität Giessen,
Germany

and

Jean-Louis Laville

Researcher in Economic Sociology
Director of LSCI, CNRS, Paris, France

GLOBALIZATION AND WELFARE

Edward Elgar
Cheltenham, UK • Northampton, MA, USA

Published by
Edward Elgar Publishing Limited
Glensanda House
Montpellier Parade
Cheltenham
Glos GL50 1UA
UK

Edward Elgar Publishing, Inc.
136 West Street
Suite 202
Northampton
Massachusetts 01060
USA

A catalogue record for this book
is available from the British Library

Library of Congress Cataloguing in Publication Data

The third sector in Europe / Adalbert Evers, Jean Louis Laville (eds.).
    p. cm.
  Includes bibliographical references.
    1. Nonprofit organizations—Europe. 2. Non-governmental organizations—Europe.
3. Cooperation—Europe. 4. Welfare state—Europe. 5. Europe—Social policy. I. Evers,
Adalbert. II. Laville, Jean-Louis.

HD2769.2.E85T48 2004
338.7'4—dc22   2003061597

ISBN 1 84376 400 8

Typeset by Cambrian Typesetters, Frimley, Surrey
Printed and bound in Great Britain by MPG Books Ltd, Bodmin, Cornwall

Contents

Figures

Tables

Contributors

Ingo Bode, private senior lecturer at the Institute of Sociology of the University of Duisburg-Essen, Germany, is currently working in a research project investigating the evolution of social enterprises in Europe. Fields of research: the sociology of organizations, of social policy and of the non-profit sector, including international comparisons. Recent publications include: *Die Organisation der Solidarität*, 1997, and *Solidarität im Vorsorgestaat*, 1999.

Carlo Borzaga is Professor of Economic Policy at the Faculty of Economics at the University of Trento and Director of the Institute for the Development of Non-profit Organizations. His main fields of research are labour economics and the economics of non-profit organizations and social enterprises. Recent publications include *The Emergence of Social Enterprises* (ed. with J. Defourny), 2001, and *Capitale umano e qualità del lavoro nei servizi sociali. Un'analisi comparata tra modelli di gestione* (ed.), 2000.

Philippe Chanial is Professor of Political Sociology at the University of Caen (France) and a member of the Directing Committee of *La Revue du MAUSS*. He mainly works on theoretical and historical analysis of associations and civil society, including international comparisons, and on social solidarities in democratic societies. Recent publications include *Justice, don et association. La délicate essence de la démocratie*, 2001, and *Association, société civile et démocratie* (co-edited with A. Caillé and J.L. Laville), 2001.

Jacques Defourny is Professor of Economics at the University of Liège (Belgium) where he is also Director of the Centre d'Economie Sociale. He mainly works on economic analysis of cooperatives and associations, work integration, social enterprises and conceptual approaches of the third sector in industrialized as well as developing countries. He is the coordinator of the EMES European Research Network which links research centres from all EU countries working on the third sector. Recent publications include *Economie sociale – The Third Sector*, 1992, and *The Emergence of Social Enterprise* (ed. with C. Borzaga), 2001.

Paul Dekker is head of the 'Participation and government' research group of the Social and Cultural Planning Office of the Netherlands in The Hague, and part-time Professor of Civil Society at the Globus Institute of Tilburg University, the Netherlands. Recent publications include *Social Capital and Participation in Everyday Life* (ed. with Eric Uslander), 2001, and *The Values of Volunteering: Cross-cultural Perspectives* (ed. with Loek Halman), 2003.

Jacques Delors, former Minister of Economy and Finance (1981–84) and then President of the European Commission (1985–94), is currently, the President of the Research and Policy Unit, Notre Europe, and the CERC (Conseil de l'Emploi, des Revenus et de la Cohésion Sociale). From 1974 to 1979, he was an associate Professor of the University of Paris-Dauphine, and directed the research centre, Work and Society. He chaired UNESCO's International Commission on Education for the 21st century (1992–99). He has written numerous books, including *Les Indicateurs Sociaux*, 1971 and *Combats pour l'Europe*, 1996.

Adalbert Evers is Professor of Comparative Health and Social Policy at the Justus-Liebig-Universität in Giessen, Germany. His research and publishing is on civil society and the welfare mix, care and personal social services and the third sector, much of it in comparative perspective. Recent publications include *Developing Quality in Personal Social Services. Concepts, Cases and Comments* (ed. with R. Haverinen, K. Leichsenring and G. Wistow), 1997, and *Von Öffentlichen Einrichtungen zu sozialen Unternehmen: Hybride Organisationsformen im Bereich sozialer Dienstleistungen* (with U. Rauch and U. Stitz), 2002.

Ralph M. Kramer is Professor Emeritus at the School of Social Welfare at the University of California, Berkeley, California, where he worked from 1964 to 2001; programmes and publishing have been on community organization, social planning and administration, research, voluntary agencies, social services and the welfare state; publications on these issues include *Voluntary Agencies in the Welfare State*, 1981, and *Privatization in Four European Countries: Comparative Studies in Government–Third Sector Relationships* (with H. Lorentzen, W. Melief and S. Pasquinelli), 1993.

Jean-Louis Laville a sociologist, is Director of the Laboratory of Sociology of Institutional Change (LSCI, Paris) at the National Centre of Scientific Research (CNRS). He also teaches at different universities in Paris. His main fields of research are civil society and plural economy, and sociology of the third sector in an historical and comparative perspective. Recent publications include *Sociologie de l'association* (with R. Sainsaulieu), 1998, and *Les services sociaux entre associations, état et marché* (with M. Nyssens), 2001.

Jane Lewis has been Barnett Professor of Social Policy at the University of Oxford since 2000. She was previously Professor of Social Policy at both the London School of Economics and the University of Nottingham. Her main research interests are in the fields of gender and social policy and family policy, as well as the voluntary–statutory relationship. She is the author of *The Voluntary Sector, the State and Social Work in Britain*, 1995 and, most recently, *The End of Marriage? Individualism and Intimate Relations*, 2001.

Peter Lloyd worked in the University of Queensland. Returning to the UK in 1964, he spent 25 years at the Univeristy of Manchester; in 1989 he was appointed Professor of Urban Geography at the University of Liverpool. In September 2001 he left full-time employment at the university for private consultancy, but continues his connections with the University of Liverpool as an emeritus professor. Publications include *Modern Western Society* (with P. Dicken), 1981, and *Location in Space: A Theoretical Approach to Economic Geography* (with P. Dicken), 1990.

Marthe Nyssens, a professor at the Catholic University of Louvain, Belgium, works in the Department of Economics and is coordinator of a research team on social and non-profit economics at the Centre de Recherches Interdisciplinaires sur la Solidarité et l'Innovation Sociale (CERISIS). Her research activities deal mainly with the third sector and the evaluation of social policies. Recent publications include 'The Social Enterprise: Toward A Theoretical Approach' (with J.L. Laville) in *The Emergence of Social Enterprise*, ed. C. Bozarga and J. Defourny, 2001, and 'Solidarity-Based Third Sector Organizations in the "Proximity Services" Field: a European Francophone Perspective' (with J.L. Laville), *Voluntas*, 2000.

Victor Pestoff was educated in Long Beach, California, as well as in Stockholm, Paris and Oslo. He taught at the Department of Political Science and then the School of Business at Stockholm University. He became Professor of Political Science at Södertörns Hgskola and is now Head of Department at the Mid-Sweden University in Östersund. Recent publications include *Between Markets and Politics. Cooperatives in Sweden*, 1996, and *Beyond the Market and State. Social Enterprises and Civil Democracy in a Welfare Society*, 1999.

Marilyn Taylor is Professor of Urban Governance and Regeneration and Director of the Cities Research Centre at the University of the West of England, Bristol, UK. Her main current research interests are in the field of community participation, neighbourhood renewal and relationships between government and the third sector. Recent publications include *Public Policy in the Community*, 2003, and *Contract or Trust? The role of compacts in local governance*, 2002.

Introduction

Adalbert Evers and Jean-Louis Laville

In the last decade of the twentieth century, it seemed as if Europe was about to rediscover itself through the eyes of an American legacy. What Tocqueville had detected in the formative process of the United States – the role of freely founded associations formed by active citizens – became an important point of reference in Europe for a broad debate on the history and role of a 'third sector', and the notion of a 'non-profit sector', a label that had been coined in the United States, became a buzzword for both research and public debate. Furthermore, in an increasingly internationalized academic sector, US-led comparative empirical research gave the concept of the non-profit sector a much higher profile.

Obviously, Europe has its own legacy of research on third sector issues, but such research has commonly been linked to national discourses and therefore, in contrast to the more recent US-led research, has had little significance at the European level. The diversity of labels and approaches mirrors the broad and different traditions of non-profit organizations in Europe – mutuals, cooperatives, associations, charities and voluntary organizations.

Bearing in mind this plurality of movements, organizations and notions, and the new European interest in what has for some years been widely referred to by the neutral term 'third sector', the influences from the United States have been of mixed utility. First, the theoretical concepts underlining US contributions to the debate mirror a history that does not correspond to contemporary European reality. In many regions in Europe, organizations with a not-for-profit orientation working within a social economy tradition have always made profits or a surplus. Furthermore, many US-led studies and debates were dominated by an economic approach that explained the so-called 'non-profit' organizations as a result of market and state failures. According to this understanding, consumers realize an institutional choice in their preference, under certain conditions, for the third sector over private business or public service. This theoretical current exemplifies an extension of neoclassic reasoning by which rational choice and methodological individualism are central and where clear frontiers are established between the three sectors, private business, public service and non-profit.

In contrast, the growing European academic interest in the third sector took, for the most part, a sociological and political science perspective. And there were reasons that had to do with developments in Europe itself for the fact that specialized studies about the third sector struck a chord and found an increasingly international public. The main points of reference for studying the third sector have been increasing concern with the structure and quality of public services that took shape in the first decades after the Second World War, and with the pioneering of new forms of services by new groups and movements; subsequently these concerns have overlapped with problems of social exclusion and the crisis of the traditional welfare state. These developments have led to questions being raised in regard to the third sector in terms of clients as 'co-producers', 'social inclusion', 'subsidiarity' and 'partnerships' which aim at the use of non-state resources and at curbing the costs of public spending. Public concern has grown more recently in view of the perception that 'old-style' social democracy has reached its limits, and with an appreciation of inequalities that have been accentuated by neoliberal globalization. Debates about a 'third way' and 'another globalization' have opened up a space for general questions about the changing relationship between the public, the market and the third sector, as well as between the state and its citizens.

In the course of these debates about the future of welfare and the contributions to be made to it by a third sector, the academic debate has also become more conscious of special national and regional legacies, the role of different welfare regimes and the different roles the third sector has to play as a part of these developments. Summing up, one can say that both in the face of and stimulated by US-led initiatives to 'measure' the European third sector according to their criteria, a debate has opened up that analyses the history and potential future of the third sector within a specifically European context.

This book is not the first to present findings about the third sector in Europe; but it is the first to present such findings within a common framework that seeks to integrate conceptually two debates that have been previously separated: the debate about a special 'social economy' of cooperatives and mutuals, and the debate about the social and political phenomena of voluntary and not-for-profit organizations. The book also brings together contributions from some of the most internationally recognized authors in the field.

In parts I and IV, theoretical concepts are debated and developed, constituting what could be seen as a specifically European contribution to an increasingly international debate.

In part II contributors recapitulate the specific history of the tight relationship between the development of national societies, public welfare and the third sector.

Part III, the third sector is debated with respect to the crucial role of the state and of public policies, including concepts and measures that have taken shape at the level of the European Union.

Within this structure there is considerable diversity in approaches. It may, for example, take some time for the reader to come to grips with the fact that there is no clear and fully shared convention as to whether to use the word 'non-profit' or 'not-for-profit'; furthermore it has to be appreciated that sub-sectors as diverse as the voluntary sector, mutuals and cooperatives all fall under the rubric of the third sector, as do many organizations that are at the margins of the discourse in this book: advocacy organizations without any service-providing role. Finally, not even recurrent key words such as 'hybrids' or 'social enterprises' always mean the same. For some authors, only some third sector organizations are hybrids; for others hybridism defines what third sector organizations essentially are. For some authors, social enterprises are the inheritances of the cooperative movement; others use the label for service providers across the third sector; the widest definition that is offered (in the last chapter of the book) uses this label for all service-providing organizations outside the core area of the business sector that manage to stabilize a multi-goal and multi-resource system which entails a strong component of social capital due to strong roots in civil society.

What an introduction can and must do in the face of such diversity is to highlight the points of convergence that constitute the central theme of this book. This may be formulated as follows: there is a special European legacy of developments and approaches that should fertilize an international debate and challenge other approaches, and this legacy should not get lost or be denied. Such communalities within the contributions to this book can be loosely categorized with respect to historical developments, theoretical concept building and the political challenges ahead.

NATIONAL SPECIFICITIES AND CHALLENGES: A HISTORICAL PERSPECTIVE

Chapters 2 to 7 consider the historical backgrounds for the development of the third sector. These encompass a Nordic country (Sweden), three Central European countries (France, Germany and the Netherlands), the United Kingdom and Italy, as a Southern European country. Besides the empirical information that is provided by these contributions, and without denying the differences in theoretical background and style of argumentation, they high-light three specific points that are featured in more analytical terms below and also in the later theoretical chapters.

First, throughout Europe, the formation of a third sector has benefited from special *contributions by organizations other than charities, voluntary organi-zations and foundations* that are also a part of the legacy of US society; these organizations are mutuals, cooperatives and other associations constituting a 'social economy'. The country studies in this book are the first ones to bring together historical evidence from these two parts of the European third sector, the social economy and the voluntary sector, that, until now, have always been discussed separately. Marilyn Taylor, for example, with regard to England, shows that only such careful wording as 'the broad and narrow voluntary sector' can help to keep these two strands under one heading. Victor Pestoff, in his discussion of Sweden, is perhaps most explicit about the consequences of measuring the third sector of one country alongside criteria taken from a different context (that of the USA). Carlo Borzaga on the historical development in Italy, Philippe Chanial and Jean-Louis Laville on the historical development in France and Ingo Bode and Adalbert Evers on Germany all demonstrate that the European third sector cannot be equated either with the narrow concept of the voluntary sector or with the US notion of a non-profit sector.

Second, the contributors highlight the specific historical and political embeddedness of the European third sector and its evolution. Besides the impact of markets and public policies and faith-based organizations or charities established by the 'better off' classes, the role of social movements, such as labour movements and popular movements as found in the history of Scandinavian countries, has to be underlined. These latter components in particular have shaped concepts, paths and organizations in ways which differ from the US legacy. At the same time, the emergence of new social movements and forms of association building reported in the contributions from all these countries point to many aspects that are shared across the Atlantic: to civil society as a point of reference, to new understandings of voluntary commitment and solidarity, but also (see Chapter 5, by Ingo Bode and Adalbert Evers) to a new entrepreneurial spirit. This raises questions of rupture and continuity between the past and future of third sectors in Europe, a point that is well reflected in Jacques Delors' chapter about his motives for putting the third sector on the agenda of the European Union, more than a decade ago.

Third, all of the contributions underline the special *importance and role of the European welfare states* for the third sector, and vice versa. This relationship has brought competition, rejection and incorporation, but besides that there has been a long history of mutual stimulation. The third sector has been built into models of welfare, and the more central role of the welfare state in the present 'welfare mixes' (as compared to the USA) can by no means simply be equated with a lesser importance of the third sector. These historical observations convey a warning for theories of social policy and of welfare regimes: the 'conspicuous absence' (Jane Lewis) of the third sector is one of their weakest points.

THEORETICAL ASPECTS

There are at least two particular theoretical innovations stemming from the European debate that are featured throughout in this book. First of all, the

European debate on the third sector, especially by including cooperatives and mutuals, has brought onto the agenda the issue of *the economic dimension of the third sector*. This is something totally different from measuring the economic impact of third sector services, or from explaining this sector – like all the others – using tools and concepts that stem from market theories. Acknowledging that moral and political dimensions are to be found in associations which provide goods and services and that these constitute specific social and solidarity-based economies opens the way to a huge theoretical challenge: to reconstruct the specificities of a third sector economy as part of a plural set of economies. Chapter 2 by Carlo Borzaga and Chapter 4 by Jean-Louis Laville and Philippe Chanial are especially instructive with respect to this pluralist vision, which has a strong overlap with concepts that have been developed in the European debate, such as 'welfare pluralism', the 'welfare mix' or 'the mixed economy of welfare'.

A second distinguishing feature of much of the European research is the emphasis placed on the fundamentally open, pluralistic and *intermediary nature of the third sector*, instead of seeing it as a kind of 'independent' sector, a special 'box' where organizations take either a residual or an alternative role with respect to state and market. Thinking in terms of 'intermediarity' means more than just acknowledging that the lines between the sectors are blurred. Paul Dekker mentions in his contribution that thinking in terms of sectors is alien to the whole history of the public debate in his country and he gives good reasons for the alternative concept of a 'social midfield' and its intermediary functions. Some authors (for example Adalbert Evers and Jean-Louis Laville in Chapter 12) take the intermediate character as an explanatory element. According to them, associations are not different by nature but have to be seen as kind of 'hybrid' (a recurrent topic in the contributions), held in a tension field, where it can never be guaranteed that state links and market elements can be outweighed by the associations' roots in civil society.

These two points provoke a theoretical question that, perhaps not by accident, has been sharply delineated in the first instance by an American scholar (Ralph Kramer) with extensive research experience on the third sector on both sides of the Atlantic; this question is: does sector matter?

The question is taken up here by the US contribution of Ralph Kramer, and by such others as Paul Dekker, Marilyn Taylor, Adalbert Evers and Jean-Louis Laville. In their respective contributions, they all raise the issue of *the degree to which sector might matter* when it comes to analysing the reasons why some organizations develop distinct and different styles of action and services. The answer that emerges is that organizations develop according to the varying impact of building principles such as democratic participation, cooperation with users, the degree of embeddedness in local spaces of civil society – or vice versa, to the degree that, for example, pure commercial and managerial principles override principles of social and professional action that had shaped social services in the public and third sector. From such a viewpoint, it becomes clear that the rationales and values that nourish civil society and the principles related to it cannot be restricted to one sector. There is no 'civil society sector', nor are the links of the third sector with values such as activating volunteers or user involvement exclusive. Municipal and state public services can demonstrate similar characteristics if they develop within a more civic society, and contrariwise, both sectors may, in part, be colonized by bureaucratic or commercial principles.

POLITICAL CHALLENGES

Considering the role of the third sector in future politics, issues of governance and concepts for recasting models of welfare in Europe there are once again three points of convergence. The first point concerns the general vision. Concepts for the future should entail *a basic 'compact' concerning the status and the contributions of third sector organizations*. Between professional politics and state administrations on the one hand and third sector organizations and their representatives on the other, visions of partnership are needed that reject instrumental attitudes towards one another. Neither the public authorities nor the contributions of third sector organizations should be reduced to a mere financial or economic dimension. A partnership has to acknowledge the moral and political value of third sector organizations, as well as the fact that those providing goods and services on such premises are not (just) economic actors like the more usual for-profit organizations. The need for such future partnerships is very well argued in Chapter 8 by Jane Lewis, while various other contributions underline the second aspect: the importance of policies that accept the intertwining of political, moral and economic concerns, the basis for the different, 'social' kind of third sector economy.

The second point prioritized in this book is the challenge of *developing a clear picture of the impact of and overall balance between values, goals and criteria that lead to support or rejection of third sector organizations*, or to building a preference for specific corporate designs such as 'social enterprises'. These are basic, sometimes contradictory, values such as equality and diversity, or the need to activate citizens and social capital resources or to provide a quick fix by well-managed services. Furthermore, there are special criteria concerning service quality, the role of the users or accountability. Third sector organizations will not manage to respond to all these forces to the same degree and, while they can develop different profiles, some of these criteria will tend to work against them. Paul Dekker explicitly discusses this.

This leads to a final point that is raised throughout the book: that *in many instances third sector organizations need rules and legal frameworks, appropriate forms of governance and networks of interaction that acknowledge and respect their special added value.* Carlo Borzaga, for example, in Chapter 2, makes it very clear to what degree the success story of Italian cooperatives has been due to the establishment of supportive legislation. And in Chapter 12 Adalbert Evers and Jean-Louis Laville present an argument for policies and legal frameworks that give more room for social enterprises both in the 'public' and in the 'third' sector. With an eye to some of the policies related to the third sector that have been carried out by the European Union, Peter Lloyd, in Chapter 9, shows how difficult it is to build stable programmes and perspectives which activate and encourage the special abilities of third sector organizations rather than reducing them to an instrument fit for just one purpose. Ralph Kramer finally, points to the fact that in various policy fields there are approaches where private business, various state authorities and third sector organizations develop interactive, mixed and intermeshed policy networks and where service systems are at work. Consequently, what counts is not the size of a sector or a single type of organization, but the ability to cultivate, by a networked governance of welfare, this kind of precarious 'ecology'.

This book largely benefits from work undertaken within the European EMES Network (www.emes.net), founded in 2002 as a non-profit organization in Brussels, composed of researchers and centres throughout Europe that are interested in research and policy concerning the third sector. Furthermore, we are grateful to the CIRIEC (International Centre of Research and Information on the Public and Cooperative Economy); the framework of research done there for the European Commission (DG V) gave the authors and co-authors the possibility for developing a first version of the overview and argument that are presented in Chapter 1 of this book. In addition, the editors of this book have to thank all those who cooperated in making it possible, obviously the contributors of papers, but also those who gave the technical, social and moral support needed for such an endeavour.

PART I

Distinct Realities and Concepts: the Third
Sector in Europe

1. Defining the third sector in Europe

Adalbert Evers and Jean-Louis Laville

(in collaboration with Carlo Borzaga, Jacques Defourny, Jane Lewis, Marthe Nyssens and Victor Pestoff)

Current academic debates about the third sector in journals and readers are to a high degree international, with scholars from various countries contributing to a seemingly shared corpus of theory. Yet the participants in that international debate know not only that the characteristics of the third sector vary from country to country but that the approaches they use are shaped by special national and regional traditions, both in the academic sphere and in regard to cultural and political development. This chapter addresses this contradiction with respect to the debate in Europe and a US-led debate whose parameters, though they often pretend to be universal, are characterized by the specific context in which they have developed. Trying to highlight some specific European features of the third sector and of a multidisciplinary approach towards it may help to establish commonalities and differences and to contribute to an international debate that is more sensitive to regional and national realities and streams of thinking.

The specific features of a European approach to the third sector can be summarized on the basis of three parameters: the type of organizations involved, the intermediary nature of the third sector within a 'welfare pluralism' or a plural economy, and a sociopolitical dimension that is as important as the economic dimension. Because of these different components, classificatory interpretations of the third sector's importance that measure its contribution to the economy of a country according to a set of definitions and criteria need to be complemented by a historical–dynamic approach, which is essential for understanding the system's potential in European societies.

SPECIFIC FEATURES OF A EUROPEAN APPROACH

Social Economy versus Non-profit Sector

A distinctive feature of the European approach is the attention given to the historical–dynamic perspective. This is less evident in the US-led approach as embodied in the Johns Hopkins project (Salamon and Anheier, 1995), the dominant international model for 'third sector' issues. This focuses on defining the main national components of a sector comprising a community of 'non-profit organizations'. In contrast, many European approaches, while not discarding the synthetic dimension, have taken a more analytical perspective, focusing on generating non-profit association typologies that highlight different modes of action and the changes in them over time. Thus recent studies conducted in a number of countries converge in observing an increase in the associations' production of goods and services, which does not mean a downturn in other functions such as representing interests and raising public awareness for specific issues (CIRIEC, 1999). Without creating any barriers between associations, since an organization's position in relation to production can change, the analytical distinction between service-delivering associations and advocacy groups/NGOs is very important for understanding the dynamics of the development in the third sector. A look at the interaction of the two parts can serve as a reliable indicator of whether the 'associative revolution' (Salamon and Anheier, 1998) 'points at an increasing asymmetry between the amount of state-based services and those provided by society or whether it must be understood as a result of the strength of the dynamic forms of social advocacy which take shape in civil society' (Evers, 1998).

The problem, however, is not only that a global survey of a third sector may mask those internal differences that are important when one attempts to analyse the reasons for its development. There is a problem also if specific types of organizations that do not belong to private business or the state are excluded, particularly if they are those which form an important part of the European legacy when it comes to the development of the third sector, as is the case with the important and influential international study carried out by the Johns Hopkins project. This excluded cooperatives and mutual aid societies on the grounds that they can distribute some of their profits to members. This operation, however, cannot be justified in a European context.

First, some cooperatives, like the housing cooperatives in Sweden, have never distributed their profits. Second, the distribution of profits is always limited, because cooperatives and mutual aid societies are a product of the same philosophy as associations; that is, they are created not for maximizing return on investment but for meeting a general or mutual interest (Gui, 1992), contributing to the common good, or meeting social demands expressed by certain groups of the population (Laville and Sainsaulieu, 1997). Taking this into account, a concept of the third sector appropriate for Europe must be broader than concepts from countries where – as in the USA – cooperatives or mutuals have never played such an important role. Furthermore, it has to be taken into account that, in contrast to charities and most voluntary organizations, cooperatives represented an attempt to create a different economy, with solidarity-based elements at their foundations.

This highlights the role of at least parts of the third sector as a different 'social economy'(Defourny *et al.*, 2000) with a different approach to dealing with surplus. The struggles waged in the nineteenth century led to compromises legalizing organizations in which a category of agents other than investors is classified as a beneficiary. The legal status of the organizations (cooperative, mutual company, association) covers a group of social economy organizations in which the determining factor is not the non-profit requirement but the fact that limits are imposed on the material interest of investors. From that perspective, the line of demarcation is not to be drawn between for-profit and non-profit organizations but between capitalist organizations and social economic organizations, the latter focusing on generating collective wealth rather than a return on individual investment.

Thus the most popular definition of the third sector, as developed by the Johns Hopkins project, has an 'American bias' (Borzaga, 1998) because it is based on the criterion of non-distribution that underlies the American configuration of the sector (Table 1.1). This does not take into account the specific legal requirements of European countries for which the distinguishing criterion is the existence of limits on profit distribution. It is this criterion that separates third sector organizations from other productive organizations. Using a term such as 'non-profit sector' as equivalent to 'third sector' is then clearly misleading. Given the European experience, with an influential 'social economy' besides charities, voluntary agencies and those associations that are primarily advocacy groups, one might say that all organizations in the third sector are 'not-for-profit', having a legal status that places limits on private, individual acquisition of profits.

Table 1.1   The organizations involved

'European' definition of the third sector	'American' definition of the third sector
Emphasis on an analytical approach developing association typoloties and changes as well as the development of the economic dimension of all 'not-for-profit' social economy organizations	Emphasis on a classificatory approach centred on a statistical interpretation of the importance of a sector comprising all non-profit organizations
Criterion of limits on private acquisition of profits: inclusion of cooperatives and mutual aid socities	Non-distribution constraint central, exclusion of cooperatives and mutual aid societies

Welfare Pluralism and a Plural Economy

Historically, the third sector in Europe is associated with the expansion of public intervention. The third sector has been the source of a number of action models that have generated public services: for example, mutual aid societies have helped to create social security systems. In addition, since the third sector has focused, to different degrees and under conditions that vary from country to country, on the production of goods and services, it has established a relationship with the market. Historically, in Europe, there has been an increasingly complex relationship between public policies, state authorities and actors within the third sector, resulting in a broad and stable area of welfare services with often shared and complementary arrangements for service provision between the sectors. Therefore it is no wonder that in Europe the intermediary dimension of the third sector is emphasized. This goes hand in hand with a strong emphasis placed on the fundamentally open, mixed and pluralistic nature of a third sector, where it is difficult to demarcate clearly the boundaries with the state sector when third sector organizations operate for the public good and as part of a guaranteed system of welfare services, or when local municipalities are involved in the provision of welfare services that are strongly embedded in local civil society.

Compared to the USA, in Europe there has been a stronger emphasis on seeing the third sector as part of a welfare mix or a mixed economy of welfare (Evers and Svetlik, 1993; Johnson, 1998). This goes along with a rejection of the notion of sectors altogether, if this notion induces a clear line of demarcation between, on the one hand, the marketplace, the political arena and the community and, on the other, the third sector (Evers, 1997). This has led to a view of the third sector as embedded in the framework of a tripolar system of market, state and informal communities and economies (like the private households) rather than understanding the 'third' as juxtaposed to other clear-cut sectors, and instead of taking into account only states and markets.

The conceptual framework for these approaches may be represented graphically by a triangle linking the extensive range of factors that compose and influence the third sector (Evers, 1997, p.52). The resulting analytical framework is used as a reference by various authors (Eme, 1991; Evers, 1990; Laville, 1992, 1994; Kramer *et al.*, 1993; Pestoff, 1991, 1996, 1998) and was referred to in studies produced by the Local Economic and Employment Development Program (LEED) of the Organization for Economic Cooperation and Development (OECD, 1996). The framework reflects two sets of closely related issues: the first (Figure 1.1) presents the components of social security and welfare, and the second (Figure 1.2) presents the components of a plural and mixed economy.

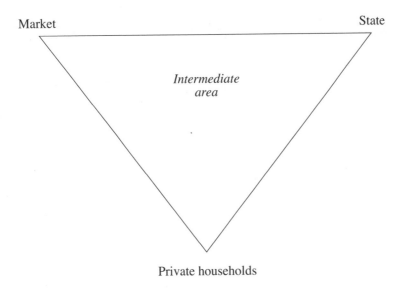

Market   State

*Intermediate
area*

Private households

Source: Evers (1990).

Figure 1.1   The welfare triangle

The 'welfare triangle', as proposed by Evers (see Figure 1.1), intends to take account of both socioeconomic and sociopolitical issues. From a socio-economic perspective the triangle highlights the plural nature of the resources that contribute to social welfare. With respect to services, it highlights an important element that is often overlooked in the tradition of the US debate, namely the role of informal and semi-formal communities, and in particular that of the family at the core, as a constituent part of 'a mixed economy of social welfare'. When new organizations and services take shape, the nature of the contributions and the role of private households and families change as well. And vice versa: changing family life and living conditions can be at the forefront of new groups taking shape, such as self-help groups.

From a sociopolitical perspective, Evers (1990, 1995) has underlined that organizations in the third sector act in a kind of tension field; they are simul-taneously influenced by state policies and legislation, the values and practices of private business, the culture of civil society and by needs and contributions that come from informal family and community life. What is different with third sector organizations, then, is the fact that they represent and balance a plural bundle of norms and values, while it is constitutive for the sectors at the 'corners' of the triangle that they are defined by the clear prevalence of either profit (market), redistribution (state) or personal responsibility (family and

Distinct realities and concepts

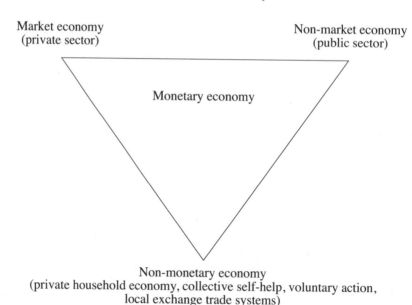

Market economy
(private sector)

Non-market economy
(public sector)

Monetary economy

Non-monetary economy
(private household economy, collective self-help, voluntary action,
local exchange trade systems)

Source: Roustang et al. (1997).

Figure 1.2   The overall structure of the plural economy

community). To what degree they can keep their special position within the triangle is then dependent both on developments in their environment, marked by state policies, governance and regulatory systems, and on the goals and strategies of their stakeholders.

Pestoff (1991) has used a similar scheme (Figure 1.3) in order to define and delimit the sphere of action of social enterprises and civil democracy in welfare societies, particularly with respect to 'post-communist' and Scandinavian countries.

The aforementioned concepts have highlighted socioeconomic as well as socio-political aspects, that is, challenges which may be called the 'governance' of mixed welfare systems. The 'plural economy triangle' in its version by Roustang *et al.* (1997) (Figure 1.2), however, focused on developing a differentiated theory of the socioeconomic aspects of the third sector and the economic system in modern democratic societies at large. It is based on the substantive approach of Polanyi's economic theory (Polanyi, 1944), which distinguishes three economic principles:

- *The market principle* allows for a convergence between the supply and demand for goods and services exchanged through price setting. The

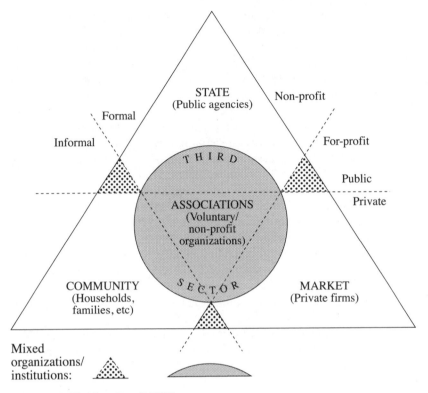

Source: Modified from Pestoff (1992).

Figure 1.3 The welfare mix

relation between the supplier and the customer is a contractual one. The market principle does not imply its immersion in social relations, 'which are now considered by western cultures as being distinct from economic institutions' (Maucourant *et al.*, 1988). It is not necessarily embedded in the social system, contrary to the other economic elements as described below.

- *Redistribution* is the principle on the basis of which the results of production are handed over to a central authority responsible for managing it. This involves implementing a procedure to define payment rules and targets. A relationship is established over time between the central authority that imposes an obligation and the agents that are subject to it. 'Cash benefits' can be distinguished from 'benefits in kind' as two different forms of redistribution. Sometimes this redistribution can be private, when the institution which is responsible is private, such as an organization whose directors have the power to take a percentage of the profits for corporate sponsorship or donations, for example by means of private foundations. But the redistribution is above all a public matter: around the welfare state a modern form of redistribution has grown up, sustained by compulsory rules and used for paying benefits according to social rights.

- *Reciprocity* is the circulation of goods and services between groups and individuals that can only take shape when all participating parties are willing to establish a social relationship. So reciprocity is an original non-contractual principle of economic action in which the social link is more important than the goods exchanged. The reciprocity cycle is based on a gift calling for a counter-gift through which the groups or persons who received the first gift exercise their right to give back or not. There is an incentive for recipients to give back but are not compelled to do so by outside forces; the decision is theirs. As a result, gift is not synonymous with altruism and free products or services; it is a complex mix of selflessness and self-interest. The reciprocity cycle is opposed to market exchange because it is inseparable from human relations that express the desire for recognition and power, and it is different from redistribution-based exchange because it is not imposed by a central authority. A special form of reciprocity, referred to as 'domestic admin- istration' by Polanyi, operates within the family, which is the basic cell of the system.

On the basis of these three basic principles, a variety of combinations have developed historically. They can also be used to define a tripolar economy (Figures 1.2 and 1.4) in today's world.

The market economy is an economy in which the production of goods and services is based on the motivation of material interest; distribution of goods and services is entrusted to the market, which sets the price that brings supply and demand together for the exchange of goods and services. The relationship between supply and demand is established contractually, based on an interest calculation that allows for increasing autonomy in terms of other non-market social relations. However, the market economy is certainly not the product of the market principle alone. Market economies are not only organized around the market; they include many non-market contributions, such as collective infrastructures and grants for businesses. Nevertheless, the distinctive feature of the market economy is the priority given to the market and the subordina- tion of the non-market and non-monetary contributions to it.

The non-market economy is an economy in which the production and distribution of goods and services are entrusted to redistribution organized under the tutelage of the welfare state. Redistribution is mobilized to provide

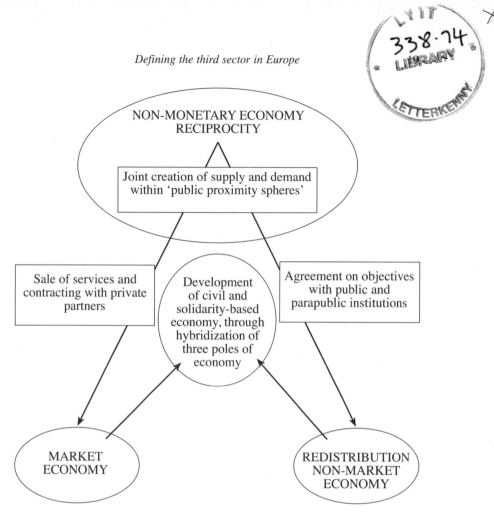

Source: Eme (1991), Laville (1992, 1994).

Figure 1.4   The civil and solidarity-based economy

citizens with individual rights, thanks to which they are entitled to social security benefits, or last-resort assistance if they are part of the most disadvantaged
groups. Public service is defined by a delivery of goods or services involving
a redistributive dimension (from the rich to the poor, from the active to the
inactive, and so on). The rules governing this dimension are laid down by a
public authority subject to democratic control. Redistribution in a broad sense
covers all forms of levy and resource allocation, whether the purpose is financing social transfers or playing the role of a macroeconomic stabilizing force.

The non-monetary economy is the one in which the distribution of goods
and services is based primarily on reciprocity and domestic administration.
Obviously, a number of reciprocity-based relationships take a monetary form

(for example, donations), but it is definitely within the non-monetary economy that the main reciprocity-based contributions are generated, be it by self-production or by the private household economy. The reciprocity cycle is the opposite of a market exchange because it is inseparable from human relationships that bring the desires for recognition and power into play. It must be distinguished from the redistributive exchange because it is not imposed by a central authority.

Each division of the economy is therefore organized around the predominance of one principle (Eme, 1993), and the main examples of the present-day economy reflect a hierarchy of these divisions, with the market economy considered as primary, the non-market economy as supplementary, and the non-monetary economy as residual. Within such a framework of understanding, the specificity of the third sector can therefore be interpreted as being a hybridization between the three poles of the economy, existing in a state of tension with this hierarchical structure. In other words, the third sector is not defined as a clear-cut sector and is approached more as a component of the economy based on solidarity and a hybridization of different economic principles. The authors of the concept call it a civil and solidarity-based economy.

It is obvious that this concept overlaps with those of Evers and Pestoff mentioned above. In all cases it is emphasized that third sector organizations are influenced simultaneously by different spheres that make up their social and historical context, and that their survival as something 'different' instead of adapting to the core values of state and market or regressing to informal settings and networks cannot be taken for granted. Despite their differences, all the approaches we have referred to emphasize a kind of 'welfare mix/welfare pluralism' and a 'mixed' or 'plural' economy.

Linkages Between the Sociopolitical and Economic Spheres

Another point of difference between the dominant part of European research on the third sector and much of what has been developed in the US debate concerns the fact that, in contrast to Europe, contributions from economic theory have dominated the debate in the USA, shaping much of the vocabulary of the discourse on the third sector.

Initially, explanations of the existence of a third sector reflected a neoclassical approach. Internationally renowned theorists like Hansmann (1987) and Weisbrod (1988) contend that the third sector emerged primarily from the market's failure to reduce informational asymmetries and the state's failure to respond to minority demands (Lewis, 1997; Nyssens, 2000). They see the state, the market and the third sector as separate entities and tend 'to place them in separate compartments' (Lewis, 1997, p.166). Their thesis is also based on the naturalization of a hierarchical structure in which the market and the state are viewed as pillars of society and the third sector as an auxiliary force.

However, history has proved the above thesis to be misleading. The emergence of a self-regulating market sparked reaction from social groups, including the creation of associations and then the development of the welfare state. Salamon (1987, 1990) referred to this historical process in his criticism of the 'failure' thesis and pointed out that associations were 'the first line of defence' (Lewis 1997, p.166) developed by society; he argued that thereafter their shortcomings (insufficiency, narrow focus, paternalism, amateurism) forced them to forge cooperative links with the state. But this kind of functionalist explanation does not cover all aspects of the subject, as recognized by Salamon and Anheier (1998). Following up the Johns Hopkins project's early research, they have adopted a 'social origins approach' in order to gain a better understanding of national situations through an analysis of their historical origins and development. They also reinforce the hypothesis that the traditional concept of the sector is outmoded. The re-emergence of the issue and the reference to civil society indicate a fundamental, intuitive grasp of the subject, and they have become an ever stronger shared point of reference for those researchers from both sides of the Atlantic who raise the issue of the third sector in other languages than that of economics.

American contributions to an economic theory of the third sector have also sought to cope with national and regional diversity. Several theories have attempted to establish relations between national macro variables: population diversity in the case of the heterogeneity theory (Weisbrod, 1977), religious competition in the case of the theory of supply (James, 1987, pp.397–415), trust in private enterprise in the case of the trust theory (Hansmann, 1980, 1987), per capita income in the case of the welfare state theory (Titmuss, 1974), and social security expenditures in the case of the theory of solidarity (Salamon, 1995). In the light of data collected in a variety of countries, these theories seem to provide a less convincing explanation than the 'social origins' theory linking the third sector's roots to national historical developments (Salamon and Anheier, 1998). This is based on the premise that the system's components are 'not only goods and services producers but also major political and social co-ordination factors' (Seibel, 1990, p.46). Yet none of these theories has identified the principal criterion accounting for the social integration of the third sector. The parallel that Salamon and Anheier draw between the third sector and civil society as a whole, integrating both issues closely under the label of a 'civil society sector', is done too hastily. Identifying the third sector and civil society too closely makes it difficult to distinguish the nature of the links between third sector organizations on the one hand and the civil society on the other. When debating the inter-relations between the third sector and civil society, one should face the fact that speaking of a clear-cut sector makes little sense for the 'third' sector, but it makes even less sense for civil society. For a 'civil' society, defined among other things by the right to associate and speak freely, democratic politics and state guarantees are constitutive. European theorists have advanced the hypothesis that the third sector is part of the public sphere of modern democratic societies, a sphere that cannot be attributed simply to a civil society 'sector' as opposed to a state sector (Evers, 1995). Concretely, the public sphere is not a homogeneous whole; in fact, there is a 'plurality of public spheres' (Chanial, 1992). Some of them have been penetrated by the power structure and are highly organized (Habermas, 1990, p.154; Eme, 1994, p.192), and others 'are emerging as independent forums for free debate and discussion' (Eme, 1996, p.7). Voluntary association partnerships take a leading role in civil society because around them 'autonomous public spheres can take shape' (Habermas, 1992, p.186). But once they are formed, their development is contingent on the recognition granted by the public authorities, knowing that they have to be integrated in the existing systems. Moreover, there is a fundamental tension between the tendency to treat the third sector as an alternative to state-based services and its importance as an expression of civil society. The relationships between the third sector and public authorities are of primary importance, because they have an impact on two political issues: first of all on the potential for action by members of the political community as a whole, and secondly on the sector itself.

So, when further developing the concept of embeddedness introduced by Polanyi (Swedberg, 1996; Granovetter, 1985), one has to take into account that the type of embeddedness prevailing at respective points in historical development has an important political dimension. It is defined by the set of interactions between public authorities and third sector initiatives, which cause effects on both sides, their intensity and character changing considerably over time. Similar to the concept of the realm of third sector organizations as a 'tension field' (Evers, 1995) the purpose of the concept of political embeddedness is to highlight the complex totality of the relations between public policy and initiatives in civil society. While the components of the third sector cannot be understood without conducting an analysis of the public regulations governing them, at the same time the forms they take cannot be entirely attributed to the policies of state authorities. Because the influence of politics on third sector organizations is something other than government intervention, public policy comprises more than the decisions of state authorities – a kind of interplay with social and political actors outside the realm of the state and of professional politics. Consequently, the third sector's structure is influenced historically by initiatives taken by a variety of social players who necessarily participate in the development of new forms of public regulation. These interactions between a variety of different initiatives in and outside the realm of state policies vary in stability over time (Eme, 1996). They are then to be seen as an important element of civil society in a society constantly constituted by politics (see Cohen and Arato, 1995, pp.425f) instead of being conceived as the opposite to the power of a kind of politics that is falsely identified with state power and institutions (Evers, 2003a).

A HISTORICAL–DYNAMIC APPROACH TOWARDS THE THIRD SECTOR

The phenomenon described before as a political embeddedness of the third sector also mirrors the fact that the European social economy as a part of the third sector can be described in legal terms (associations, cooperatives, mutual aid societies and foundations). Law represents the outcome of a legacy of politics. However, the third sector perspective, understood in a welfare pluralism or plural economy framework, also deals with the question of the development model in which these legal structures operate. The approach proposed here focuses on the special kind of political embeddedness of the third sector in order to understand the ways in which it is affected by the dynamics of institutionalization and re-emergence. Three major periods can be identified in terms of a political embeddedness of the third sector.

Emergence and Institutionalization

Once democracy took hold in Europe, modern associations started to emerge. Associationism was initially viewed as being both citizenship-related and fundamentally sociopolitical (Evers, 1997, p.51). This reference to citizenship brings out what national concepts of the third sector have in common while at the same time making it easier to understand differences. Popular definitions of citizenship can conflict, as the English and French examples show.

In the United Kingdom in the nineteenth century, the concept of charitable organizations was linked to the debate on citizenship; charity was a social principle, an essential component of a democratic society that helped to regulate it through the establishment of moral objectives and altruistic voluntary commitment. The objective of government in Victorian England was 'to provide a framework of rules and directives to enable society to manage itself to large measure'. As a result, associations and their charitable activities were not funded by the government but run with a high degree of autonomy; at the same time they forged cooperative links with the authorities responsible for legislation on poverty. In addition, a large portion of the benefits was financed and managed locally, with limited central government assistance, giving rise to a host of 'institutions that acted as intermediaries' between the state and the citizens while being at the same time 'an integral part of the state fabric' (Lewis, 1997, p.169).

In France, on the other hand, while some of the community of associations arose from a philanthropic desire for social peace, an influential philosophy was the republican egalitarianism reflected in a broad-based appeal to the multifaceted concept of solidarity. After the Revolution, the solidarity principle eventually led the country beyond the dichotomy between liberalism and statism. In the nineteenth century, two popular solidarity theories emerged: solidarity as a democratic voluntary social link, as proposed by Leroux, and solidarity as a debt to society, as proposed by the solidarity theorists. Leroux ([1851]1997) believed in the value of solidarity networks based on the work of associations and of the press as means of ensuring that the public spirit essential to democracy was kept alive. The solidarity concept, as it was supported by politicians, legal experts and sociologists such as Bouglé, Bourgeois, Duguit and Durkheim, took on a new meaning at the end of the nineteenth century. Going beyond Leroux's theory of collective involvement in human activity, the new discourse on solidarity spoke of a debt that generations owed to one another, a debt that would take the form of a contract (Dubois, 1985). This concept of solidarity laid the philosophical foundations of social law and legitimized the first compulsory social insurance schemes of the twentieth century.

These two examples bring back onto the agenda in terms of principles what has been debated already by pointing to the importance of two different realms of organizations: the ones belonging to the social and solidarity-based economy and the ones that belong to the realm of voluntary organizations and charities. For the latter, the dominant source is altruism, the commitment to others: the promoters of charities created a general-interest organization for the benefit of a distinct class of beneficiaries. For the former, mutual-interest organizations that provided services for their members, the solidarity within a class or group was decisive.

All these actions gradually won greater acceptance from public authorities and led to the development of legal frameworks that acknowledged the different forms of altruism, solidarity and other forms of self-organization by communities and citizens. The legal provisions all placed limits on the organizations. In Italy, the major social service associations were forced to become public agencies at the end of the nineteenth century. In France, the associations' capacity for economic action was controlled by the government, which was concerned with preventing the Church from consolidating its power. In the United Kingdom, criteria defining 'charities' introduced a form of discrimination against mutual-aid activities and restricted them to traditional philanthropy. In Germany, at the time of the Weimar Republic, the state acknowledged that, when it came to social service provision, the big welfare associations, related to the churches or the social democratic movement, should be called upon first, while simultaneously regulating their operation (Sachße, 1996). In Sweden, 'ideal associations', which were model exponents of the self-management concept, were given a different status from economic associations.

Development by Sub-sectors

From the end of the nineteenth century, the development of legal frameworks and forms of economic integration contributed to the emergence of various sub-divisions and a multiplicity of different arrangements (Vienney, 1994) within a third sector that comprised three different types of organizations providing goods and services: cooperatives, mutual societies and associations. In each sub-sector historical development differs, depending on the contextual framework of the welfare regime wherein it took shape.

Cooperatives
Cooperatives have been largely integrated into the market economy, occupying sectors in which capitalist activity remained weak. They helped a variety of players to mobilize their own resources for the activities that they needed to carry out and which prospective investors had dropped. Historically, cooperatives such as agricultural cooperatives were set up in almost every country, but other types of cooperatives were consolidated in specific countries: consumers' cooperatives in the United Kingdom, housing cooperatives in Germany, the United Kingdom and Sweden. In countries such as France and Italy, where industrialization was slower, workers' production cooperatives took root; they were helped along in the 'third Italy' by the establishment of industrial districts.

While the cooperatives benefited from special provisions negotiated with the state, they had to operate in a competitive environment for the most part. In general, the logical consequence was to concentrate the means of production, and this prompted them to specialize in a major activity connected and identified with the work of their members. The end result was market isomorphism (Di Maggio and Powell, 1983; Enjolras, 1996). Concern for business durability meant that the broader political objectives had to be scaled down, and the transformation process continued to such an extent that financial groups appear as the typical cooperative institutions inside capitalist developed economies.

Mutual aid societies and welfare states
The emergence of the welfare state brought about a profound change in the role played by mutual aid societies and by associations like voluntary agencies, charities and others active in health care and social services.

In the case of mutual aid societies, a number of initiatives were launched in the early nineteenth century to handle the problems of work disability, sickness and old age on the basis of solidarity principles by organizing the members of a profession, branch or locality in a group. These forms of self-organized mutual insurance were considered by socialists as a means of worker emancipation and by liberals and conservatives as barriers against social conflicts; the mutual-benefit organizations were tolerated and controlled by the authorities, as was the case in Belgium and in France from the middle of the nineteenth century onwards. Later, with the mutual insurance organizations becoming part of the broader architecture of social security of the respective country, contribution and benefit levels and conditions were standardized nationally. The nature of the economic activities involved created a dependence on the state for all the benefits they provided. The risk inherent in these benefits could be better controlled because of the involvement of a large number of members at the national level and the additional support of statistical techniques. With the institution of compulsory insurance schemes, the system became more stable and mutual-benefit organizations became complementary insurance sources for compulsory plans and, as for example in Belgium and Germany, managers of the social security system. They were integrated into the non-market economy, even if this meant amending the principle of voluntary membership in order to meet the criteria for supplementary group social insurance. This process of institutionalization was consistent with, on the one hand, the Bismarckian or corporatist concept of social insurance for wage-earners in Germany, Belgium and France and, on the other, with Beveridge's concept of national solidarity, which makes no reference to professional activity (Merrien, 1997, p.82), taking a universalist approach that focuses on welfare rights for all or on providing assistance of last resort in the event of family and market failures (Titmuss, 1974; Esping-Andersen, 1990).

Associations and welfare regimes
Analysing the development of different welfare state regimes also raises the need to include a historical analysis of the relationships between associations of various kinds (voluntary organizations, charities, and so on) and public authorities (Kuhnle and Selle, 1992). As feminist critics (Orloff, 1993; Hernes, 1987; Lewis, 1992) have shown with regard to social and health care services, the public authorities have adopted two contrasting attitudes to social relations between the genders: the first aimed at women's independence and gender equality; the second established a hierarchical relationship between men as being responsible for household income and women as being responsible for domestic chores (Jenson, 1993; Lewis, 1998; Sainsbury, 1994). The gender criterion then finds its expression either in the emphasis on the development

of services for all (as in the first case) or in the priority given to monetary transfers at the expense of services, with women being encouraged to perform domestic work (as in the second case).

By combining the above features, one can identify three types of relationships between associations and public authorities. The first type is the universal or social–democratic system of Scandinavian countries like Sweden and Denmark. Broad reliance on the state as organizer of national society finds expression in a 'collectivization of needs' (Leira, 1992) in the social services sector and a concomitant promotion of social integration and gender equality. In this context, associations have exerted social pressure by acting as a channel through which to voice demands and they have mobilized networks to foster the delivery of services by public organizations. These services are the responsibility of government, for which gender equality is an official objective.

The second type covers liberal and dual systems. Here, services are generally not provided by the state. In the liberal welfare state system typified by the United Kingdom, public assistance is concentrated on the most disadvantaged sectors of the population. Successive governments have maintained this pattern of service delivery. The corollary of this is a lack of such services as child care, as a result of which a high proportion of women have to work part time (Lewis, 1992). The weakness of non-market services regulated by public authorities is also characteristic of the dual system in southern Europe, as can be demonstrated in Spain, Italy and Portugal. This system emphasizes monetary transfers, neglects services and provides social insurance for those who have successfully become integrated into the labour market at the expense of groups who do not have employment security, who have little hope and who are trapped in the underground or informal economy. According to Ferrera (1996), 'access to rights is neither universal nor egalitarian, but operates on the basis of personal knowledge, privilege and patronage'.

In both of these welfare regimes the third sector, as a goods and services provider, is very limited, albeit for diametrically opposed reasons. In the universalistic model, there is a strong impetus from the public authorities to create services and take over tasks that were formerly performed by the market or the third sector. In the liberal and dual models, public service delivery is generally limited, services are for the most part the responsibility of women and remain in the private domain of markets and households. Once gender is taken into account, it is impossible to subscribe to the somewhat surprising conclusion reached by Salamon and Anheier (1998), who describe the Italian system as a social–democratic system akin to that of Sweden on the grounds that, in both countries, there are 'high levels of public social expenditure and relatively weak nonprofit sectors'. In this context, the distinction between monetary transfers and services is essential if we are to avoid equating national systems with a given model solely on the basis of public expenditures and associations. As has been pointed out by Borzaga and Santuari (1998), the apparent similarity of systems is contradicted by the fact that the financial means of the Italian welfare state are swallowed up by pension payments. The Italian model has focused traditionally on monetary transfers and, as a result, tends to neglect the implementation of social services. This is where the Italian and Swedish models differ.

The third type of association–state relationship is the corporatist regime. In contrast to the other two, it assigns a significant role to the third sector. In this system of interaction between initiatives and public authorities, services are considered as an integral part of social policy based on taxes or social security resources. Services are not exchanged for a price to cover most of the production costs because the state provides the major part of the funding. Besides its role as a service-financing and guaranteeing institution, the state sets rules for service delivery procedures as well as for the working conditions in the sector. In Germany, Austria, France and Belgium, associations were therefore mostly service pioneers, identifying emerging social requirements and then responding to them within their own associative contexts while at the same time being increasingly supported and regulated by the state. Conglomerates of organizations took shape, grouped together in national association federations that interacted with the public authorities. The establishment of a regulated service regime gave rise to a non-market isomorphism of third sector structures that brought them closer to government and prompted them to form large national federations. They were linked to political parties, churches, the Red Cross and non-aligned organizations in Germany, they were lay and Catholic bodies in France, and they were socialist and Christian bodies in Belgium and the Netherlands. In the two latter countries, these systems of large associative 'pillars' were coupled with mutual organizations active in family assistance and home care services (Leblanc and Paulet, 1989).

While mutual organizations have become in many ways 'para-state' organizations (Evers *et al.*, 2001, p.2), an analysis of the relationships between associations and public authorities shows that the relationships are particularly strong in health care and social services and manifest themselves in three ways: demand for public services, support for the household economy, and the 'merger' of associations and public authorities through trusteeship and regulation. Only the third element has led to a greater volume of third sector service delivery, and that increase has prompted a weakening of the lines of division between the state and the third sector that is mirrored in strong centralization and increasing reliance on the state for funding and regulation.

THE NEW DYNAMIC

The identity of what in analytical terms can be called the third sector has thus been affected by the differences in paths taken by the various components in the course of their interplay with the respective welfare regime. The present situation, however, cannot be understood simply as an organic evolution, determined by a foundational setting at the outset of welfare state developments. In the subsequent periods of transformation, new circumstances and forces have served to redefine the character of national welfare systems and of the kind of social and political embeddedness of the third sector. That is, the future of the welfare state and of the third sector seem to be interrelated questions even if the former tends to be treated autonomously in some major contributions, as, for example, by Merrien (2002) and by the classical and recent work of Esping-Andersen (1990, 2002). For reasons of simplicity only a few features that have had a strong impact in the last decades will be enumerated below.

Evolving Forms of Commitment

First of all, the shift in forms of commitment in the public sphere must be considered. On the one hand, general-interest activism associated with a desire for social change, involving long-term action and strong delegations of authority within federative structures, has lost impact, as illustrated by the weakening of trade union and ideological affiliations. On the other hand, the crisis in voluntarism, evident in some of the most institutionalized associations, has been paralleled by short-term, specific commitments by associations focusing on providing quick solutions to particular problems (Ion, 1997; Barthélemy, 2000). One of the questions that arises here concerns the interrelation between voluntary work and political and social participation. After the increasing professionalization of social services in the period preceding the revitalization of the third sector from the early 1970s onwards, people had begun to question a perspective which suggested equating the citizen in the realm of health and social services with a mere patient, client or taxpayer. Groups started to take action outside the traditional social movements, combining social cooperation, mutual aid and protest. The third sector's role from this point of view was no longer the mere delivery of services and jobs. Even though today a strong consumerist view has become dominant, there is still a point of view which insists on the relationship between service work and quality and issues of social cohesion and an active society. This cooperative and participatory approach, however, differs from traditional concepts of involvement by occupational or political participation that had been influential before new social movements and initiatives arose.

The Change in the Structure of Productive Activities

The labour structure in developed countries is going through profound changes. Two major categories with contrasting orientations can be distinguished. On the one hand, there are industries for standard products and services, covering logistical services (transport, large-scale distribution, waste treatment, and so on) and administrative services (banks, insurance companies, government, and so on), which have moved towards mass production activities. Dealing primarily with material goods, technical systems and the processing of coded information, these services were changed by new information technologies. Thus their development has been similar to that of industrial activities, which have been characterized by two trends: their job creation capacity is less than it was during the period of prosperity from 1945 to 1975, and there is a demand for workers with higher qualifications.

On the other hand, there are what can be called 'relational services'. As pointed out by Baumol (1987) and Roustang (1987), these give service relationships a pivotal role because the activity is based on direct interaction between supplier and customer. The purpose of such services is either to support business organizations they respond to or to improve the physical, intellectual or moral state of individual customers or users. In this context, new technologies are only relational support systems offering additional options in terms of the variety and quality of services. Innovation in the production process does not necessarily lead to standardization. It can lead to another form of innovation, with complex work being displaced, not eliminated. Greater variety and better quality will offset the effect on capital and labour, thus relational services can generate new jobs. Moreover, in spite of the problems caused by the way organizations are categorized in national accounts which do not present relational services as a separate group, the available figures show that these services are at the centre of job creation. Overall, in the member countries of the Organization for Economic Cooperation and Development (OECD), trade, services to business, the hotel–restaurant industry, personal and domestic services, education, health care, social action and public administration account for most jobs, and their share is steadily increasing. Some sub-sets such as education, health care and social action, social and personal community services and domestic services show a significant increase in employment (Borzaga, 1998).

Proliferation of Initiatives

In this new context, innovative ideas have been developed in civil society networks throughout Europe. The various sub-sectors of a third sector that have been sketched before have taken part in this search for innovation to different degrees. Usually the debate tends to focus on the role of associations such as voluntary agencies, local initiatives and so on, but we should not lose sight of developments linked to the cooperative current (Defourny, 1999). Their reorientations within recent decades can be seen as an attempt to adjust to the changes in public action in different ways, depending on the welfare state system in their particular country.

In the Scandinavian countries, new organizations adopted a mode of operation that was different from that of traditional associations. Moving away from the hegemonic political and cultural approach of the 1970s, they proposed 'new organizational forms and solutions to local social problems' in the 1980s (Klausen and Selle, 1996). In Denmark, organizations called 'project developers' arose out of the strong involvement of one or more individuals. Day care cooperatives emerged in Sweden, where already in 1994 non-municipal child care accommodated more than a tenth of children cared for in day care centres (Pestoff, 1998). In this context, cooperatives and associations contributed to a redeployment of existing services as much as to the creation of new services. The 'cooperatization' of social services (Pestoff, 1998) is designed primarily to increase the role of users, such as parents, in the organization of child care services, and has been accepted because of the financial pressures on the public sector.

Paradoxically, at the other end of the scale, the same form of organization took shape in Mediterranean countries with a dual system: the legal status of cooperatives was used to propose services that the public sector was unable to provide. In Italy, social cooperatives became popular in many areas because of their ability to perform new functions: providing jobs for people from sectors of the population that had been excluded from the labour market and creating a variety of services for individuals. They emerged in the 1970s and grew rapidly. In 1996, there were about 3000 of them, representing approximately 100 000 associates and providing services for several hundred thousand people (Borzaga, 1998). Until recently, the third sector in Italy had been smaller than elsewhere because the state played a dominant role in services such as education and health care instead of incorporating, as other countries had done, a significant third sector dimension (Gui, 1996). In recent years the section has grown considerably. This illustrates well that, instead of relying on the non-redistribution principle as the only guarantee for a not-for-profit orientation (Hansmann, 1980; Ortmann and Schlesinger, 1997, pp.97–119), cooperative characteristics, such as the involvement of stakeholders and the actions of entrepreneurs and workers, can also be seen as principles which help to safeguard the dominance of a not-for-profit orientation (Young, 1983; Borzaga and Mittone, 1997). The 1998 legislation on social solidarity cooperatives in Portugal brings together 'salaried' members, the recipients of services and 'voluntary' members, the non-salaried providers of goods and services.

Socially oriented cooperatives appeared in Spain at the same time. The general law of 1999 refers to social service cooperatives providing education, health care and integration services as well as other social needs not covered by the market. On a regional level one can find mixed cooperatives for social integration in Catalonia and the Basque country and cooperatives for social integration in the region of Valencia, where traditional workers' cooperatives comprising for the most part home care employees developed into a mixed organization of producers and consumers (Espagne, 1999; Sajardo-Moreno, 1996).

Similarly, though to a lesser degree, the voluntary sector in the United Kingdom has been replaced in some areas by social cooperatives providing such services as help for social and cultural integration of disadvantaged populations, child care and home care. The number of initiatives may be no more than a few dozen, but there are also many community enterprises to be found, particularly in Scotland. At the same time, voluntary organizations have a strong role in covering some of the shortages that are left by the state and municipal authorities. An example may be taken once again from the area of child care: in 1986, more than half of the children in England and Wales who benefited from community day care services attended playgroups, part-time day care services for children under five years of age that were the result of measures taken by parents to counter the shortage of child care programmes (Macfarlane and Laville, 1992).

The expansion of cooperatives for the above activities is partly due to the fact that cooperatives, which had traditionally been homogeneous entities, had been allowed to involve a variety of stakeholders (volunteers, workers, consumers, local communities, and so on) in the decision-making process. The 1991 legislation in Italy provided for precisely that kind of expansion. Obviously, the varying balance between innovations that were cooperative-based and others that came from local associations and voluntary agencies is linked to the fact that, depending on the respective welfare state system, the role of both sub-sectors has differed. In some of the Scandinavian countries, for example, the public authorities have by tradition sought very little assistance from associations as service providers, and there has been an agreement to see them mainly as advocates for special groups and concerns. The situation is different in countries with corporatist regimes, where government authorities have established close partnerships with associations as service providers.

In Germany and Austria, initiatives were termed 'self-help' in an effort to reflect a desire to empower the people involved. The initiatives can be divided into three sub-sectors: semi-informal groups outside the third sector, 'self-help' groups of individuals affected by the same problems, and finally groups taking up the needs of others and providing help and services for people outside the group. These 'self-help' groups and small associations are formed on a voluntary basis, and paid professional work is used only in a back-up role. There have been about 70 000 of such initiatives in Germany, involving approximately 2.65 million people, and the formalized half of them can be considered as a part of the third sector (Evers *et al.*, 2001). In the 1980s they enjoyed a period of strong growth, especially in health care and social action: between 5000 and 10 000 groups became active in the health services field alone. They have since stabilized and have changed the landscape of associations. A large number of them joined one of the major charitable federations, and as a result of this process a kind of generation and cultural change has arisen, resulting in the fact that today it is a widely shared opinion that the modernization of operations of voluntary service providers cannot simply be equated with a 'marketization' and a 'managerial revolution'. Issues of social entrepreneurship and of a new cooperative orientation towards the users are also part of this discourse on modernization (see Bode and Evers, in Chapter 5).

The practical criticism that is represented by the movements of the 1970s and 1980s and by what has survived from them in organizational and cultural terms until today must, however, also be seen as a kind of self-criticism. As in Germany and the Netherlands, in Belgium and France the issue was one of accepting the fact that the lack of a profit motive does not suffice to guarantee user respect and, accordingly, of devising new ways of providing associative services. As major, long-standing service providers, associations benefited from local quasi-monopolies during the trusteeship and regulation period. Since there was a tradition of cooperation between public authorities and associations in those countries, new groups adopted the same legal status, but at the same time they intended to build on new foundations and focused on the mode of operation of associations as a central issue. According to their promoters, the legitimacy of service delivery by associations strongly depends on their ability to give users a voice, to elicit voluntary commitment from a variety of sources, to mobilize and cultivate the social capital that stems from supportive relations in civil society (Evers, 2003a) and to find a new financial balance geared to a context offering less protection.

Many associations, including both older organizations that are re-evaluating their traditional practices and more recent groups that are proposing new approaches, are trying to adjust to the new context. Taking up once again illustrative examples from the sector of child care, one can say that in France groups have achieved models for community child care services involving parents, such as day care centres with parent participation promoted by the 'Association des collectifs enfants–parents–professionnels' (Association of professional–child–parent initiatives). Initiated by parents, they were later taken over by professionals, who saw them as both an employment opportunity for themselves and a means of ensuring and monitoring quality of service through close relations with the parents. These community child care facilities experienced the highest growth of all such services in the 1980s. Globally, association initiatives over the past ten years have helped to create two-thirds of the collective day care spaces.

Setting aside national differences, the survey of new actors and developments highlights two key factors that concern the use value of new forms of cooperatives and voluntary associations. First of all, third sector experiments have proved capable of creating original ways of fostering the trust required for certain activities to succeed. Building trust often depends on the commitment of the stakeholders (Ben-Ner and Van Hoomissen, 1991), a commitment which is facilitated by rules and frameworks that limit the opportunities for deriving individual financial advantages from the operations. Within such a 'multi-stakeholder' dynamic (Borzaga and Mittone, 1997; Pestoff, 1998), mutual trust is built through the development of reciprocity-based spheres of activity in which strategic, instrumental and utilitarian factors are secondary and where there is room for collective reflection. Such spheres have been described as 'proximity public spheres' (Eme and Laville, 1994; Laville, 1994). Issues and concerns that have formerly been limited to the informal sector of families and communities (such as issues of personal care for frail elderly persons) can then be brought into such an environment with a view to defining a common good and an approach which can then be used as a frame of reference for users and professionals. Expressed, for example, in a charter, such an arrangement can reinforce the mutual trust that helped in the first instance to find a more public solution to what had been seen before as an entirely private problem.

There is an often-reported reluctance to use public solutions for health and medical problems or for child minding and elderly care. Perhaps the importance of the experience of social cooperatives in Italy, of child care cooperatives in Sweden, of community care associations in the UK, and of self-organized service providers in Germany, France and Belgium concerns precisely this critical point of active trust building. This is because what is taking shape is a joint development of supply and demand for services (Laville and Nyssens, 2000), which becomes possible where one addresses users and stakeholders not only as clients, consumers and payers but also as citizens, community and family members in a specific local environment. However, such new forms of institutionalizing services will need space for experimentation and discussion (Eme and Laville, 2000) and they will need new forms of governance, comprising networking and partnerships between social actors and public authorities (Evers, 2003b). A top-down approach that 'implants' new services may fail in this requirement even if it promotes high professional standards.

Underlining the importance of a process of joint service development wherever the respective services are related to issues of trust building does not mean that the various stakeholders are equally involved or that the initiative will always belong to the same side or group. Sometimes professionals who are critical of their traditional methods will dominate; in other cases administrators seeking to bring about change in their institutions may take the leading role. A mixed, pluralistic model involving a variety of stakeholders (professionals, volunteers, users, institutions and so on) takes shape. By establishing an intermediary, third, sphere this pluralistic model, in varying combinations, can make it possible to counteract what it is proposed here to call 'informational uncertainty', something which goes beyond the well-known topic of 'informational asymmetry' as it is used in economic debates on markets and services. In 'relational services', which involve close contact with the users, there is not simply informational asymmetry but a lack of definition of tasks and concepts, something that is even more disturbing to the stakeholders. This points towards the challenge in imagining a new third sector-based dynamic for such processes of institutionalizing service systems. It is defined by its focus on the impact of the participatory social and political dimension of development concepts for new spheres of service activities. Both researchers and practitioners are concerned here. In practice this means that beyond organizations and initiatives there is a need for entrepreneurs. Adopting the label of entrepreneurship does not deny the social and political dimension of the challenge. An efficient balance of collective and individual commitments would reflect an entrepreneurship that includes a social and civic dimension.

This leads to the second crucial factor to be underlined here. In the course of their emergence, based on the use of non-monetary resources, such as voluntary commitment, supportive partnerships, donations and sponsorships, third sector innovations seek a balance which draws to a considerable degree on resources other than state support and sales to customers. Their goal of self-management prompts them to return to public support not only by public authorities but also by organizations and partners in the public sphere constituted by civil society. They seek a certain degree of independence by maintaining a plurality of dependencies, and they try to cultivate a rich set of goals and effects by their services and activities, some of them for special and particular groups and needs, others more broadly for the common good. However, a 'social enterprise' (Borzaga and Defourny, 2001) with a multi-resource and multi-goal approach (Evers, 2001) is an unknown quality within the institutional and legal setting of most welfare states. It runs up against the careful and tight divisional line that is drawn in so many countries between resources that 'count' and others that are not taken into account, between effects that are easy to measure and others that are less measurable and easily neglected; that is, between economic and social purposes, market and non-market economies. Hence, very often the limits imposed by legal status lead to a proliferation of experiments based on a combination of various legal forms.

CONCLUSION

It has been argued that there are peculiar theoretical contributions that stem from the European debate and which are linked to a specific legacy when it comes to discussion of a third sector in Europe. Four features have been identified which allow one to speak of a 'European way' of conceiving the third sector.

First, throughout Europe, the formation of a third sector has benefited from special contributions by organizations other than the charities, voluntary organizations and foundations, which are also a part of the US legacy; these contributions have come from *mutuals, cooperatives and other organizational features of a 'social economy'*. They are in a large part linked to movements and ideologies that were historically stronger in Europe than in the USA, such as the labour movement and a range of political and economic ideas to create mechanisms for the production of wealth and welfare other than market exchange or state protection. They represent a wide spectrum of collective actions coming from civil society, based on various forms of solidarity.

Second, a European definition of the third sector, especially including cooperatives and mutuals, opens a debate about the role of economies – reformatory economies – that differ from the market, the state economy and the moral economy of private households. The theoretical challenge taken up by the European debate has been to reconstruct the peculiarities of a third sector economy as part of *a plural set of economies* rather than explaining the economic dimensions of the sector with tools and concepts that stem from market theories. Their specificity is not only a question of collective entrepreneurship, of being owned by stakeholders instead of shareholders. It is also related to the institutional framework in which these organizations operate, balancing and intertwining different economic principles.

Third, a considerable part of the European research places the emphasis on the fundamentally open, mixed, pluralistic and *intermediary nature* of the third sector. This differs from contributions that set it apart from state and market as a kind of 'independent' sector, or as a natural feature of a 'civil society sector'. The concept of the civil society background as an intermediary sphere underlines the impact of the effects of market action, state action and changing behaviours of private households and communities on civil society as a contested ground, and on third sector organizations. Thus they may become more commercial, more similar to welfare state organizations, or find ways to keep their specificity by intermediating successfully between the influences that come simultaneously from other sectors of society. Thinking in terms of an 'intermediary space' makes one aware of the fact that there is no clear line of demarcation between, on the one hand, the marketplace, the political arena, communities and state organizations, and on the other, the third sector.

Finally, this pluralist vision, alongside the strong historical impact of welfare politics in most European countries, has to be seen in conjunction with the fact that it was in Europe that the debate incorporated such notions as *'welfare pluralism'*, *'the welfare mix'*, *'the mixed economy of welfare'* or *'the plural economy'*. Such approaches all suggest an analysis of the third sector linked to the history of welfare regimes, socially and politically 'embedded' in the political action, institutions and legal frameworks of welfare politics. Especially in European social–democratic or corporatist welfare regimes, the various parts of the third sector have adopted a special status. Cooperatives, mutuals and associations/voluntary agencies have been integrated and developed in ways and to degrees that are quite different from the US experience. Such European legacies must, however, be regarded when one tries to recast future European models of welfare and the role to be given therein to a third sector.

Keeping these elements of a 'European way' in mind, the second part of this chaper sketched economic, social and political shifts that can be observed on both sides of the Atlantic.

The forms and faces of social and political movements that have a strong impact on the emergence of third sector organizations have changed, from largely class-based and closed 'camps' to more open and fragile coalitions where common interests, differences and particular concerns other than social class play a more important role. The *new forms of cooperation and participation* that emanate here and contribute to the structure of civil society must not be confused with the traditional repertoire of forms of engagement. New forms of association, projects and initiatives seem to be increasingly the product and expression of cooperation among *various stakeholders*: 'corporate citizenship' from the business side can join the social action of other groups, of professionals, citizens and public authorities.

But even if there is a strong element of state action and support, a role for the business community and a defined economic purpose, new associations and services as kinds of 'social enterprises' are peculiar to the degree to which they mobilize and cultivate the *'social capital'* of lively roots in civil society, through partnerships, support networks, trust building, donations and voluntary action. Thus, as 'hybrids', they can possibly create a 'win–win' situation in which markets as well as civil society and community-based resources supplement state resources for services.

These features have a special impact today, given the fact that the *roles of personal services, marked by their proximity* to daily life and needs of peoples, households and families, are gaining importance in various areas of urban and social life: child and elderly care, education, health and welfare. To the degree that these services are a field of growing importance in terms of economics, well-being and politics, the link between this field and the role of the third sector becomes crucial.

With this in mind, a hypothesis has been developed concerning the specific role and impact of third sector organizations when involved in the development of these personal services. They could be crucial for joint development strategies and networked forms of governance that endeavour to *cope with the uncertainties and issues of active trust building* between various sides and partners that arise when one wants to transform private needs into public issues, restructure provision and cooperation and give shape to appropriate service arrangements.

When individual capacity, action and responsibility come to the fore, this leads to the aim of freeing entrepreneurship from its traditional exclusive link with economic action. Politics are needed that open the way for social and civic entrepreneurs. There is a tension in modern economics: the necessity of creating new links between public action and civil society contrasts with the increasing tendency to turn human services into commodities.

REFERENCES

Barthélemy, M. (2000), *Associations: un nouvel âge de la participation?*, Paris: Presses de Sciences Po.

Baumol, W.J. (1987), 'Microeconomics of unbalanced growth: The anatomy of the urban crisis', *American Economic Review*, June, 415–26.

Ben-Ner, A. and T. Van Hoomissen (1991), 'Non profit organisations in the mixed economy', *Annals of Public and Cooperative Economy*, 4, 519–50.

Borzaga, C. (1998), 'The economics of the third sector in Europe: The Italian experience', Department of Economics, University of Trento.

Borzaga, C. and J. Defourny (eds) (2001), *The emergence of social enterprise*, London: Routledge.

Borzaga, C. and L. Mittone (1997), 'The multistakeholders versus the nonprofit organization', Università degli Studi di Trento, draft paper no. 7.

Borzaga, C. and A. Santuari (eds) (1998), *Social Enterprises and New Employment in Europe*, Trentino, in cooperation with European Commision-DGV, CGM-Consorzio nazionale della cooperazione sociale.

Chanial, P. (1992), 'Espace public, sciences sociales et démocratie, introduction au débat: Les espaces publics', *Quaderni*, 18, Autumn, 61–73.

CIRIEC (1999), *Les entreprises et organisations du troisième système. Un enjeu stratégique pour l'emploi*, Action pilote 'troisième système et emploi' de la Commission Européenne, Brussels: CIRIEC.

Cohen, J.L. and A. Arato (1995), *Civil society and political theory*, Cambridge, Massachusetts: MIT Press.

Defourny, J. (ed.) (1999), 'The emergence of social enterprises in Europe', EMES European Network, Brussels.

Defourny, J., P. Develtere and B. Fonteneau (eds) (2000), *Social economy north and south*, Liège: Centre d'économie sociale, Université Catholique de Louvain, Hiva.

Di Maggio, P.J. and W.W. Powell (1983), 'The iron cage revisited: Institutional isomorphism and collective rationality in organizational fields', *American Sociological Review*, 48, April, 147–60.

Dubois, P. (1985), 'Le solidarisme', Thesis, Université de Lille II.

Eme, B. (1991), 'Les services de proximité', *Informations sociales*, 13, August–September, 34–42.

Eme, B. (1993), 'Lecture d'Habermas et éléments provisoires d'une problématique du social solidariste d'intervention', roneo, CRIDA-LSCI, IRESCO-CNRS, Paris.

Eme, B. (1994), 'Insertion et économie solidaire', in B. Eme and J.L. Laville, *Cohésion sociale et emploi*, Paris: Desclée de Brouwer, pp.157–94.

Eme, B. (1996), 'Politiques publiques, société civile et association d'insertion par l'économique', roneo, CRIDA-LSCI, Commissariat Général du Plan, Paris.

Eme, B. and J.L. Laville (eds) (1994), *Cohésion sociale et emploi*, Paris: Desclée de Brouwer.

Eme, B. and J.L. Laville (2000), 'L'enjeu de la confiance dans les services relationnels', in M. Orillard (ed.), *La construction de la confiance*, Paris: L'Harmattan, pp.281–322.

Enjolras, B. (1996), 'Associations et isomorphisme institutionnel', *Revue des études coopératives, mutualistes et associatives*, 261 (59), 3rd term, 68–71.

Espagne, F. (1999), 'Les coopératives à but social ou d'intérêt collectif et le multisociétariat', roneo, Paris.

Esping-Andersen, G. (1990), *The three worlds of welfare capitalism*, Princeton: Princeton University Press.

Esping-Andersen, G. (2002), 'The sustainability of welfare states: Reshaping social protection', in B. Harris-White (ed.), *Globalization and insecurity. Political, economic and physical challenges*, London: Palgrave, pp.218–32.

Evers, A. (1990), 'Im intermediären Bereich. Soziale Träger und Projekte zwischen Hanshalt, Staat und Markt', *Journal für Sozialforschung*, 2 (30), 189–210.

Evers, A. (1995), 'Part of the welfare mix: The third sector as an intermediate area', *Voluntas*, 6 (2), 119–39.

Evers, A. (1997), 'Le Tiers secteur au regard d'une conception pluraliste de la protection sociale', in MIRE (ed.), *Produire les solidarités. La part des associations*, Paris: Fondation de France, pp.51–60.

Evers, A. (1998), 'Sur l'étude Johns Hopkins. Un commentaire critique', in 'Une seule solution, l'association? Socio-économie du fait associatif', *Revue du Mauss*, 11, first term, 11–118.

Evers, A. (2001), 'The significance of social capital in the multiple goal and resource structure of social enterprises', in C. Borzaga and J. Defourny (eds), *The emergence of social enterprise*, London: Routledge, pp. 298–311.

Evers, A. (2003a), 'Social capital and civic commitment: on Putnam's way of understanding', *Social Policy and Society*, 2 (1), 1–9.

Evers, A. (2003b), 'Origins and implications of working in partnerships', in L. Kjaer, P. Abrahamson and P. Raynard (eds), *Local partnerships in Europe*, Copenhagen: The Copenhagen Centre.

Evers, A. and I. Svetlik (eds) (1993), *Balancing pluralism. New welfare mixes in care for the elderly*, Avebury: Aldershot.

Evers, A., I. Bode, S. Gronbach and A. Graf (2001), 'The enterprises and organizations of the third system: A strategic challenge for employment', national report Germany, in CIRIEC (ed.), *The enterprises and organizations of the third system in the European Union*, Liège: University Liège and Derouaux Ordina Editions.

Ferrera, M. (1996), 'The southern model of welfares in social Europe', *Journal of European Social Policies*, 6 (1), 17–37.

Granovetter, M. (1985), 'Economic action and social structure: The problem of embeddedness', *American Journal of Sociology*, 91 (3), 481–510.

Gui, B. (1992), 'Fondement économique du Tiers secteur', *Revue des Études Coopératives, mutualistes et associatives*, 72 (247), 160–73.

Habermas, J. (1990), *Écrits politiques*, Paris: Le Cerf.

Habermas, J. (1992), 'L'espace public, 30 ans après', *Quaderni*, 18, Autumn, 161–91.

Hansmann, H. (1980), 'The role of nonprofit enterprise', *Yale Law Journal*, 89, 835–98.

Hansmann, H. (1987), 'Economic theories of nonprofit organizations', in W.W. Powell (ed.), *The nonprofit sector. A research handbook*, New Haven: Yale University Press, pp.27–42.

Hernes, H. (1987), *Welfare state and woman power: Essays in state feminism*, Oslo: Norwegian University Press.

Ion, J. (1997), *La fin des militants?*, Paris: Les éditions de l'atelier.

James, E. (1987), 'The nonprofit sector in comparative perspective', in W.W. Powell (ed.), *The nonprofit sector, A research handbook*, New Haven: Yale University Press, pp.397–415.

Jenson, J. (1993), 'Representing solidarity: class, gender and the crisis of social–democratic Sweden', *New Left Review*, 201, 76–100.

Johnson, N. (1998), *Mixed economies of welfare: A comparative perspective*, London: Prentice-Hall Europe.

Klausen, K.K. and P. Selle (1996), 'The third sector in Scandinavia', *Voluntas*, 7 (2), 99–122.

Kramer, R.M., H. Lorentzen, S. Pasquinelli and W.B. Melief (1993), *Privatization in four European countries*, Armonk, New York: M.E. Sharpe.

Kuhnle, S. and P. Selle (eds) (1992), *Government and voluntary organisations*, Aldershot: Avebury, pp.99–122.

Laville, J.L. (ed.) (1992), *Les services de proximité en Europe*, Paris: Desclée de Brouwer.

Laville, J.L. (ed.) (1994), *L'économie solidaire*, Paris: Desclée de Brouwer.

Laville, J.L. and M. Nyssens (2000), 'Solidarity-based third sector organizations in the "proximity services" field: a European francophone perspective', *Voluntas*, 11 (1).

Laville, J.L. and R. Sainsaulieu (eds) (1997), *Sociologie de l'association*, Paris, Desclée de Brouwer.

Leblanc, S. and T. Paulet (1989), 'Les mutualités', *Courrier Hebdomadaire*, special issue, 1228–9, CRISP, Brussels.

Leira, A. (1992), *Models of motherhood: Welfare state policy and Scandinavian experiences of everyday practices*, Cambridge: Cambridge University Press.

Leroux, P. ([1851]1997), *A la source perdue du socialisme français*, anthology compiled and presented by B. Viard, Paris: Desclée de Brouwer.

Lewis, J. (1992), *Women in Britain since 1945. Women, family, work and the state in the post-war years*, Oxford: Blackwell.

Lewis, J. (1997), 'Le secteur associatif dans l'économie mixte de la protection sociale', in MIRE (Rencontres et Recherches avec la collaboration de la Fondation de France) (ed.), *Produire les solidarités – la part des associations*, Paris, pp.164–72.

Lewis, J. (ed.) 1998, *Gender, social care and welfare state restructuring*, Aldershot: Avebury.

Macfarlane, R. and J.L. Laville (1992), *Developing community partnerships in Europe. New ways of meeting social needs in Europe*, London: Directory of Social Change and Calouste Gulbenkian Foundation.

Maucourant, J., J.M. Servet and A. Tiran (1988), *La modernité de Karl Polanyi, introduction générale*, Paris: L'Harmattan.

Merrien, F.X. (1997), *L'état-providence*, collection Que sais-je?, Paris: Presses Universitaires de France.

Merrien, F.X. (2002), 'États-providence en devenir', *Revue française de sociologie*, 43 (2), 211–42.

Nyssens, M. (2000), 'Les approches économiques du tiers secteur. Apports et limites des analyses anglo-saxonnes d'inspiration néo-classique', *Sociologie du travail*, 42 (4), 551–65.

OECD (1996), *Reconciling economy and society. Towards a plural economy*, Paris: OECD.

Orloff, A.S. (1993), 'Gender and the social rights of citizenship: The comparative analysis of gender relations and welfare states', *American Sociological Review*, 58 (3), 303–28.

Ortmann, A. and M. Schlesinger (1997), 'Trust, refute and the role of non-profit enterprise', *Voluntas*, 8 (2), 97–119.

Pestoff, V.A. (1991), *Between markets and politics: Cooperative in Sweden*, Frankfurt am Main and Boulder, Colorado: Campus Verlag and Westview Press.

Pestoff, V.A. (1992), 'Third sector and co-operative services. From determination to privatization', *Journal of Consumer Policy*, 15 (1), 21–45.

Pestoff, V.A. (1996), 'enterprises and civil democracy in Sweden: Enriching work environment and empowering citizens as co-producers', School of Business, Stockholm.

Pestoff, V.A. (1998), *Beyond the market and state: Social enterprises and civil democracy in a welfare society*, Aldershot: Ashgate.

Polanyi, K. (1944), *The great transformation*, New York: Rinehart & Company.

Roustang, G. (1987), *L'emploi: un choix de société*, Paris: Syros.

Roustang, G., J.L. Laville, B. Eme, D. Mothé and B. Perret (1997), *Vers un nouveau contrat social*, Paris: Desclée de Brouwer.

Sachße, C. (1996), 'Verein, Verband und Wohlfahrtsstaat: Entstehung und Entwicklung der "dualen" Wohlfahrtspflege', in T. Rauschenbach, C. Sachße and T. Olk (eds), *Von der Wertgemeinschaft zum Dienstleistungsunternehmen*, 2nd edn, Frankfurt: Suhrkamp Verlag, pp.123–49.

Sainsbury, D. (ed.) (1994), *Gendering welfare states*, London: Sage.

Sajardo-Moreno, A. (1996), 'Economie sociale et services sociaux en Espagne', *Revue des études coopératives, mutualistes et associatives (RECMA)*, 261 (59), third term.

Salamon, L.M. (1987), 'Partners in public service: The scope and theory of government–nonprofit relations', in W.W. Powell (ed.), *The nonprofit sector. A research handbook*, New Haven: Yale University Press.

Salamon, L.M. (1990), 'The nonprofit sector and government. The American experience in theory and practice', in H.K. Anheier and W. Seibel (eds), *The third sector. Comparative studies of nonprofit organizations*, Berlin and New York: Walter de Gruyter, pp.219–40.

Salamon, L.M. (1995), *Partners in public service: Government–nonprofit relations in the modern welfare state*, Baltimore, Maryland: Johns Hopkins University Press.

Salamon, L.M. and H.K. Anheier (1995), *Defining the nonprofit sector*, Manchester: Manchester University Press.

Salamon, L.M. and H.K. Anheier (1998), 'Social origins of civil society: Explaining the nonprofit sector cross-nationally', *Voluntas*, 9 (3), 213–48.

Seibel, W. (1990), 'Government/third sector relationships in a comparative perspective: The cases of France and West Germany', *Voluntas*, 1 (1), 42–60.

Swedberg, R. (1996), 'New economic sociology: What has been accomplished, what is ahead?', Department of Sociology, Stockholm University, Stockholm.

Titmuss, R. (1974), *Social policy*, London: Allen & Unwin.

Vienney, C. (1994), *L'économie sociale*, collection Repères, Paris: La Découverte.

Weisbrod, B. (1977), *The voluntary nonprofit sector*, Lexington, Massachusetts: Lexington Books.

Weisbrod, B.A. (1988), *The nonprofit economy*, Cambridge, Massachusetts: Harvard University Press.

Young, D.R. (1983), *If not for profit, for what?*, Lexington, Massachusetts: D.C. Heath.

PART II

Social Economies, Voluntary Agencies and the
Civil Society: the Third Sector in Various
European Countries

2. From suffocation to re-emergence: the evolution of the Italian third sector

Carlo Borzaga

INTRODUCTION

Italy is undoubtedly one of the European countries that in the last ten years have experienced the most intense and unexpected development of the third sector and of some interesting organizational innovations. In fact, just over ten years ago, it was still believed that 'the sector of private, nonprofit activity, the third sector did not play a dominant role in the Italian public sphere, and moreover that, although the role of the third sector was gradually increasing, it was unlikely that it would come to play a very significant part in Italian society' (Perlmutter, 1991, p.157). Contrary to these predictions, in little more than ten years Italy has seen the birth of tens of thousands of voluntary and social associations, more than 6000 social cooperatives and hundreds of new foundations, among them 88 bank foundations with assets estimated at 30 billion euros. The sector's workforce, which at the beginning of the 1990s stood at just over 300 000 (Borzaga, 1991; Barbetta, 1996), has almost doubled over the past decade (ISTAT, 2001). Moreover, in recent years, the third sector has worked closely with institutions, and interest in it among researchers, policy makers and the media has grown exponentially.

This recent growth of the third sector has come about following a long series of measures in the last century which sought to restrict its role and action. Its growth has been due less to the strengthening of already existing organizations than to the birth of completely new ones largely induced by the 'institutional creativity' of their promoters, and only subsequently incorporated into legislation. There seem to be two distinctive features of these innovations: a constant endeavour to involve stakeholders directly through forms of democratic management, and the widespread use of the cooperative form in the production of social services, which in other countries are usually undertaken by associations and foundations.

Throughout this period the attitude of the public authorities towards the third sector has been hesitant and contradictory. Some policies have certainly fostered its development by repeatedly intervening to recognize and regulate the new organizational forms, and by increasing the involvement of third sector organizations in the implementation of social policies. At the same time, however, the attitude of the public institutions towards the third sector has been one of suspicion, as evidenced by the contradictory nature of numerous legislative provisions, the failure to grant any significant form of tax relief, excessively stringent regulations, and attempts to reduce the autonomy of third sector organizations by means of funding procedures intended more to curb public spending than to increase and upgrade the supply of social services.

These contradictions have been due to the predominance of a statist political culture, the lack in Italian law of well-defined non-profit legal forms, and the distinctive organization of Italy's welfare system. In fact, until innovations were introduced in the 1990s, the legal forms of association and foundation were envisaged by the civil code, but they had limited autonomy and could only pursue economically significant activities with difficulty. Moreover, the Italian welfare model has always given priority to monetary transfers, neglecting the supply of social services and assigning a residual role to private organizations.

Precisely because the third sector has managed to develop despite these difficulties and contradictions, it has, especially during the 1990s, contributed to the evolution of social policies by bringing neglected situations of need to light by proposing and experimenting with new services and by encouraging changes in social expenditure in favour of the introduction of a wider range of services.

Proper understanding of the unexpected re-emergence of the Italian third sector, however, requires more than analysis of its recent evolution. It is necessary to retrace its history and examine its relationships with public welfare policies, linking these various aspects with the social movements that characterized Italy in the years between the end of the 1960s and the 1980s. This reconstruction is the main purpose of this chapter.

Before the analysis begins, the next section describes the interpretative model that will be used. The third section describes the size and features of the non-profit sector at the end of the eighteenth century, when the first measures intended to restrict its action were introduced. The fourth section describes the various stages in the progressive scaling down of the third sector between the late 1800s and the 1970s. The fifth section analyses the re-emergence, and then the consolidation and growth, of the Italian third sector from the 1970s onwards. The sixth section 5 provides some recent data on the quantitative dimensions of the sector since 2000.

THE INTERPRETATIVE MODEL

Broadly speaking, one may say that the well-being of a community results from the joint action of five actors: the family, for-profit enterprises, public organizations, mutual benefit organizations or enterprises and non-profit or public benefit organizations of philanthropic–altruistic type.[1] On the combined action of these depends both the overall production of goods and services, and their distribution among individuals and social groups.

Each of these institutions handles transactions between economic agents on the basis of distinct principles: exchange between equivalents for for-profit enterprises (in other words, the market), authority for public organizations, reciprocity for the family, solidarity for mutual organizations, and altruism or philanthropy for public benefit or charitable organizations. In other words, each of these institutions organizes itself by selecting among the motivations for action those most coherent with its characteristics and goals. In so doing, each of them also restricts its range of action, and it restricts the activities in which it can guarantee satisfactory levels of efficiency and effectiveness – or at least better levels than those achieved by the other institutions.[2] Consequently, the spread and importance of each of these organizational types evolves according to the extent of labour division and the level of economic development.

Yet the role and economic and social importance of these various institutions is also determined by the attitudes and actions of policy makers, and the latter in their turn are influenced by the social, political and economic theories and ideologies that happen to predominate at a particular time.

During the twentieth century, until the Second World War, the social sciences, economics in particular, often took for granted that economic and social development coincided with the growth of for-profit enterprises (and therefore of the market as a transaction-governing device). Only with the advent of welfare economics and Keynesian theory was it recognized that the state, and therefore authoritarian forms of transaction governance, were important as well. It was thus believed that market and state, on their own and each of them acting within its area of jurisdiction, were able to maximize economic and social well-being.

This conviction had two main consequences. The first was an undervaluing of the role of the family and of unpaid work by women in the production of essential goods and services.[3] Secondly, justification was provided for the gradual scaling down of the third sector and the promotion of for-profit enterprises and the public institutions as alternatives to it. In those countries, mainly European, in which these convictions were widely embraced (with the conservative parties in favour of development of the market, and socialist political forces in favour of an extension of the state's role), the third sector's freedom of action and its development were progressively cut back. The same did not happen, for instance, in the United States, where resistance to any increase in the functions of the state, deemed prejudicial to individual freedom, led to the maintenance of a larger non-profit sector. In the course of the twentieth century, in fact, third sector organizations were either incorporated into the public sector or eliminated and replaced by public bodies and enterprises.

Until the 1970s, this institutional framework, which hinged essentially on the state and the market, worked efficiently. But thereafter, and especially following the marked and persistent slowdown of economic growth, it grew increasingly evident that for-profit enterprises and the public authorities were unable to cope on their own with numerous social needs, and that the family was unable to continue in its role as the provider of most personal services. New spaces for the re-emergence of non-profit institutions, both public and for mutual benefit, were opened. However, just as the needs of what was by now a post-industrial society differed from those of the late nineteenth and early twentieth centuries, so the non-profit organizational forms used, and types of action implemented, also differed from those of the past.

The years since the 1990s have seen an increasingly evident shift towards a model of society and the economy in which economic and social well-being springs from the action of a wider range of institutions. This evolution, however, is still in its early stages. Its consolidation requires a careful over-haul of the roles assigned in the last 50 years to the various institutions, of their boundaries, and of the forms of interaction and collaboration among them.

Yet looking at this evolution from a historical perspective, taking as a benchmark a country like Italy, which during the twentieth century drastically reduced – indeed, almost eliminated – the third sector, it becomes clear that its re-emergence is an entirely unexceptional occurrence. More exceptional were those few decades in the twentieth century when growth and well-being were achieved through almost exclusive reliance on the combined action of for-profit enterprises and public institutions. The history of recent years seems instead to show that the marginalization of certain types of institution may produce substantial social and economic damage (Zamagni, 2000).

THE THIRD SECTOR AT THE END OF THE EIGHTEENTH CENTURY

In Italy, until the end of the eighteenth century, the market and the state still played a minor role in the production and distribution of income, for which other actors, especially the family, were mainly responsible. Outside the household, social protection was largely provided by private not-for-profit organizations, many of them endowed with considerable assets and financed by both private citizens and local authorities. The most important of them were the *Opere Pie* (charities), mutual benefit societies, cooperatives, the savings banks and the *Monti di Pegno* (provident loan societies).

The *Opere Pie* were the most widespread of the organizations considered. With traditions stretching back for centuries, they were present throughout the country even prior to unification, providing benefits to the poor as well as social and health services. At the time of the 1880 census there were around 22 000 *Opere Pie* operating in 33 different areas of activity. In order to standardize the management structures of these institutions, immediately after unification of the country Parliament passed the so-called 'Great Act' on *Opere Pie*, which was the first item of legislation relating to non-profit organizations in Italy: Law No. 753 of 1862, in fact, was an attempt both to preserve and to reorganize the *Opere Pie*. It granted them administrative autonomy and reduced the supervision measures provided by previous laws to a significant extent, especially those in force in Piedmont and Lombardy (Farrell-Vinay, 2000). Also the savings banks and *Monti di Pegno*, which were aimed at encouraging saving by workers and the middle class, and at providing them with loans, had the legal status of *Opere Pie*.

Mutual benefit societies were also relatively common at the end of the nineteenth century. Having arisen in the second half of the nineteenth century, following dissolution of the corporations of medieval origin and the simultaneous appearance of new forms of manufacture (Allio, 2000), these societies insured their members against illness, injury, disability and joblessness. First restricted to specific occupational categories, their coverage subsequently extended to all the workers resident in a particular area. At the beginning of the twentieth century there were more than 6500 of these mutual benefit societies, with more than one million members. Besides monetary benefits they also provided subsidized housing, promoted cultural activities, organized vocational training and were generally managed democratically (Gheza Fabbri, 2000).

Credit cooperatives (especially in rural areas) and consumer cooperatives were also widespread. The former played an important role in stimulating investment in agriculture, while the latter ensured the country-wide availability of goods and endeavoured to keep prices low, protecting the incomes of the poorer classes and ensuring their survival by extending credit to their members. In 1885 there were 4896 cooperatives in the country, with more than 570 000 members, 904 of whom were credit cooperatives.

However, the diffusion of these organizations, their economic and financial resources, as well as their managerial structures, varied considerably across the country. They were mainly located and better managed in the northern regions.

FROM 1890 TO 1970: THE PROGRESSIVE SCALING DOWN OF THE THIRD SECTOR

The scaling down of the Italian non-profit sector began at the end of the nineteenth century. The first stage in the process was revision of the legislation on the *Opere Pie*, which the government and Parliament undertook primarily because the reform law of 1862 had not been uniformly applied or respected in the country's various regions. Numerous *Opere Pie*, especially in the central region and the south, had proved unable to handle the autonomy granted them by the law, and they had failed to comply with the rules on management and accounting.

Moreover, it had grown increasingly difficult to coordinate the activities of a myriad of independent organizations, with the risk that the most unscrupulous people might obtain more subsidies, to the detriment of the poorer ones. In other words, the *Opere Pie* increasingly displayed the failure typical of the third sector which subsequently came to be called 'particularism' (Salamon, 1987) .

Overlapping these objective reasons were both the conception of the modern state deriving from the French revolution, and the German model of 'social democracy'. According to the French model, intermediate organizations like the *Opere Pie* constituted a third party between the government and the individual which obstructed the direct relationship between the state and the citizen. They were consequently regarded with suspicion. The German model of social democracy maintained instead that direct public intervention was necessary in order to insure workers against disability and illness.

In this climate, the Italian government, in 1888, first enacted a law which reorganized health care provision (the first step towards construction of a public welfare system) and then, in 1890, transformed the *Opere Pie* from private and independent organizations into public institutions, changing their name to *Istituzioni Pubbliche di Assistenza e Beneficienza* (IPABs). The new Act introduced forms of public control over them and sought to direct their activities towards goals that the public authorities deemed of importance. By enacting these laws, the Italian state assumed regulatory responsibility for private social welfare for the first time in its history. The autonomy of non-profit organizations, not only in the choice of objectives and activities but also in their day-to-day management, was drastically reduced.

In the years that followed, construction of the public welfare system continued simultaneously with retrenchment of the third sector. In 1903, Parliament passed an Act on public housing, and in 1904 a law on industrial accidents and the relevant insurance; in 1910, a national maternity fund was established. This expansion of the state's functions in the field of welfare services was strengthened even further during the Fascist period. Compulsory insurance against invalidity and a public pension system were introduced in 1923. The National Institution for Maternity and Childhood was created in 1926; and in 1937 social provisions were extended to all individuals and families in particularly needy circumstances.

Reduction of the role of third sector organizations was accelerated by the centralized and authoritarian character impressed upon social policy by

Fascism. Not only did the introduction of compulsory insurance against invalidity spell the demise of the mutual benefit societies, but it also eliminated any form whatsoever of self-management by the new institutions. Moreover, the regime's determination to maintain close social control and build consensus meant that even more stringent centralized and political control was exerted over the IPABs, with their resources being used increasingly for political ends. According to Fascist doctrine, in fact, not only was civil society to play no part in the implementation of social policies, but the Fascist Party itself should assume direct responsibility for the delivery of welfare (Preti and Venturoli, 2000). The regime also attacked the cooperative movement that had continued to grow during the early years of the century, particularly that part of it most closely associated with the workers' movement (the workers' cooperatives), and the second-level organizations, which were replaced by a single body closely controlled by the state and the Fascist Party.

The Civil Code approved in 1942[4] confirmed the residual role to which the third sector organizations were then confined. The main purpose of the Civil Code was to foster and support for-profit companies. Hence organizations pursuing objectives other than profit were treated as marginal and less important. Associations and foundations were (and still are) dealt with by the First Book of the Code, most of the provisions of which concerned the control that the state authorities should exert over these organizations. Although a certain degree of freedom of association was granted, the First Book of the 1942 Code set out the incorporation procedure that associations and foundations should follow in order to gain legal personality. Simultaneously, the Code's intention was to ensure that these organizations engaged in non-economic activities.

The end of Fascism and the approval of the Constitution of the Italian Republic in 1948 marked a profound change in the conception of both social policies and the role of third sector organizations, though only in theory. The Constitution delineated a universalist type of welfare model and envisaged direct commitment by the state to providing the resources required by social policies. It also explicitly and repeatedly recognized the role of civil society and of non-profit organizations, which were granted freedom of action especially in social welfare work, within a framework of collaboration between public institutions and private organizations (Roberti, 2000).

However, the welfare model set forth by the Constitution was ignored at least until the end of the 1970s. Contrary to its provisions, in fact, the domination of the Italian public sphere by the political parties gave rise to a particularistic and clientelistic welfare system in which values and principles differed according to the social group concerned, and generally worked in favour of the middle classes. The welfare system created after the Second World War was also strongly biased towards cash benefits and showed little concern for the provision of services. The central component of the social security system was pensions, which were dispensed by a highly fragmented and corporatist system. Moreover, health services, and the few non-family delivered social services that existed, were managed by public institutions under the direct control of the political parties, and therefore at the expense of the civil society organizations (Perlmutter, 1991).

Even after 1948, therefore, despite the intentions of the Constitution, third sector organizations were further curtailed, being restricted mainly to the role of intermediators between the parties and their areas of influence. With the exception of the law on cooperatives enacted in 1948, no significant legislative measure was introduced with the intention to revive third sector organizations and to expand their role in social policies until the end of the 1980s. Thus, among the general public, the conviction was fostered that the only institution responsible for social welfare was the state.

FROM THE 1970s ONWARDS: THE EMERGENCE OF THE NEW THIRD SECTOR

At the end of the 1960s, the Italian welfare model began to show signs of crisis, and the political system came under fire from both the trade union and the student movements. Increasing dissatisfaction with the political situation in general and with social policies in particular gave rise to the protest movements that burgeoned in 1968. These involved both students and workers and they continued well beyond the mid-1970s. However, the demands advanced by these movements were met by only partial political responses and their members were only in part reabsorbed into the traditional political parties, or into the ones newly constituted at the time.

The slowdown of economic growth caused increasing unemployment, especially among young people and women. At the same time, the role of the family in providing social support declined as a consequence of increased female participation in the labour market. The elderly population expanded, and new needs connected with so-called 'post-materialist poverty' (for example mental disability, homelessness, drug abuse, immigration and long-term unemployment) emerged. These new needs could not be tackled using traditional cash benefit policies, and demand for both traditional and new social services grew.

The public sector, mainly the local authorities, sought to meet this demand by increasing the supply of services, but they were hampered in doing so by the high costs associated with public units and by the continuing financial crisis of the welfare state. Cash benefits automatically grew as a consequence, with the result that, between the mid-1980s and mid-1990s, the proportion of GDP consisting of public resources allocated to social welfare rose from just over 20 per cent to more than 25 per cent. By contrast, financial manoeuvres to curb public spending resulted in a freeze on recruitment in the public sector which prevented adjustment of the supply of social services to demand.

Given this situation, some of the discontented activists of the student movements shifted to more direct social commitment by creating new civil organizations. They were assisted in this endeavour by sections of the Catholic Church which sought to give concrete embodiment to the Second Vatican Council's message of human promotion that aimed at a better integration of the 'new poor', especially by action to be taken by voluntary organizations. It was in this context that some groups of people sought to bridge the gap between the demand for and the public supply of social services by inventing new provisions and new organizational forms. It was the action of these groups, indeed, that restored an autonomous role to civil society and to the third sector in Italy.

The emergence of the new third sector can be divided into three phases: start-up, recognition and consolidation.

The Start-up

The start-up phase occurred between the end of the 1970s and the end of the 1980s. It was brought about mainly by a growing number of small organizations tied to specific local contexts and principally concerned with the 'new poor': teenagers with family problems, the elderly, the handicapped, the homeless and drug addicts. These initiatives were initially organized mainly as associations, and since they relied more on voluntary work than on donations they took the name of 'voluntary organizations'. Public support was limited to the provision of financial aid, which was generally small, sporadic and unrelated to the amount of services delivered.

The success of many of these organizations in assisting the new poor accounts for their growth in size and number. After some years, partly as a result of increased public funding, several of them reorganized themselves into more efficient units, providing services on a stable basis and employing paid social workers. This development, however, came up against a legal obstacle: in Italy, associations may not engage fully in production or in economically significant activities. This restriction mainly affected those organizations that had begun to employ workers, and those that had been set up to integrate the disadvantaged (mainly the handicapped) into work. The idea thus arose of using the legal form of the cooperative to manage these activities, given that a cooperative had the legal status of an enterprise but, in accordance with the Constitution, pursued social ends. Moreover, cooperatives were the only organizations with quasi-non-profit status and not liable to tax on undistributed profits. They were also characterized by member participation and democratic management, like most of the new voluntary organizations.

Although by law a cooperative could not have members who did not benefit from its activities (and the volunteers did not), the new cooperative form spread, especially after the mid-1980s. The most innovative of them took the name of 'social solidarity cooperatives'. So that these new cooperatives might gain recognition by the courts and public authorities, their advocates emphasized the contradiction between the 1948 law on cooperatives, which confined the benefits of their activities to members, and the Constitution, which recognized that cooperatives might pursue broader social aims and be used to provide services in the interest of the community.

However, during the 1980s, the creators and managers of both voluntary associations and social solidarity cooperatives continued to regard themselves as pioneers compensating for temporary failure by the public authorities. They believed that their efforts would no longer be necessary when the state recovered from the fiscal crisis.

The Recognition

The stage when formal recognition was accorded to the new third sector began with Decision no. 396 handed down by the Constitutional Court in 1988. This decision declared that Section 1 of the 1890 Act on the IPABs (according to which organizations providing social services must have public status, so that only public bodies might engage in such activities) was contrary to Section 38 of the Constitution and its stipulation that 'private care is free'. Section 1 of the 1890 Act was thus declared unconstitutional because it did not provide that charities furnishing social and health services could pursue their activities in the form of private non-profit organizations. This decision had even wider impact, however, in that it permitted citizens to establish and manage private organizations providing social services.

In compliance with this ruling by the Constitutional Court, Parliament approved a number of laws over the next few years granting recognition to the third sector organizational forms that had developed. The two most important of these laws, the Act on Voluntary Organizations and the Act on Social Cooperatives, were enacted in 1991. The Act on Voluntary Organizations (no. 266) acknowledged and regulated the role of organized voluntary work allowing voluntary organizations to use a small number of paid employees. It also provided for enrolment on special registers and granted some tax benefits to both the organizations themselves and to donors (although the main provisions were not implemented until 1997).

The Act on Social Cooperatives (no. 381) recognized the new form of cooperative operating in the social services sector. The law altered some of the restrictions on traditional cooperatives, most notably the requirement that they engage in activities beneficial to their members only. The 1991 Act stated that social cooperatives operate 'in the general interest of the community and for the social integration of citizens' and that they may have voluntary members, but only to a maximum of 50 per cent of their memberships, which could also comprise workers, consumers and legal persons (including municipalities).

The law provides that social cooperatives may be of two types:[5] cooperatives delivering social, health and educational services, and cooperatives producing goods and services other than social ones, in order to integrate disadvantaged or hard-to-place workers into employment. At least 30 per cent of the workforces of social cooperatives of the latter type must consist of disadvantaged workers, for whom the cooperative is exempt from payment of social contributions.[6]

Approval of these two laws constituted the first important political recognition of the third sector in the twentieth century, thus acknowledging the right of private individuals to organize services to the benefit of other citizens, and the possibility that organizations other than public ones might organize the provision of social services on an autonomous and stable basis. At the same time, by recognizing the voluntary organizations and social cooperatives set up after the 1970s, the public authorities also began to recognize that the groups of people who used the services provided by these new organizations were entitled to protection and to social services. Those years thus saw the onset of a process, still going on, by which perceptions of the welfare system's functions, the role of private non-profit organizations and the relationships between these and the public authorities have undergone radical change.

A clear example of the increased importance attributed by the Italian political class to non-profit organizations is provided by the reform of savings banks and public banks. In 1990, the government began the privatization of these banks by dividing each of them into two entities: a company responsible for traditional banking activities and a foundation which was to act as the main owner of the bank. The reform process was completed in 1999 with Law Decree 153/1999, which was concerned almost exclusively with the role and governance of private foundations as non-profit organizations. Contrary to intentions in 1990, these foundations are now required to sell the property of their banks and to pursue socially useful ends. They must use the profits from their assets to support actions and projects in such typically non-profit areas as scientific research, education, promotion of the arts, health and social care. Interestingly, this outcome was not one of the initial purposes behind the privatization of saving and public banks. Rather, it came to the fore in the course of the decade amid growing awareness of the importance of the third sector and of the need to encourage its development.

However, recognition of the new organizational forms and of their social role did not suffice to ensure the consolidation of the third sector. This, in fact, was conditioned by the limited availability of funding for social services and by a widespread tradition of organizing the provision of social services through public units.

The Consolidation

Decisive, therefore, for consolidation of the new third sector organizations was reform of the public administration, which also began in the 1990s. Of particular importance were the changes made to the forms and modes of collaboration between the public authorities and third sector organizations. Both the laws on voluntary associations and on social cooperatives allowed the central and local authorities to contract for the production of services with these third sector organizations. But the Italian public administration, traditionally characterized by an authoritarian stance towards both citizens and the organizations of civil society, was not immediately able to establish effective partnership relations. In fact, the two laws did not define the form that the contracts should take, and they did not change the rules which already regulated contractual relations between private providers and public financers in the field of social services. These problems were addressed at the beginning of the 1990s by legislation to reform the public administration. Law no. 142 of 1990 allowed the municipalities to establish systematic relationships with private associations for the first time and recognized the right of citizens' associations to be consulted by the municipal administrations, to lodge appeals, to submit petitions and proposals, and to have access to administrative acts. In the same year, Law 241 authorized the municipalities and the provincial and regional administrations to grant subsidies and economic aid to public and private bodies engaged in the delivery of services of benefit to the community. Although the changes introduced by these laws were still not sufficient to engender stable partnership, they marked the beginning of an important cultural shift.

Following these legislative measures regarding both non-profit organizations and the public administration, the 1990s were a time in which the new third sector and a new culture of social policies were consolidated. Approval of the above laws by Parliament was followed by regional laws intended to support the development of the new organizations and to regulate their contractual relationships with the public authorities. A growing number of local authorities decided to finance third sector organizations, in the belief that one way to cope with growing demand for services was to help the independent organizations that provided them. At the same time they could avoid the expense of creating new public units.

Moreover, other organizational forms were recognized during the decade: for instance, in the year 2000, the 'social promotion associations' which regulate non-profit organizations that mainly promote social rights, solidarity, equal opportunities, the arts, sport and research.

Apart from these specific laws, increasing reference to third sector organizations was made by national and regional laws issued to implement and finance services for specific types of users (the handicapped, drug addicts, the elderly and so on). Undoubtedly the most important of these was the law enacted on 18 October 2000 to reform social policies (the Social Care Reform Act). Almost as if to wind up the debate and conclude the experience of the 1990s, this law radically overhauled Italy's social policies. It recognized the right of all citizens in difficulty to receive care and acknowledged the need to boost the provision of social services. For the first time in Italy, it created a national fund specifically intended to finance the supply of social services. Moreover, though confirming that the planning of social policies was still the task of the public authorities, it recognized the right of third sector organizations to take part in both the planning and the management of those policies.

Following these changes to the law and to social policy, the leaders of the third sector grew increasingly aware of the economic, social and political role of their organizations. This awareness gave rise to a proliferation of discussion, analysis and collaboration among third sector organizations and between them, the public authorities and the political parties. As a result, various second-level non-profit organizations were created which performed advocacy functions and produced services for their members (research, training, participation in European projects and so on). Efforts were also made to increase the political and institutional visibility of the sector as a whole. These efforts led to the creation in the mid-1990s of an organization with the function of representing the entire sector: the Third Sector Forum (Forum del Terzo Settore). As a result of lobbying, ten representatives of the organizations belonging to the Third Sector Forum have recently been appointed to the National Council on the Economy and Work (Consiglio Nazionale dell'Economia e del Lavoro).

However, this consolidation of the third sector has not been without its contradictions. Despite attempts over a number of years, Parliament and the government have not yet been able to approve a general law on the third sector as a whole. The legislative fragmentation caused by piecemeal recognition of individual organizational forms has led to a situation in which organizations engaged in similar activities receive different treatments and benefits. The persistence of a certain suspicion towards the new organizations among both government and opposition parties, combined with a need to maintain tax revenues at their previous levels, has prevented any systematic and incisive reform of taxation on third sector organizations, and the granting of tax relief comparable to that available in the United States and many European countries.

Finally, contracting-out practices developed within a still ill-defined legal framework, and without the adequate preparation of both the local authorities and the third sector organizations, has reduced the autonomy enjoyed by many of the latter. Particularly deleterious has been the proliferation of contracting-out practices designed solely (or largely) to minimize the cost of the service, with little concern shown for the quality of the services or the nature of the organizations involved.

The final outcome of this process of recognition and consolidation has been an increase both in the supply of social services, mainly financed by local authorities, and in the number of third sector organizations and of their employees. This growth has principally come about in the case of social cooperatives, whereas voluntary organizations have tended to consolidate their positions. Among social cooperatives, however, those which are exclusively composed of worker-members have had the largest increase in numbers because they are the easiest to set up. Since the third sector has increasingly come to depend on public financing, during the 1990s the mix of services supplied by third sector organizations has also changed: services designed to satisfy mainly public demand and consequently the needs of the median voter (mainly the elderly)[7] have grown at the expense of those groups affected by social exclusion which were served by third sector organizations at the end of the 1980s.

THE QUANTITATIVE DIMENSION OF THE THIRD SECTOR

There are no statistics and therefore no reliable analyses of the size and features of the third sector in Italy prior to the beginning of the 1990s. Because the sector was residual and on the brink of extinction, it inevitably failed to attract the interest of scholars and statistical institutes. The first studies on the third sector or on groups of similar organizations (especially voluntary ones and social cooperatives), as well as the first estimates of their size, were carried out during the 1990s. Since then the interest of researchers and knowledge about the size and features of the third sector have grown apace.

The first attempt to estimate the size of the third sector was made on the basis of national accounting and census data (Borzaga, 1991). It was concluded that, at the end of the 1980s, the sector employed around 310 000 people, 1.3 per cent of the total labour force. There had been a 38.9 per cent increase between 1980 and 1998, compared to only a 7.4 per cent increase in total employment.

The first direct survey (Barbetta, 1996) was conducted as part of the project coordinated by Johns Hopkins University (Salamon and Anheier, 1995) and made it possible not only to measure the size of the sector in Italy, and its articulation, but also to compare it with those of the other more developed countries. The survey estimated that, in the early 1990s, employment in the third sector amounted to 418 128 standard units of labour (1.8 per cent of total employment), in addition to which there were 302 950 full-time voluntary workers.

The ratio between current expenditure of third sector organizations and GDP was 1.9 per cent. Distribution by sector shows that more than half of the employees (61.9 per cent) worked in social services, education and research. Moreover, 35.3 per cent of all voluntary workers operated in social services.

International comparisons confirm that the Italian third sector was relatively undersized in terms of both employment and value added. With respect to both criteria, it ranks behind the USA, Japan and other Western European countries.

In 2000, the National Statistics Institute finally conducted the first census of Italian non-profit organizations, which showed the existence, at the end of 1999, of 221 412 active third sector organizations staffed by 630 000 paid workers (of whom around 51 000 were part-timers) and 3.2 million volunteers,[8] and with total earnings amounting to 38 billion euros. The census data enable verification of the arguments put forward thus far. They confirm that the development of the third sector in Italy is a recent phenomenon: 23.3 per cent of the organizations in the census had begun operations during the 1980s, and fully 55.2 per cent had been set up after 1990.

Of the more than 220 000 organizations surveyed, the majority used voluntary workers, while only 33 600 (15.2 per cent) also had paid employees. Most of them (91.3 per cent) were constituted as associations, the majority without legal personality. However, it was social cooperatives, foundations and the organizations run by religious orders which employed the majority of paid workers. In particular, social cooperatives, which numbered around 1000 at the beginning of the 1990s, totalled 4651 in 2000, employing more than 22 per cent of paid workers.

The organizations surveyed worked mainly in the sectors of culture, sport and recreation (63.1 per cent) and social services (18.7 per cent). However, this distribution changes radically if paid workers are considered. In this case, the sector with the largest percentage is social welfare (27.6 per cent), followed by health (22.8 per cent) and education (private schools) and research (18.9 per cent). These three components also account for around 60 per cent of earnings by the entire third sector. More generally, 87.1 per cent of the organizations surveyed were mainly financed by private resources, while only 12.9 per cent received their funding from public institutions. Sectoral differences are very marked in this case as well. Consistent with the information given in previous sections, in fact, 58.8 per cent of social cooperatives, almost all of which work in the social welfare sector, are mainly funded by public bodies.

Finally, the census data confirm the weakness of the third sector in the southern regions of the country, which comprise only 27.7 per cent of the total number of organizations in the census, compared to 51.1 per cent in the north. There are 29.4 organizations for every 1000 inhabitants in the south, compared to 44 in the northern regions and 42.3 in those of central Italy.

CONCLUSIONS

The evolution of the third sector in Italy, with its distinctive features, shows that a well-balanced society cannot do without these organizations, and that attempts to replace them with public ones may prove a failure. The re-emergence of the third sector in Italy, especially during the 1980s, has been due to the reaction of civil society against the rigidities and crisis of the public welfare system. It has come about in a context of, first, the hostility and, then, the suspicion, shown towards it by all the political parties and a large proportion of the public institutions.

The political and cultural significance of this re-emergence is much greater than suggested by the data on the organizations and their number of employees. The action of the new third sector organizations has in fact helped to alter the Italian welfare system, both by redirecting resources to social services and by bringing recognition of needs neglected by the public welfare system created between the 1950s and the 1970s. A constant endeavour to combine the production of social services with advocacy explains several of the features assumed by the third sector organizations which arose in the 1980s and 1990s, most notably the emphasis given to the involvement of stakeholders and to forms of democratic management. Insistence on these organizational aspects has helped renew the sector, which today is tied much less closely to the Catholic Church and much more closely to civil society. Its communitarian dimension is more accentuated, and it addresses the political system on an equal footing, even though a large part of its resources is of public origin.

Nevertheless, the evolution of the Italian third sector is still far from complete. Numerous changes are still in progress, and one cannot exclude further shifts whereby the sector loses some of its autonomy, ending up as the executor of decisions taken by the public administration. The outcome of this evolution will depend on the maturity and intelligence of both the political forces and the leadership of the third sector organizations.

NOTES

1. This classification remains valid even if the distinctions among these institutions are not always clear-cut. In fact, there may be non-profit organizations which pursue aims both mutual and public, or for-profit enterprises which pursue explicitly social goals.
2. As economic theory has done with reference to the market and government, the concept of 'failure' can be used to denote situations in which each of these institutions is unable to guarantee satisfactory levels of efficiency.
3. This undervaluation is demonstrated by the fact that family work has never been included in the national accounts.
4. This code is still in force.
5. Subsequent government circulars sharpened this distinction by stating that individual social cooperatives may not undertake both activities.
6. The fact that organizations in the Italian third sector have opted to become cooperatives and associations, instead of other well known forms, highlights the differences between the European and the American models. From a theoretical perspective, Italian experience seems to demonstrate that, in creating trust-based relations (Hansmann, 1980; Ortmann and Schlesinger 1997), the non-profit distribution constraint can be replaced by other organizational characteristics, such as stakeholder participation and democratic management. Italian experience also shows that analysis of the non-profit sector should pay closer attention to the role of 'non-profit entrepreneurs' (Young, 1983) and of the worker's behaviour (Borzaga and Mittone 1997).
7. The role of the median voter in influencing public goods provision and the development of non-profit organizations is discussed in Weisbrod (1977, 1988). See also Kingma (1997).
8. These figures are not comparable with those given by Barbetta (1996), which refer to the early 1990s. The latter show, for both paid and voluntary workers, the units of full-time labour, while ISTAT surveyed the number of people employed, independently of the employment relationship or the number of voluntary hours worked per week.

REFERENCES

Allio, R. (2000), 'Le origini delle società di mutuo soccorso in Italia', in V. Zamagni (ed.), *Povertà e innovazioni istituzionali in Italia. Dal Medioevo ad oggi*, Bologna: Il Mulino.

Barbetta, G.P. (ed.) (1996), *Senza scopo di lucro. Dimensioni economiche, storia, legislazione e politiche del settore nonprofit in Italia*, Bologna: Il Mulino.

Borzaga, C. (1991), 'The Italian Nonprofit Sector. An Overview of an Undervalued Reality', *Annals of Public and Cooperative Economics*, 62 (4).

Borzaga, C. and L. Mittone (1997), 'The Multi-stakeholders versus the Nonprofit Organisation', discussion paper no. 7, University of Trento.

Farrell-Vinay, G. (2000), 'Le legislazioni preunitarie sulle opere pie e la legge del 1862', in V. Zamagni (ed.), *Povertà e innovazioni istituzionali in Italia. Dal Medioevo ad oggi*, Bologna: Il Mulino.

Gheza Fabbri, L. (2000) 'Le società di mutuo soccorso italiane nel contesto europeo fra XIX e XX secolo', in V. Zamagni (ed.), *Povertà e innovazioni istituzionali in Italia. Dal Medioevo ad oggi*, Bologna: Il Mulino.

Hansmann, H. (1980) 'The Role of Nonprofit Enterprise', *The Yale Law Journal*, April.

ISTAT (2001), *Primo Censimento delle Istituzioni e imprese nonprofit*, Rome: Istituto Centrale di Statistica.

Kingma, B.R. (1997), 'Public Good Theories of the Non-profit Sector: Weisbrod revisited', *Voluntas*, 8 (2).

Ortmann, A. and M. Schlesinger (1997), 'Trust, Repute and the Role of Non-profit Enterprise', *Voluntas*, 8 (2).

Perlmutter, T. (1991), 'Italy: Why No Voluntary Sector?', in R. Wuthnow (ed.), *Between States and Markets. The Voluntary Sector in Comparative Perspective*, Princeton: Princeton University Press.

Preti, A. and C. Venturoli (2000), 'Fascismo e Stato sociale', in V. Zamagni (ed.), *Povertà e innovazioni istituzionali in Italia. Dal Medioevo ad oggi*, Bologna: Il Mulino.

Roberti, P. (2000), 'Analisi dei modelli ed obiettivi della politica sociale italiana attuale', in V. Zamagni (ed.), *Povertà e innovazioni istituzionali in Italia. Dal Medioevo ad oggi*, Bologna: Il Mulino.

Salamon, L.M. (1987), 'Of Market Failure, Voluntary Failure and Third-Party Government: Toward a New Theory of Government. Nonprofit Relations in the Modern Welfare State', *Journal of Voluntary Action Research*, 16 (1–2).

Salamon, L.M. and H.K. Anheier (1995), *The Emerging Sector: The Nonprofit Sector in Comparative Perspective. An Overview*, Baltimore: The Johns Hopkins University Institute for Policy Studies.

Weisbrod, B. (1977), *The Voluntary Nonprofit Sector*, Lexington, MA: D.C. Heath.

Weisbrod, B. (1988), *The Nonprofit Economy*, Cambridge, MA: Harvard University Press.

Young, D.R. (1983), *If Not For Profit, For What?*, Lexington, MA: D.C. Heath.

Zamagni, V. (ed.) (2000), *Povertà e innovazioni istituzionali in Italia. Dal Medioevo ad oggi*, Bologna: Il Mulino.

3. The development and future of the social economy in Sweden

Victor Pestoff

This chapter is the Swedish contribution to a collective effort to define and delimit the social economy in Europe. Sweden is the sole example of a country with a universal welfare state and a Social Democratic welfare state regime included in these efforts. As such it presents some unique features of the European social economy, including a large public sector, a strong etatist tradition and a weak but growing role for third sector providers of personal social services. However, it is sometimes wrongly assumed that Sweden lacks a thriving third sector: nothing could be farther from the truth.

Ever since the days of de Tocqueville ([1832] 1996) and Bryce (1888), Americans have taken pride in themselves as a 'nation of joiners' (Key [1942] 1958; Truman [1951] 1971; Zetterberg, 1961; Lipset, 1963). However, by the 1970s, it became apparent that the highest levels of membership in voluntary associations were not found in North America, but in the Scandinavian/Nordic countries. A comparison of the results of diverse election studies in the 1960s and 1970s ranked Sweden, Denmark, Norway, Canada and Finland as the five countries with the greatest propensity to join voluntary associations, all well ahead of the United States (Pestoff, 1977, Table 6.1.A, p.65). Four-fifths of the Swedish electorate claimed one or more memberships in a voluntary association in 1971 (ibid.). In 2000, some 30 years later, nine out of ten Swedish adults claim one or more memberships, a slight decline of 2 per cent from eight years earlier (SCB, 2001, Table 1). Thus Sweden is truly a 'nation of joiners'.

However, early American research on voluntary associations often excluded membership of churches and trade unions, on the grounds that it was not truly voluntary. One could be born into or forced by 'closed shop' laws to join these types of organizations (Babchuck and Edwards, 1965; Babchuck and Booth, 1969). More recent American research on the non-profit sector excludes cooperatives, mutual aid societies and so on, on the basis that they distribute a limited part of the surplus to their members and therefore do not conform to the non-distribution constraint. Both these tendencies underreport memberships in American organizations but, if applied to Europe, would exclude many social economy organizations.

Moreover, the exclusion of any type of organization in international quantitative projects with a comparative aim produces a skewed sample of the organizational landscape and leads to biased comparisons. The point of making comparisons is not only to look for similarities but also to explain the differences between countries. Thus, in the Johns Hopkins comparative project on non-profit organizations, some NPOs which have never distributed a surplus to their members, such as the Swedish building and tenant cooperatives, were excluded 'for reasons of comparability' (Lundström and Wijkström, 1997). But this excludes nearly a third of all multiple family dwellings in Sweden and all the members and resources associated with cooperative housing since 1925. This is just as questionable as the earlier practice of excluding church and trade union membership in US studies and does not promote reliable and unbiased comparative results.

In spite of this, the voluntary sector in Sweden proved similar to that found in the other western industrialized countries in terms of membership, activity and economy (Salamon et al., 1996). However, the Swedish voluntary sector was less dependent on public support and more self-sufficient than in most other countries (ibid.). What really makes it different in Sweden is its distinctive structure: membership-based and democratically governed popular movements that are mostly a result of a combination of unique historical and political factors in the Scandinavian countries. The Swedish voluntary sector may be weak in areas like health care, higher education and social activities, but it is strong in sports, leisure and culture activities, and in adult education (Rothstein, 2001), as well as housing cooperatives in multiple family dwellings and of course the labour market.

This contribution begins by discussing the development of non-profit organizations, popular movements and the social economy from a Swedish perspective. Then it considers some of the major challenges facing the welfare state. Finally, some recent developments promoting the potential expansion of the social economy, both locally and regionally, are mentioned briefly. On the basis of this, certain conclusions are reached about the future of the social economy in Sweden.

VOLUNTARY ASSOCIATIONS, POPULAR MOVEMENTS AND THE SOCIAL ECONOMY

The concepts of voluntary associations and non-profit organizations are not widely used in Sweden and the neighbouring Scandinavian countries. Rather the concept of *folkrörelse* or popular movement is used, but this refers to a different type of organization with quite different historical roots. The concept of popular movement is a historical category that lacks legal status but usually connotes membership-based and democratically governed social movements. However, it should be noted that the Swedish concept of *ideell förening* refers to the legal status of organizations promoting non-lucrative goals, and perhaps comes closest to the US concept of non-profit organization. Many popular movements register as *ideell förening*, a status which distinguishes them both from an *aktiebolag* or incorporated firm and an *ekonomisk förening* or economic association, which is the form normally chosen by cooperatives. The latter two legal forms carry no personal financial responsibilities for their board members for debts incurred by the organization, while board members of an *ideell förening* have full responsibility for all such debts. Therefore many popular movements that produce goods and services prefer to take the legal status of *ekonomisk förening*, while those with limited commercial activities retain the legal status of *ideell förening*.

The concept of social economy, as generally used and understood in Europe, includes organizations that have open membership and are democratically run. The principle of one member one vote applies to their internal decision making. Normally cooperatives, mutuals and associations are included in this category. Further distinctions exist between established and new types of organizations belonging to the social economy. Together the consumer, building and tenant and agriculture cooperative movements comprise the established or old social economy organizations in Sweden. They only provide sporadic or intermittent support for the new social service cooperative movement. The newer adherents often have highly visible and socially relevant motives or aims for providing services to their members or to special client groups. They also represent needs not currently catered to by the public sector, such as parent cooperative day care services, cooperative elder care and so on.

Social economy is a new concept that lacks a natural translation into Swedish. As a new member of the European Union, the Swedish government initiated a parliamentary or official investigation of the concept in order to stand on firm ground when applying for EU funds or projects related to the social economy. The 95 page report of this parliamentary committee summarizes Swedish and international experience of the usage of this concept and concludes with a proposal for an official Swedish definition of the term 'social economy'. Thus Sweden is now the first country in the European Union with an officially sanctioned definition of the social economy. This report weighed various aspects of the social economy and mentioned various segments of it. However, the definition it proposed is more akin to 'non-governmental organizations' or NGOs than to 'non-profit organizations' or NPOs. Unfortunately, it fails to include the more specifically economic aspects of the activities of such organizations. But the term 'social economy' is often understood in Sweden as the economic and/or social activities of popular movements.

Popular movements in Scandinavia differ from voluntary associations in most other countries, in several respects (Klausen and Selle, 1996; Rothstein, 2001). First, they were established and run as democratic organizations for ordinary citizens, rather than exclusive clubs of the well-to-do. Second, although they had strong and active local branches for mass participation, they are also national movements that effectively coordinate the activity of their local branches. Third, popular movements considered themselves protest movements against the bureaucrats, clerics, aristocrats and capitalists that dominated Sweden in the nineteenth and early twentieth century. The very concept of movement implies social change due to movement from below. Fourth, popular movements were not single organizations, but often whole networks of organizations. So the labour movement not only comprised trade unions and the Social Democratic Party, but also organizations for consumers' cooperatives, lodgers, building and tenant cooperatives, pensioners, scouts and adult education. A similar network of popular movements developed among the rural agricultural population. This included an independent political party, formerly the Agrarian but now the Centre Party, a wide network of agricultural/farmers' cooperatives and banks, and folk high schools for promoting the social and cultural identity of the rural population.

Fifth, popular movements that both protested against existing conditions and promoted self-help were often opposed to middle and upper-class charitable organizations. Sixth, a corporatist pattern of lay representation on the executive bodies of public administration boards, initiated at the beginning of the twentieth century, incorporated representatives of many major popular movements. This not only provided them with privileged access to policy making as well as legitimacy in the eyes of the elite, but also promoted popular influence over public policy prior to the breakthrough of universal suffrage. This pattern of corporatist lay representation persisted until the early 1990s. The privileged access, legitimacy and influence in turn helped to set the tone for the relationship between popular movements and the state in terms of cooperation and collaboration, rather than the competition and conflict found in many other countries. Finally, popular movements in Sweden are also considered important schools for democracy and organizational training, which helped the transition to democracy.

The uniqueness of the third sector in Scandinavia has to do with the way in which, historically, it grew out of, and was a part of, broad and politically significant social movements. At the same time it became an integrated part of the development of the welfare state, making the Scandinavian countries the prototype of 'state-friendly' societies. The Scandinavian countries share the rise of popular movements, in particular the labour movement and the Social Democratic Party, the peasants' movement and their political allies, the Agrarian or now Centre Party (Klausen and Selle, 1996). The third sector in the Scandinavian countries has played a crucial and distinctive role both in nation building (Rokkan [1967] 1970) and in the growth and development of the modern welfare states. Thus the development of modern Scandinavian society from the mid-1800s is closely linked to the growth of social movements and numerous associations organized in and around them. Therefore this period has been called the 'Age of Associations' in Scandinavian history (ibid.). In particular, the development of the agrarian and labour movements is related to the rise of two distinct new social classes and their gradual integration into society. These two social movements have had a major impact on political, economic, social and cultural developments in the Scandinavian countries for more than a hundred years.

The role of the peasants' movement is unique in the Scandinavian countries because of its large impact on political developments via independent political parties, its economic importance via the agrarian cooperatives and its social, cultural and ideological importance via folk high schools. It has also maintained close relations with the temperance, religious and sports movements. This clearly weakened the base of the Conservative Party in Scandinavia. These agrarian parties played an important role in the struggle for parliamentary democracy in the late nineteenth and early twentieth centuries, as well as in the 'historical compromises' with the Social Democrats during the 1930s that led to the development of the modern welfare state (ibid., pp.103–4).

The second pillar, the labour movement, developed alongside the peasants' movement from the end of the nineteenth century. The workers, who met great resistance in the beginning, organized themselves into political parties, trade unions, consumer cooperatives, building and tenant cooperatives, a scout and youth movement, a pensioners organization and a number of cultural associations, including temperance and religious organizations as well as folk high school and adult education organizations and even a burial society or cooperative. They eventually became the dominant political force and ruling party in all the Scandinavian countries in the twentieth century (ibid., p.105).

In addition, several other unique historical and political factors are also important for understanding the development of the welfare state in Sweden and its relations with popular movements and voluntary associations. First, the Social Democratic Party (SDP) ruled Sweden alone or in coalition with other parties during most of the formative period in the development of the universal welfare state. The SDP was only in opposition for two periods during the post World War II era, that is, between 1976 and 1982, and again between 1991 and 1994. This unusually long rule has provided the party with unparalleled influence on the type of welfare state developed in Sweden and its relations with popular movements and voluntary associations. Second, Sweden lacked a strong independent religious movement like the Catholic Church which provided the backbone of many continental welfare states (Esping-Andersen,

1996). It also lacks the concept and institution of subsidiarity that are so important in Germany and which assign a clear role to voluntary associations. Third, the Swedish Lutheran Church only separated from the state in 2001.

Fourth, unlike most other European countries, Sweden also lacked a strong Christian Democratic movement and/or political party until quite recently. In fact, the Christian Democratic Party did not clear the minimal 4 per cent threshold necessary to enter the *Riskdag* until the 1991 General Election. Taken together, these unique historical and political factors meant that there were no clear independent religious champions of individual charity, benevolent activities or subsidiarity which are found in many other European countries. Thus there was no effective opposition to the dominance of the more universal and collectivist approach promoted by the popular movements and the Red/Green (SDP/Agrarian Party) coalition, during and after World War II. Rather, the Confederation of Swedish Employers (SAF) served as the main force challenging the extension of the universal, tax-based welfare state for economic reasons and frequently called for its privatization during the 1990s (Pestoff, 1995, 2001).

HISTORICAL DEVELOPMENT OF THE RELATIONS BETWEEN VOLUNTARY ASSOCIATIONS, POPULAR MOVEMENTS AND THE SWEDISH WELFARE STATE

Lundström and Wijkström (1997) maintain that there are four main periods in the development of the Swedish voluntary associations and popular movements. (I would hasten to add a fifth and possibly even a sixth period.) They include (a) the period prior to the emergence of voluntary associations (up to the beginning of the 1800s); (b) the period of emergence of the voluntary sector (1810–70); (c) the period of industrialization and development of popular movements (1870–1930s); and (d) the period of the emerging welfare state (1940–70). The fifth period is the period of new social movements and a growing welfare mix (1970–2001), and we are now perhaps witnessing the initiation of a sixth period, the introduction of a new (American) non-profit category of organizations for the production of health care and education (2002–?).

In the *first period*, prior to the Reformation, organized charity and poor relief were a matter for the Church. Then, after the Reformation, when the Church became a national concern, the responsibility for poor relief followed the ownership of church properties and became a matter for the Swedish Crown. In the *second period* the early 'societies' or associations were not open or democratic organizations but an exclusive expression of the elite of the emerging capitalist society. Many of them were social clubs and were oriented to charitable activities, often working closely with local poor relief boards.

From a historical viewpoint, in areas like poor relief there was no clear boundary between the state or municipalities and the voluntary sector; rather 'intimate mutual cooperation' can best describe the fight against poverty in the early nineteenth century, particularly among the urban proletariat. Later one can note a transition of voluntary social work to more professional and bureaucratic modes that gradually also came to characterize municipal social care. When many voluntary charitable organizations later became marginal, one main reason was that the material grounds for their activities had changed so radically. The periodic waves of poverty had been replaced as the conditions of the urban proletariat slowly improved, so the reason for the marginalization of charitable organizations was the naturally diminishing need for their services, as poor relief and child welfare in towns became a professional municipal undertaking (Lundström, 1996, p.131).

Sweden experienced late but rapid industrialization, and also late democratization, compared to many other European countries. Sweden dissolved the guild societies in the middle of the nineteenth century (1846). The freedom of association was introduced a few years later (1864). These two developments interacted and overlapped in such a fashion as to reinforce the collective efforts of many ordinary people with very few resources, privileges, rights or alternatives and who were not able to organize themselves earlier. Thus, in the *third period*, we find the growth and development of 'popular movements' in the latter part of the nineteenth century, which often had an anti-establishment emphasis. The labour movement (which included both the trade unions and the Social Democratic Party), the temperance movement and the non-conformist churches were all against one or more aspects of the privileges of the establishment. Many popular movements and their Social Democratic allies rejected established ideas about poor relief as an expression of class oppression and also viewed charity as the poor being forced by circumstances to accept gifts from the rich. Such views still have strong support in certain segments of Swedish society today. Rather than relying on charity, the popular movements developed and put into practice ideas of self-help, which decades later became the nucleus of general welfare state programmes, such as sickness and life insurance, unemployment insurance and so on.

Popular movements were all mass organizations, based on ideas of open membership and democratic control. They actively challenged the existing society and helped to change it in a more democratic direction. They gained enormous legitimacy from their early years and are still considered by many today as synonymous with the democratization of Sweden. They are also considered by some as an expression of collectivism and perhaps also socialism. They became important as schools for organizational and democratic training for the growing working class, long before universal suffrage. They encouraged their members to learn to read and write and also taught them how to run meetings, write resolutions, argue for their proposals and promote their interests in a democratic fashion. The leaders of many popular movements became local, regional and national political leaders at the turn of the nineteenth century (Ambjörnsson, 1988). Newer popular movements grew in the wake of their predecessors, and often followed their example in terms of open membership and democratic decision making. They included the consumer cooperatives, the building and tenant cooperatives, the farmer cooperatives, the women's movement, trade unions for salaried employees and persons with academic credentials, the sports movement, the pensioners movement, the environmental movement, and so on.

The Social Democratic Party and the trade unions, with support from the Liberal Party, were the major political forces promoting universal suffrage and breaking the power monopoly of the Conservatives and the employers. Sweden adopted near universal suffrage as late as the 1921 *Riksdag* election. By 1932, the Social Democratic Party was the largest party, and it formed a minority government for a brief time. Then, when it returned to power in 1936, it formed a coalition with the Agrarian Party (now the Centre Party), referred to as the Red/Green coalition. Both of these parties were and are still known as the 'popular movement parties' (Pestoff, 1977). Their most solid base for many decades comprised the rank-and-file members of the trade union movement and the agricultural cooperatives respectively. These two parties governed Sweden together from 1936 until 1957, but also with the other noncommunist parties in a Grand Coalition during the World War II period. Thus these two popular movement parties together helped to transform Swedish society in a fundamental way and to plan and develop the welfare state that makes Sweden one of the leading nations in providing universal social services and social insurance on the basis of citizenship or residence (Esping-Andersen, 1996; Stephens, 1996).

In the *fourth period* the social policies adopted by the national government during this Red/Green coalition were often based on the demands, activities and programmes promoted by popular movements. These were years of great scarcity due to the Great Depression, World War II, and the postwar reconstruction. First and foremost, the basic needs of ordinary citizens and collective means for providing them with security were promoted by popular movements and the government. The ambition of the Social Democratic/Agrarian Party coalition governments during the post-World War II period was to provide all citizens with certain basic social services and to insure them against economic loss due to sickness, unemployment, old age and so on.

Based on a labour movement ideology of self-help, the Social Democrats supported the development of social insurance based on solidarity between equals. The combined impact of the Depression in the 1930s and the Red–Green parliamentary coalition in the *Riksdag* laid the groundwork for an active crisis policy of state intervention in social and economic matters. Popular movements and non-profit organizations promoted many social reforms and helped to elevate social problems to the national agenda, which then resulted in their being assumed by the state and provided by the public sector. In many areas where the voluntary associations had previously been active, state subsidies were only available for municipal services. Such services were directed towards broad groups of citizens. Motives given for governmental intervention were that the importance of the activities was such that their execution needed to be guaranteed by the state, that such services could now be made more widely available, and that quality and professionalism could be better controlled in the public sector. Thus many services were turned into rights and made available to most citizens. The voluntary sector did not oppose these developments, but on the contrary often supported and championed an expansion of government involvement. This can be seen as an extension of the process of integration and cooperation between the voluntary and public sectors which began as early as the nineteenth century, and it reflects a strong tradition of friendly relations between these two sectors (Lundström, 1996, pp.133–5).

This served to eclipse the purpose and activities of many voluntary associations based on charity from the period prior to the advent of the welfare state. However, some voluntary associations still provide services today, and in some cases they are financed by public funds. They include limited elements of health care, education, recreation and leisure activities, sports, and so on. They are discussed more below. In addition there are various types of foundations in Sweden, but they comprise solely autonomous property administered to accomplish specific objectives. They are seldom involved in welfare services. In general, voluntary associations and foundations have not only become marginalized by the development of a universal welfare state, but they are also isolated from the major promoters of a universal welfare state and the popular movements associated with it.

In the *fifth period* we note that new social movements based on new or unmet social needs, identity, socializing or recreation, rather than class, provide the basis for growth of new social movements and for a growing welfare mix (Evers, 1995). As previously noted, for historical and political reasons popular movements cooperated closely with the state in the development of universal welfare rights and services for all inhabitants. The corporative channel provided popular movements with influence and resulted in collaboration and cooperation between them and the state rather than conflict and competition over the delivery of social services. The space available for independent initiative in terms of providing social services or health care has been restricted by active state provision, and universal provision has margin-alized the need for and role of charitable organizations. However, in some well-defined areas, voluntary associations still play today an important role in providing some services, such as education, health care and social services. As regards education, they are mostly found in adult education and residential colleges or *folkhögskolor*, and in study circles. Also several of the national education organizations are part of popular movement networks, including the labour movement, agricultural movement, sport movement, and so on. In health care they are usually found in small niches such as epilepsy, tuberculo-sis, cancer (Lundström and Wijkström, 1997) and diabetes (Werkö, 2002). In the later years of the twentieth century, client organizations also began to develop for newer health care needs, such as those for persons afflicted by HIV/AIDS (Walden Laing and Pestoff, 1997; Walden Laing, 2001).

In terms of meeting new social needs, such as providing advice and shelter to battered women, services were initiated by a variety of women's organiza-tions in the 1980s. Such groups exist in most parts of Sweden, and today nearly half of the municipalities have also established some kind of public help activities for women. Provision of shelter for the growing number of homeless is an activity taken on by various religious groups, including the Salvation Army. Even prior needs like caring for alcoholics are met in a new way by the spread of Alcoholics Anonymous groups. Handicap organizations provide an example of a strong client organization, but they have negative atti-tudes towards charity, and prefer to emphasize the rights of handicapped persons to work, housing and even personal assistance. Their demands are met by a growing mix of public and third sector efforts, including the Independent Living movement. Several of these examples demonstrate the international spread of successful models from the USA.

Non-municipal child care services also provide an illustration of new or unmet social needs. In the late 1970s and early 1980s, when demand for child care services largely outstripped the public supply for many years running, the Social Democrats reluctantly conceded the right of parents to form their own pre-school child care cooperatives and receive a public subsidy covering about 85 per cent of the expenses. This put them on a similar economic footing with the municipal child care services. Then, in 1991, all restrictions were removed concerning the legal status of the provider of pre-school services, and private for-profit providers could receive public subsidies for their day care services. Today 15 per cent of all pre-school children are enrolled in non-municipal day care facilities (Pestoff and Strandbrink, 2002). The major providers of such services are in fact the parent cooperatives, while worker cooperatives and voluntary associations are also significant providers (Pestoff, 1998).

However, the popular movements, established cooperative movements and trade union movements do not have much in common today with the new social movements or with the old voluntary associations in terms of their stance towards the developing welfare state. The voluntary associations are not generally viewed as active defenders or promoters of an expanded welfare state, while some of the popular movements still are, at least occasionally. In particular, both the blue-collar trade unions, under the umbrella of *Landsorganisationen* (LO), and the white-collar trade unions, under the mantel of *Tjänstemannens Central Organisationen* (TCO), actively support a universal welfare state, while calling for changes or reforms to make it more in tune with major social and demographic changes in the 1990s. For example, TCO in its new social policy programme, 'The Welfare State 2.1, Developing Welfare', reiterates its support for a general tax-based welfare state (TCO, 2001). But it also draws attention to some of its shortcomings in terms of the amount and quality of welfare services. Among other things it points to the decrease in spending for health services during the 1990s and to the ceilings for public expenses that have become part of the budget process since 1997. Now any increase in one area must be matched by decreases in another. The OECD has warned that this will serve to amplify the ups and downs of normal economic cycles. TCO also warns that it may impair the high level of public support for general welfare programmes (ibid.).

Some of the popular movements associated with the Social Democrats in the earlier period, such as the housing cooperatives and labour unions, continue to play major economic and social roles for the well-being of their members, while others, such as the consumer and agricultural cooperatives have been transformed into big businesses. For example, at the beginning of the twentieth century, the consumer cooperatives played an important role in breaking the hold of local factory magnates on the sale of daily goods, and even in breaking the production monopoly on basic staples, such as margarine. However, growing urbanization, industrialization and international competition have diminished the importance of such activities for the well-being of ordinary citizens. Moreover, through a process of extensive amalgamations starting in the 1960s, the consumer cooperatives grew into large bureaucratic organizations, well beyond the reach of ordinary members (Pestoff, 1991).

In 1992 the Swedish consumer cooperative movement changed its legal status from that of an economic association to a limited company, and with it eliminated the last remnants of democratic control. The Swedish consumer cooperative movement has thereby become an ordinary commercial wholesale and retail chain (Pestoff, 1999a). Then, in 2001, the Danish, Norwegian and Swedish consumer cooperative movements amalgamated to create *Co-op Norden*, in order to protect their market shares in the respective Nordic countries against foreign competitors. The agricultural cooperative movement has also become 'big business' and is now involved in a series of amalgamations in neighbouring countries, hoping thereby to become an important actor in the

European Union. Thus both these popular movements have been transformed into huge commercial conglomerates, operating successfully in several countries, but far removed from their origin as popular movements that promote social values, and that are democratically run.

The two major building and tenant cooperatives, HSB and Riksbyggen, established in 1924 and 1930, respectively, also played an important social role, by building low-priced but good-quality housing for working class inhabitants (Pestoff, 1991). They contributed to resolving problems brought on by the major demographic changes and urbanization of Sweden and to the urban renewal of major urban areas in the 1960s and 1970s. They are still democratically run by their members and continue to expand and to provide high-standard housing, but not always as low-priced as many young people would like today. HSB also supports a general tax-based welfare state. Moreover, it has engaged itself in the field of home care for the elderly in recent years and has recently expressed concern about the future of public services and the welfare state, owing to increasing marketization of services, and the threat this poses to third sector alternatives (*Dagens Nyheter*, 2001, 1 September).

Also the trade unions have traditionally played and still play an important role when it comes to providing unemployment insurance. Unemployment insurance in Sweden is primarily organized and administered by the trade unions themselves, through separate organizations known as an *Erkänd arbetslöshetskassa* or 'Recognized Unemployment Fund'. Employees may opt out of membership in a trade union, but non-members cannot be excluded from the 'Recognized Unemployment Fund'. Many argue that union control of unemployment insurance provides the unions with strong arguments in recruiting new members. Membership is indeed very high in Sweden, with nearly 85 per cent of the labour force belonging to a trade union. When unemployment began to exceed 5 per cent in the early 1990s, some groups began to demand that unemployment insurance should be taken over by the state, to avoid any unnecessary links between the unions and their unemployment insurance. In particular, the employers and groups close to them demanded this. As a compromise, a public unemployment insurance was initiated, but only for those not covered by the union-managed schemes.

FUTURE CONSIDERATIONS: TRANSFORMING THE WELFARE STATE IN SCANDINAVIA AND SHIFTS IN THE WELFARE MIX

Both the political and financial constraints on the Swedish welfare state during the 1990s have fundamentally changed the relationship between the state and its citizens, and this change has important implications for the role of the third sector and social economy. Privatization, the 'Freedom of Choice Revolution', brought about by radical reorientation of politics during the Bildt coalition government (1991–4) and the austerity policy pursued by the subsequent social democratic governments (1994–9) have already resulted in sweeping changes in the Swedish welfare state. The current crisis of the welfare state also has its origins in far-reaching ideological, political, financial, economic and demographic changes in Sweden during the 1990s (Pestoff, 1999b). In addition, the political struggle between the central government and the City of Stockholm and some other non-socialist municipalities in Stockholm County illustrate the risk of 'the good being the enemy of the best'. The third sector and social economy easily gets lost in the mega battle between those supporting a monopoly of public provision and their opponents who want to privatize as much as possible and as quickly as possible.

One important element of the Swedish social model so far has been its public nature: the responsibility of ensuring social solidarity and cohesion lies with the government; public funds, public schemes and public bureaucracies are the main pillars of the welfare state edifice. However, mass unemployment during the 1990s has not only been a major economic, financial, political and social burden on continued public provision of major social services. It has also challenged the legitimacy of public provision of social services and opened the way for privatization and contracting out of these services owing to sharp cutbacks in public budgets and a notable deterioration in the quality of public services in many important areas. Thus it is necessary to ask if monopoly public provision can be maintained in core areas, or whether there are alternatives which might be more effective. Such crucial questions are often discussed in terms of a changing 'welfare mix' between the various spheres and actors involved in social policy: not only the state and the market, but also the third sector, regarded by many as a sphere which could play a more prominent role in the future of Swedish social protection. The debate on changing Swedish company law reflects this.

Three Challenges Facing the Welfare State in Sweden

As a result of the changes in the 1990s, the Swedish welfare state now faces at least three major challenges to the continued public provision of personal social services. The first is a threat to the quality of the services provided, due primarily to the rapid deterioration of the work environment of the front-line staff providing such services. This is a result of sharp cutbacks in public funding and the numerous reorganizations of the public sector in the 1990s. In addition, the shortage of work experienced in the 1990s will soon be transformed into a shortage of skilled workers in the twenty-first century. In the future, competition for workers will not only exist between public and private employers in Sweden, but between all types of employers in most countries in Europe. The second is the challenge posed by shifts in the welfare mix, and in particular the changing role of the third sector. Contracting out threatens to transform some third sector organizations from advocates and/or innovators into professionalized service providers, thereby reducing their internal democracy. The third challenge is the growing democracy deficit stemming from changes in basic political institutions in the 1950s and 1970s and the rapid economic and political internationalization or globalization in the 1990s, following Sweden's membership of the European Union and probable membership of the European Monetary Union. This may also erode public support for a universal welfare state.

The dramatic increase in 1998 and 1999 of the costs of sick leave and disability led the government to initiate a top level investigation into these highly negative developments. The first report came in the autumn of 2000 (Regeringskansliet, 2000). After a general overview of recent developments in working life stress in the 1990s, it devotes a special chapter to personal care and education. It notes that stress-related ill-health in the public sector is found at all levels of government, from the top to the bottom.

This is explained primarily in terms of far-reaching budget reductions, as well as numerous reorganizations during the 1990s (ibid.).

The economy of the counties and municipalities was hard pressed during the 1990s, owing to extensive budget reductions (ibid.). For example, the National School Board notes that the costs per pupil in elementary schools decreased by 9 per cent between 1991 and 1998; and by 1997 resources for teaching were only 80 per cent of what they were in 1991. Thus the ratio of teachers per 100 pupils decreased from 9.1 in 1991 to only 7.5 in 1998 (ibid., p.65). Since many of the activities in care and education are staff-intensive, such savings and reorganizations have direct effects on the staff and their work environment (ibid., p.61). In these areas of employment, women are in the majority, so these negative changes have special implications for women's work environment.

Unless the working life and work environment of the staff providing personal social services are rapidly and dramatically enriched and improved it will be hard to attract the qualified and motivated staff necessary to meet the growing need for such services. As a consequence, quality-conscious clients will flee publicly provided services, choosing instead private for-profit ones where they can top up the minimum provided by service checks in order to obtain an acceptable standard. The staff will be even less motivated to provide good quality services and so on. However, one way to improve the quality of personal social services and to attract the qualified staff necessary to provide them in the future is to enrich the working life of the staff and to improve their work environment. Research on social enterprises in Sweden shows that the staff in social enterprises were more motivated by gaining control over their working conditions and improving them than by instrumental rewards (Pestoff, 1998).

Second, one way to ensure the survival of the third sector organizations and the social economy is to promote their role as advocates of various interests and/or innovators of new services not currently provided by the public sector or the market. This strategic goal is, however, conflicting with the aim of giving the third sector and social economy a greater role in the provision of publicly financed personal social services. Contracting out the provision of personal social services to third sector organizations may, in fact, contribute to transforming them into routinized service providers. These conflicts need to be explored more closely, and a better understanding of what social values various types of third sector providers actually promote is necessary in order to evaluate their contribution more accurately. Social accounting provides a good tool for developing such an understanding.

Third, the growing democracy deficit in Sweden threatens to undermine both democracy and support for major political projects and publicly financed personal social services. Sweden experienced two waves of amalgamations by municipalities, in the 1950s and again in the 1970s, resulting in a decrease in the number of municipalities from approximately 2500 to merely 290 today. They were initiated by the central government and based on proposals for more rational organization of the social services provided to citizens. However, the creation of larger local units of government eliminated many of the part-time, non-professional politicians, and the number of elected officials decreased dramatically, from about 200 000 in 1950 to fewer than 50 000 at the end of the amalgamation process.

More recently, the growing use of market models for providing local services accentuated this democracy deficit. During the past decade an additional 9000 non-professional or free-time politicians have been relieved of their responsibilities; decisions have been delegated to local bureaucrats; purchaser–seller models have taken over a growing part of public services and contracting out to private for-profit suppliers has increased dramatically. Moreover, municipal limited companies have restricted both public accountability and their employees' possibilities of informing the public about their operations. Thus empowering citizens as co-producers of some of the major personal social services they demand will help to offset this democracy deficit and to rejuvenate the dwindling stock of social capital. It will provide citizens with a clear stake in the collective provision of personal social services and with an active role in ensuring the quality of such services. It will legitimate the continued provision of personal social services by collective and political channels, rather than individual market ones.

Over the past two decades public support for general welfare programmes was strong and stable, but the public's attitudes towards the public administration providing personal social services remained surprisingly negative (Rothstein, 2000). There was also general support for contracting out 'soft' or personal social services, but the Swedish public was more favourable to introducing 'freedom of choice' in some types of personal social services than in others. Enriching the work environment of the staff and improving the dialogue between the staff and clients are measures that could win public support in terms of greater alternatives in the production of personal social services. A greater welfare mix and greater role for the third sector would more easily receive support if public financing for such programmes continued at current levels, if coverage was maintained and if quality was improved.

Recent Developments in Stockholm

The ruling non-socialist majority in the municipality of Värmdö, a rural suburb in the archipelago of Stockholm County, broke up in the spring of 2001. It was replaced by a rainbow coalition that included the Social Democrats, Centre Party, Christian Democrats, Leftist Party and Environmental Party. The new coalition declared its intention to become Sweden's first municipality to adopt an integrated social economic policy. It organized a well visited half-day conference on the theme of the social economy at the end of October 2001, with seminars on such diverse topics as leisure time activities and youth, sports and health, pre-schools and schools, activities for seniors, cultural activities, social care and help, and civil defence. Possibilities for engaging the local social economy in the provision of services and activities in each of the above areas were discussed in these seminars. Following this conference Värmdö has been busy exploring ways to implement its intention of letting organizations from the social economy play a greater role in providing a wide range of services to its inhabitants, including libraries, child care, schooling, elderly care, health care, culture and so on. It initiated a 'Council of Associations' in 2002 to make proposals for increasing the role of the third sector in the political, social and economic life of Värmdö.

The *Länsstyrelsen* (County Administration Board) of Stockholm adopted a 'Programme of Action' in 2001 to promote the social economy in Stockholm County in the coming years. It calls for several steps to promote the role of the social economy in providing its inhabitants with services and to promote the economic development of the county as a whole. In particular, it points to the need to develop elderly care as part of the social economy. It also plans to initiate an annual quality prize for the best social economic organization in the country. The Stockholm County Administration Board also emphasized the importance of developing techniques for advancing a social audit as a quality provision and as a means of securing the legitimacy of various actors in the social economy and of promoting their marketing efforts. It also proposed to develop back-up administrative services not always available or affordable to small groups of third sector female entrepreneurs (Länstyrelsen i Stockholms län, 2001).

The Development Partnership for Promoting the Social Economy in Stockholm County successfully applied for grants by the European Social Fund in June 2002. It formed a transnational partnership with similar projects in Finland, Italy, Greece and the Netherlands. Together they will promote the role of the third sector and social economy in their respective countries for a period of two years. The Stockholm Project for the Social Economy is working to promote the creation of elder care cooperatives for people of foreign background, to provide education for foreign women who lack a base in the Swedish labour market and to provide help for them in starting elder care cooperatives. It will also try to provide the basic infrastructure for promoting cooperative development in the field of personal social services in Stockholm County and is initiating a training course for spreading methods related to social accounting and auditing for small social enterprises.

CONCLUSIONS

The social economy in Sweden is more closely associated with *folkrörelser* (popular movements) than with voluntary associations, even if the latter are not negligible. Voluntary associations and popular movements have gone through several stages in their development and relationship with the state. The etatist nature of the Swedish welfare state has also contributed to eclipsing the role and contribution of voluntary associations and popular movements in the production of personal social services. Several of the established organizations in the Swedish social economy still pay lip service to a general, tax-based welfare state, but few contribute actively to its development or renewal. The limited role of third sector providers of various personal social services in Sweden stands in sharp contrast to the extensive use of them in providing various social services in other European countries. In particular, Germany and the United Kingdom illustrate the contrast well, as the country chapters in this book clearly demonstrate.

I agree with Klausen and Selle's conclusion that the relationship between the third sector and the state is facilitated by the pattern of third sector participation in public policy making in Sweden and the Scandinavian countries. This pattern can be called institutional cooperation with the state and cooption into public policy making. Many third sector organizations participate actively both in the public debate and in the political process. Traditionally, third sector organizations have the role of pressure groups vis-à-vis the political and administrative system. They argue their case in the press, at public meetings, via petitions, demonstrations and other events. Increasingly, they have also been directly coopted into the state and policy-making process. This is done through intensive lobbying and professional networking, primarily because organizations participate in the work of the parliamentary commissions preparing the laws. Finally, they often help oversee and even administer the distribution of public funding without extensive outside control or involvement by public authorities. In this sense they take part both in the preparatory work of public decision making and in implementation of these decisions, a phenomenon known as corporatism (Klausen and Selle, 1996, p.117).

It is the new popular movements and voluntary associations, those found in the new social economy, that are the most dynamic part of the Swedish social economy today. They actively help to develop and rejuvenate the welfare state in line with broad social and demographic changes in the post-industrial, urbanized society that comprises Sweden today. They are able to renew working life in a stagnant public sector, to improve the quality of personal social services provided for by public funding, to engage citizens as co-producers of such services and to rejuvenate the social capital that is rapidly diminishing in the growing democracy deficit in Sweden.

However, there is little room for a third sector or the social economy in the highly polarized and ideological struggle between the ruling Social Democrats and their non-socialist opponents, who were in power in many cities and municipalities between 1998 and 2002 and who seemed determined to privatize as much as possible before the elections in 2002. So the third sector and social economy were largely ignored, forgotten or, even worse, were crushed in the power struggle between the central and municipal governments in major urban areas like Stockholm. Uncertainty also reigns concerning the long-term intentions of the Social Democrats to introduce new legislation to promote non-profit status for organizations or companies in Sweden. Will this result in yet another category that confuses matters for social enterprises, or will it strengthen the third sector and social economy? No certain prognosis is possible, but etatist traditions of the past and a lack of interest in alternative solutions to ailing public services do not bode well for the third sector or the social economy in the future. It should be kept in mind, however, that there are some rays of light in the cloudy picture painted here, in particular as seen in recent developments in the County Administration of Stockholm and the municipality of Värmdö, where the social economy is seen as the wave of the future.

REFERENCES

Ambjörnsson, Ronnie (1988), *Den skötsamma arbetaren*, Stockholm: Carlssons.
Babchuk, Nicholas and Alan Booth (1969), 'Voluntary Associations & the Integration Hypothesis', *Social Inquiry*, 35.

Babchuk, Nicholas and John N. Edwards (1965), 'Voluntary Association Membership: A Longitudinal Analysis', *American Sociological Review*, 34, 31–45.

Bryce, James (1888), *The American Commonwealth*, New York: Macmillian Co.

de Tocqueville, Alexis (1832), *Democracy in America*, reprinted 1956, New York: The New American Library, Mentor Book Edition, abridged by Richard D. Heffner; reprinted 1996, New York: Harper & Row.

Esping-Andersen, Gösta (ed.) (1996), *Welfare States in Transition. National Adaptations in Global Economies*, London, Thousand Oaks and New Delhi: Sage Publications.

Evers, Adalbert (1995), 'Part of the Welfare Mix: the Third Sector as an Intermediate Area', *Voluntas*, 6 (2), 159–82.

Key, Vladimir Orlando Jr. (1942), *Politics, Parties and Pressure Groups*, reprinted 1958 (4th edn), New York: Crowell.

Klausen, Kurt Klaudi and Per Selle (1996), 'The Third Sector in Scandinavia', *Voluntas*, 7 (2), 99–122.

Länsstyrelsen i Stockholms län (2001), *Handlingsplan för socialekonomin i Stockholms län*, Stockholm: Länsstyrelsen.

Lipset, Seymour Martin (1963), *Political Man*, New York: Doubleday Books and Anchor Books.

Lundström, Tommy (1996), 'The State and Voluntary Social Work in Sweden', *Voluntas*, 7 (2), 123–46.

Lundström, Tommy and Filip Wijkström (1997), *The Nonprofit Sector in Sweden*, Manchester: Manchester University Press.

Pestoff, Victor (1977), 'Voluntary Associations and Nordic Party Systems. A Study of Overlapping Memberships and Cross-Pressures in Finland, Norway and Sweden', Studies in Politics, No. 10, Stockholm.

Pestoff, Victor (1991), *Between Markets and Politics. Co-operatives in Sweden*, Frankfurt am Main, New York and Boulder, CO: Campus Verlag and Westview Press (republished in 1996).

Pestoff, Victor (1995), 'Towards a New Swedish Model of Collective Bargaining and Politics?', in Colin Crouch and Franz Traxler (eds), *Organized Industrial Relations in Europe: What Future?*, Aldershot, UK, Brookfield, USA, Hong Kong, Singapore and Sydney: Avebury.

Pestoff, Victor (1998), *Beyond the Market and State: Social Enterprises and Civil Democracy in a Welfare Society*, Aldershot, UK: Ashgate.

Pestoff, Victor (1999a), 'Konsumentkooperationens framtid i post-industriella samhällen', *Kooperatören*, and 'The Future of Consumer Cooperatives in Post-Industrial Societies', *Journal of Co-operative Studies*, 32 (3), 208–19.

Pestoff, Victor (1999b), 'Social Enterprises and Civil Democracy in Sweden: Developing a Participatory Welfare Society for the 21st Century', in William Halal and Kenneth Taylor (eds), *21st Century Economics. Perspectives of Socioeconomics for a Changing World*, New York: St Martin's Press.

Pestoff, Victor (2001), '*Globalization, Business Interest Associations and Swedish Exceptionalism in the 21st Century*', Conference paper, Florence.

Pestoff, Victor and Peter Strandbrink (2002), 'The Politics of Day Care in Sweden', CRIDA conference paper, Milan.

Regeringskansliet (2000), *Ett föränderligt arbetsliv på gott och ont*, Stockholm: Regeringskansliet.

Rokkan, Stein ([1967] 1970), 'Geography, Religion and Social Class: Crosscutting cleavages in Norwegian Politics', in Seymour M. Lipset and Stein Rokkan (eds),

Party Systems and Voter Alignments; Cross-National Perspectives, New York and London: The Free Press and Collier–Macmillan Ltd.

Rothstein, Bo (2000), 'Future of the Universal Welfare State', in Stein Kuhnle (ed.), *Survival of the European Welfare State*, London: Routledge, pp. 217–34.

Rothstein, Bo (2001), 'Socialt kapilal i den socialdemokratiskastaten. Den svenska modellen och det civila samhället', *Arkiv*, 79, 1–55.

Salamon, Lester M., Helmut K. Anheier, S. Wojciech Sokolowski *et al.* (1996), *The Emerging Sector. A Statistical Supplement*, Baltimore: Johns Hopkins Institute for Policy Studies.

SCB (2001), Table 1, 'Medlemskap och aktiviteter i olika organisationer, 1992 & 2000', private communication.

Stephens, John D. (1996), 'The Scandinavian Welfare States: Achievements, Crisis and Prospects', in Gösta Esping-Andersen (ed.), *Welfare States in Transition. National Adaptations in Global Economies*, London, Thousand Oaks and New Delhi: Sage Publications.

TCO (2001), *Välfärdsstat 2.1. Utveckling välfärd*, Stockholm: TCO.

Truman, David (1951), *The Governmental Process*, reprinted 1971 (2nd edn), New York: Knopf.

Walden Laing, Dagmar (2001), *HIV/AIDS in Sweden and the United Kingdom Policy Networks 1982–1992*, Stockholm: Dept of Political Science.

Walden Laing, Dagmar and Victor Pestoff (1997), 'The Role of Nonprofit Organizations in Managing HIV/AIDS in Sweden', in Patrick Kenis and Bernd Marin (eds), *Managing AIDS: Organizational Responses in Six European Countries*, Aldershot, UK and Brookfield, USA; Ashgate.

Werkö, Sofie (2002), 'Patient Empowerment through Patient Organizations', seminar paper, School of Business, Stockholm.

Zetterberg, Hans (1961), 'National Pastime: Pursuit of Power', *Industria International, 1960–61*, Stockholm: Confederation of Swedish Employers.

4. French civil society experiences: attempts to bridge the gap between political and economic dimensions

Philippe Chanial and Jean-Louis Laville

INTRODUCTION

From the nineteenth century on, the principle of solidarity in Europe has been a major feature in the continuing effort to curb the debilitating effects of an expanding market economy. More than mere philanthropy, this principle originated in deep-rooted habits of self-help and mutual organization, through which the pattern of modern citizenship, based upon freedom and equality for all human beings, could be turned into a valuable economic asset.

This model of association based on self-organization paved the way for the rise of a civil and solidarity-based economy in the middle of the nineteenth century, notwithstanding that the combination of the industrial revolution, the ideological triumph of liberalism and the sheer force used against various labour organizations had ushered in a steep decline in the belief in the solidarity-based economy. However, remains of this belief could be found in the various social economy organizations set up during the second half of the nineteenth century. These organizations, which remained different from capitalist associations in their legal structures, proved unable to transcend the clear-cut distinction between a market and a non-market economy, a distinction which resulted in both competition and cooperation between market and welfare state throughout Europe. Recently, however, this situation has changed with a growing number of initiatives. During the last quarter of the twentieth century, various attempts were made to reclaim the tradition of active citizenship which lies at the heart of the yearning for a solidarity-based economy.

The aim of this chapter is to recount the convoluted history of this other pattern of 'economic behaviour' by interpreting it in the light of the tradition of French associationism.[1] It will then show how this attempt to reclaim a degree of democratic control over the economy is leading towards a model of development that challenges the hegemony of corporate governance by pitting the demands of a rejuvenated civil society against the growing threat from the assertiveness of the market (Polanyi, 1944). The chapter ends with a question about what these efforts will amount to.

ASSOCIATIONISM, ECONOMY AND DEMOCRACY

To reflect on the history of association is, first of all, to be reminded that the rights of man and representative government do not amount to democracy's last word. The historical process that gave birth to modern democracies cannot be described simply as a 'movement towards individualism', but was also, and perhaps more accurately, a 'movement towards association', as Dewey was keen to emphasize. Effective though the great revolutions of the seventeenth and eighteenth centuries were at destroying the ancient, hierarchical social order, they did not prevent what he called the 'social molecules' that remained from immediately proceeding to create new kinds of organizations and associations. The new organizations were no longer based on mandatory, authoritarian participation but rather on voluntary, open membership, in accordance with democratic ideals. Thus the whole democratic process has been irretrievably associated with the flourishing of manifold political, cultural and scientific associations; indeed, association itself should be considered as the second, forgotten catalyst of the democratic revolution.

Yet the connection between association and democracy is not as clear and unambiguous as Dewey seems to imply (Cefaï and Chanial, 2000). Before the French Revolution, as early as 1780, a myriad of societies began to try to implement a new order based upon brotherhood and egalitarianism, in accordance with the spirit of Enlightenment. Obviously, association provided the vehicle through which the French Revolution could grow and mature. Up to a point, it was ruled by political associations, and yet, paradoxically enough, those very associations were ultimately swept out of the public realm: academies and women's societies were banned in 1793, followed by the clubs in 1795. Most famously, all economic and professional associations were prohibited as early as 1791. The Allard and Le Chapellier Acts were greeted with unanimous approval, from the radical revolutionaries to the conservative liberals and onwards. This universal agreement bore testimony to the widespread fear of seeing the rebirth of old-style guilds, with their anti-democratic flavour: hence the denial of the right to convene and found free, professional associations, a right previously granted by the Constituent Assembly in the name of the Declaration of the Rights of Man. It looks as if individual freedom and the principle of sovereignty were unable to cope with the survival of those guilds, even though a number of them had already decided to embrace secularism and democracy, through free membership and representative government, wholly according with the new revolutionary creed (Sewell, 1983, p.141).

It is against this background of crackdown and repression, interrupted by the occasional breathing space, that the French labour and socialist movements came into being, in the guise of various associative models.

The Labour Movement: a Testing Ground for Association

Quite apart from the theoretical breakthroughs achieved by the likes of Fourier and Saint-Simon, a pattern of workers' associations was slowly emerging. Among their distinctive features were their openly political motives. A new concept of solidarity was gradually being defined, which blended solidarity with a democratic kind of social relations. Or, as Leroux, a former follower of Saint-Simon, puts it: 'Nature did not fate one single human being to mere self-obsession. . . . It meant them for one another, and bound them together by a reciprocal solidarity' (Leroux, 1997). To escape competitive individualism and state authoritarianism, Leroux has to fall back on the solidarity networks fostered by the workshop, as well as on associations and a public-spirited press. In accordance with these ideas, a cluster of constitutional projects were framed in the 1830s and 1840s, all aiming at the foundation of a 'brotherly' and 'solidarity-based' economic model. The concept of solidarity was conceived as the ideal recipe to combine reciprocal relations and a modern public sphere. This principle emphasizes the interdependent nature of all social intercourse and the positive liberty comprised in the practice of association and mutual cooperation. It then provides the theoretical framework within which an alternative to the liberal project of an individualistic society built solely upon the defence of negative liberty and the all-encompassing paradigm of interest can be thoroughly thought out.

It is within this framework that labour associations founded by skilled workers began to ditch their corporatist habits. Various groups, coming from guilds, mutual aid societies and productive associations, became firmly committed to secularism and democracy. Building on revolutionary associationism, they helped to create an associative utopia which was inseparable from the vision of a democratic republic.

The old-fashioned guilds had been steadily growing since the fifteenth and sixteenth centuries and had managed to outlive the most repressive pieces of legislation. Between 1815 and 1848, when they reached the height of their power, they benefited from a mood of tolerance, without being able to reform themselves. During this period, many voices, including Leroux and Tristan, expressed the yearning for a post-corporatist order, for the merging of all these guilds into a new 'Labour Union', a federation allowing all workers to stop fighting each other, to reach agreement and to take part in a single project of moral improvement and economic protection. Bound together by a strong feeling of brotherhood and sympathy, the guilds were viewed as free associations, 'bodies' in which each worker is entitled to claim membership and contribute to their management.

As for the mutual aid societies, heir to religious confraternities, they filled their ranks with new unskilled members. Since 1815, they had been subjected to government attempts to turn them into law enforcement agencies. The aim was to restore the lower classes' shaken sense of loyalty towards King and Church. But the strategy backfired: some societies, without ever forfeiting their commitment to philanthropy, did indeed become political. This meant granting unemployment benefits and providing financial support to various strikes, and they thus became barely disguised pockets of resistance, foreshadowing full-fledged unions where corporatism, mutual insurance and republican feelings would be irreversibly blended together.

In the 1830s, yet another meaning of 'association' gradually emerged. Going beyond the limited reference to corporate solidarity or the demands of mutual insurance, it tended to point towards a broader picture. The labour movement's primary goal became the foundation of productive associations in which the association itself would become the symbol of freedom from being forced to live as wage earners. The theory is expounded by Buchez, one of the first theoreticians of workers' associationism, as early as 1831. It suggests that the workers, now the only source of wealth creation, share their tools and their working force so as to build an indefeasible collective asset, thus depending on nobody but themselves. Sharing equal rights and duties, they would gain the ability to submit industry to their will and end competition between workers. Born out of labour's practical experience, this project was greeted enthusiastically by the republicans of the day as well as the utopians of various stripes. All these new overlapping modes of association had their glory days as well as their fair share of dreams.

1848: From Workers' Association to Labour Republic

Between March and June 1848, Paris was bustling with associations. As the ideal recipe for a comprehensive reorganization of society, association was understood to mean two things. Universal franchise meant that the state was now ruled by political association. The attempt at reorganizing and thinking labour issues anew meant that the economy, too, should be ruled by association. Such was the double meaning of a democratic and social republic. Following Gossez (1967), Desroche mentions 39 professions, each with its own associative projects, partly drawing their inspiration from theoretical utopias. These were truly practical ventures. Breathing new life into their old professional associations, exploring new modes of labour organization, the workers strove to reconcile the principle of political equality with the glaring social inequality generated by the economic system. Whatever their inclination, these attempts shared two distinctive features: first, voluntary membership, whether religious or secular, was rooted in the claim to belong to a community strengthened by a certain economic activity; second, the action took place within the framework of a democratic society; its aim was deliberately political.

The year 1848 will always be remembered as the moment, foreseen from the 1830s on, when the world of labour, the pioneers of socialism and the framers of the republican ideal finally came together. Association provided the ground for the meeting. Political and social reformation walked hand in hand: man cannot be the master of politics while remaining a slave in the industrial order. Or, as Corbon, a follower of Buchez, puts it, 'political democracy and economic tyranny are not to coexist any longer'. The symbol of 1848 was the Committee of Luxembourg, nominated by the government to treat the problems of 'work organization' and establish rules (Laville, 1999a, 1999b).

Thus, under the guidance of the Committee, a number of old-fashioned guilds were turned into small professional organizations, ruled by universal suffrage, committed to the sovereignty of labour in accordance with the principle of association. Designed to promote and defend corporate interests (wages, welfare, working time, prevention of unemployment, regulation of competition and so on), the unions were coming into being as the child of a new synthesis (Gossez, 1967). Barely a few months later, a trend towards the amalgamation of these various associations into one was gaining momentum. It became necessary to move beyond those small, corporate bodies. The vision of a workers' republic, of an elected government of industry, republican heir to the tradition of workers' association, began to emerge. Various projects (Leroux, 1997, pp.440f; Proudhon, 1848) were aiming at transforming national parliament into a congress of workers of all specialisms, at reframing the electoral colleges on a professional basis; in short, to rebuild the polity through new democratic institutions of labour.

The obvious failure of those projects did not prevent the associationist inspiration of 1848 from fostering a political motivation, from outlining a new meaning of citizenship, legitimacy, representation and sovereignty. This 'policy of association' was aimed at reviving public spirit and renewing democratic practices by extending the republican ideal into the realm of the economy. Such is the legacy of 1848 which, under various guises, would determine the orientation of labour politics, right up to the end of the Third Republic (Moss, 1980). The rebirth of mutual insurance and cooperation under Napoleon III, the sheer peculiarity of the Commune of Paris, in 1871, the maturation (against the centralism prescribed by Marx and Guesde) of municipal socialism (Brousse) and of a decentralized and democratic kind of collectivism

(Jaurès, Malon, Fournière), the federalist feeling of French trade unionism, the rise and fall of revolutionary unionism – all bear testimony to the strength of this legacy. Association was indeed the mould of subsequent labour and socialist political movements, and, through various evolutions, proved congenial to the spirit of the Third Republic as well (Chanial, 2001).

Market, State and the Social Economy

Throughout the second half of the nineteenth century, the association pattern resulted in various legal breakthroughs. Struggles which had been lingering on for many years finally produced legal compromises recognizing organizations in which investors' power was limited. Progressively they became labelled as social economy organizations. In other words, social economy includes all the statuses (cooperative, mutual insurance, association) defined as limited profit making. So the French-speaking tradition of social economy diverged from the English definition. According to the first, the real boundary is not the one which separates profit making from non-profit making, but the one which separates capitalist societies from organizations of social economy whose primary goal remains the settlement of a collective patrimony as opposed to the guarantee of benefits to the individual shareholder. The criterion is not the absence of profit making but the existence of binding rules ensuring that capital should not prevail (Bidet, 2000, p.38). The original movement towards association thus resulted in the legalization of organizations combining stakeholder membership and economic activity, all of which were freed from shareholders' dominance.

Focusing on a specific organizational structure, the social economic approach nevertheless fails to come to grips with the institutionally enforced separation of a market-oriented 'economic' realm, including private for-profit enterprises, and a 'social' realm regulated by public bodies. This concrete separation has its roots in analytical distinctions that began with Walras. His attempt to define economies as a 'pure', value-free science, whose laws mathematics could successfully establish, is logically linked to his definition of the social economy, dedicated to respect for principles of justice and the resolution of social questions. In his view the market economy ensures the production of goods and the social economy is dependent on it because it is devoted to the redistribution of goods. The social economy was thus emerging as subservient to the 'natural' laws of the market economy, its only remaining goal being to atone for the social wrongs committed in the name of the market.

The Welfare State Comes into Being

Apart from the above events, the concept of solidarity was evolving. As a consequence of the traumatic experience of repression that resulted from the events of 1848, it was not until the end of the century that solidarity re-emerged as a republican device with the ability to reconcile individual rights and state responsibility. Promoted by a number of politicians, jurists and sociologists (Bouglé, Bourgeois, Duguit, Durkheim and others), the new concept was no longer understood to encompass the whole of mankind, but to emphasize what binds together past and future generations. As Bourgeois puts it, social commitment is not a commandment of conscience, it is a right and lawful duty, neglect of which means the violation of a definite rule of justice. The state should enforce this rule, 'by force if necessary' so as to 'grant everyone his legitimate share of work and products' (Bourgeois, 1992, pp.22–3). Striking a balance between the conflicting demands of liberty and equality is achieved through the functional separation of the economy and 'the social', defined as 'the ideal of civil service merged with the concept of solidarity'. The democratic state, the expression of the general will, becomes the appointed guardian of the general interest, but must admit the prevalent role of the market economy in wealth creation. Civil service, legitimized by political representation, allows a 'neutral' state to deliver services to its subjects.

Since the end of the nineteenth century, though remaining a key notion for organizing society, solidarity has come to refer less to horizontal relations between citizens and more to vertical relations based on law and protecting the citizens through the social state. Consequently, the supreme ability of state intervention to reshape society is fully recognized (Lafore, 1992, pp.261–3). As a kind of vertical solidarity based on law, state intervention is hailed as a very practical way to avoid 'individualism' and 'collectivism'.

Within this framework, state intervention is considered to be not so much a threat to the market economy but rather a natural complement. The end of World War II and the need to foster national unity made this complementary relationship all the more compelling. Keynesianism attempted to direct economic development through new means of knowledge and intervention. Meanwhile, the welfare state extended previous patterns of the social state in the field of social security. The status granted by wage earning resulted in an unprecedented alliance between work and protection, which thus became a major tool for social integration, thanks to the guarantee of employment and high productivity gains allowing recurring wage negotiations (Castel, 1995).

To summarize: from the first half of the nineteenth century to the 1960s the rush towards association was a natural reaction of society to the disruptions caused by the expansion of the market which gradually paved the way for state intervention. The state generated a peculiar mode of organization, called 'the social', which makes it possible to reconcile the existence of the market economy and workers' citizenship. The social issue resulted in the separation of the market economy and legally granted welfare. The body of social laws, comprising the rights of workers within both the company and the welfare state, arose from the need to heal the wounds inflicted by the market economy upon society.

The Evolution of the Social Economy

It is in this context that the famous Act of 1901, which finally recognized the legal existence of non-profit associations after decades of debate, should be considered. This Act, and more generally all the rules regulating social econ- omy, can be seen as the end of an era of grand visions and daring attempts. The legal achievements being finally secured, the heroic age of association, that of revolutionary clubs, secret societies and of workers' cooperation, came to an end.

Throughout the twentieth century, the dual effect of intricate institutional- ization and integration resulted in a dispersal of the social economy. The three statuses, cooperative, mutual and association, became dependencies of the social and economic pattern of which they are part and parcel, especially through the separation of the market economy and the welfare state. Within this framework, all three of them are subjected to institutional isomorphisms, defined as constraining processes which compel the members of a group to act and look like the other members who have to face the same constraints (Di Maggio and Powell, 1983, p.150). Such isomorphisms explain why those enti- ties are 'witnessing the standardization of their economic behaviour' (Vivet and Thiry, 2000).

Cooperatives are components of the market economy and allow various actors to mobilize for themselves the resources which they need and which are shunned by more conventional investors. Even though they benefit from a measure of state regulation, it is competition which constitutes their distinctive feature. This means that, internal differences notwithstanding, the broad logic of productive concentration has ushered in a process of specialization. The cooperatives survive chiefly in the various sectors where capitalist intensity remains weak. The desire for self-perpetuation has led these enterprises to blur their more militant political visions.

The advent of the welfare state has proved a turning point for *mutuals*. For most of the nineteenth century, attempts had been made to address the issues of accidental death, illness and old age. The basis for these attempts was provided by solidarity between members of the same profession or the same place. The very nature of the economic activities involved prompted coopera- tion with the various post-1945 social security systems, and mutual insurances became complementary to the mandatory welfare state. They duly submitted to the rules issued by governments, even when the framework laid out by social policies happened to conflict with the principle of voluntary member- ship. In France, this process of institutionalization espoused a corporatist pattern first set out by Bismarck, linking social insurance with wage earning (Esping-Andersen, 1990). However, the stiffening of competition in the field of insurance has produced hardship among commercial and mutual company insurances.

The corporatist kind of welfare state implemented in France leaves much room to the *associations* willing to provide social services. Those associations had previously entered the uncharted territories of social demands, and the state later provided the legal and financial framework within which this legacy could be kept alive and well. The government provides what can be called a tutelary regulation dictating what professions should be included and, so long as those rules are abided by, granting the necessary financial resources through budgetary expenditures. Such a regulation leads them to unite into great national federations, either secular or religious. A close scrutiny of the relationships between these two partners reveals the sheer level of involvement of a great number of associations in furnishing social services. The upshot of it all is a strong centralization and a dependency on the financial and legal might of the state (Laville, 2000).

A Common Identity?

Overall, whereas in the realm of the economy the importance of the social economy has been steadily growing since the beginning of the twentieth century, the same cannot be said of the realm of politics. The choice of members according to their relation to the activity has vastly reduced the sense of belonging upon which the original associations relied so heavily. The specialization, the competition of cooperatives and mutual insurances with other companies and the constraints imposed upon the associations by national social policies have raised new, more technical, issues in the field of the social economy. The influence wielded in public debate has been weak at best, and the associations have given up their public ambitions to concentrate on their managerial and law-abiding tasks.

Thus, to a large extent, the political dimension has been forgotten. This loss is revealed by the growing separation of the various components of the social economy. For instance, the connections are very hard to establish between cooperatives and associations when cooperatives behave and consider themselves as market-oriented enterprises, while the associations remain stuck in the social world. The existence of not-for-profit organizations does not appear to be sufficient to generate common identity and aims. It then becomes difficult to preserve even a measure of consistency inside a so-called 'social economy sector'. Such is the effect of the integration of social economy organizations within a general framework based upon the separation of market economy and social policy.

THE LIMITS OF THE SOCIAL ECONOMY

The practical limits of the social economy relate to the theoretical problems inherent in the conceptual approach of social economy found throughout francophone tradition. Five points are particularly noticeable: the institutionalization process, the definition of a model of reference for the social economy, implicit utilitarianism, the simplistic view of democracy and the pattern of development.

Institutionalization is seen merely as the natural and positive result of the process initiated by the pioneering associationism during the first half of the nineteenth century (Gueslin, 1989). Yet this process is much more ambiguous than that. The legal recognition of social economy goes hand in hand with a selection of its initiatives. Throughout the second half of the nineteenth century, governments frightened by workers' movements discriminated against self-organized bodies as compared with philanthropic actions. Societies for mutual help were closely held in check and subjected to the supervision of local elites. The suppression of the workers' organizations, the growing role of charity it involved and the fact that its zealots kept emphasizing its moral role earned the social economy the nickname of 'compassionate' political economy and aroused radical controversies inside a labour movement where Marxism and its scepticism towards associations were steadily gaining ground. Marx himself dismissed social economy as 'vulgar economy' because it contented itself with the search for a way to maintain law and order by reducing poverty without contesting social order.

With Fauquet (1965) and Vienney (1981–2), the cooperative model became the standard of social economy, which narrowed its range, among associations, to those deeply involved in permanent economic activities. Social economy organizations were now recognized only in so far as they performed some managerial tasks. So their economic activity tended to be considered as mere market activity and their relations to the market were conspicuously displayed in order to prove that social economy was genuinely concerned with economy (Jeantet, 1999). At this point, social economy ceased to be more than a non-capitalist kind of market enterprise. Any surge in its market activities was hailed as proof of its success, forbidding any question about isomorphism and non-market branches of the economy. Thus, for those associations whose financial health was heavily dependent on redistribution and voluntary service, it remained difficult to endorse the French charter of social economy which states that social economy organizations 'live in market economy and develop institutions which traditional market economy fails to generate'.

To conceive social economy in this way is tantamount to assuming empirical facts as underlying the rational and utilitarian actions of those involved in the process. While perceiving the actors through the prism of rational choice, this analysis 'leaves aside a whole world of non-consuming and non-instrumental motives' (Evers, 1993). To focus on rational choice means to reduce mental processes to discursive reason, and discursive reason to strategic calculation. Yet the actors involved in the process are just as much concerned with values; they want to take real life and its modes of socialization into account, which makes it impossible to neglect the symbolic component of their action. Summing up, one could say that by referring to a narrow paradigm of 'interest' the theory of social economy gets deprived of the intersubjective dimension of organized action. Moreover, while acknowledging the role of cooperatives, mutual insurance companies and associations, this theoretical framework appraises them only in reference to the evolution of the relations between members and the economic results. Their broader public role, including collective action which may provide the basis for future policy actions, is forgotten in the process. For instance, an institutional change such as the way in which organizations of mutual help generated and gave rise to the subsequent welfare systems remains invisible. So it does not allow us to understand how in this case the impact of the resulting innovation was felt much beyond the borders of the market economy.

At the same time, formal equality between members is too easily equated with democratic functioning, whereas all the reports show that status alone is unable to guarantee anything of the sort (Demoustier, 1984; Laville, 1994; Meister, 1974; Sainsaulieu *et al.*, 1983). It is important to acknowledge the differences that exist within social economy organizations: between various logics, interests and various groups. The assumption that status will be enough to ensure internal democracy can prevent enforcement of checks and balances or deter a search for other modes of labour organizations and employment conditions more in favour of the employees (Bidet, 2001, p.101).

Finally, social economy theory is unable to forget the cliché equating the modern economy with the market. In this respect, a number of other authors have to be considered (Boulding, 1973; Mauss, 1989; Perroux, 1960; Polanyi, 1944; Razeto Migliaro, 1988) because they open another debate by emphasizing the three channels of exchanges of goods and services irrigating the modern economy as well as more ancient ones: market, redistribution and reciprocity. The pattern of development based upon the synergy between the market and the state, and within the framework of which the social economy grew and matured, can thus be described as a pattern in which the market is the primary economic principle, redistribution organized by the social state being merely an auxiliary. The economy is considered as a market economy, public redistribution slowly becoming an expression of abstract solidarity, the lively dimension of solidarity being thus forgotten (Gauchet, 1991, p.170).

One could say that such a pattern stops just short of defining reciprocity as an independent principle, distinct from market as well as from redistribution; or, when reciprocity is acknowledged, one could say that it is confined to a residual role, 'subordinate and secondary, content with filling the vacuums left by the other principles' (Salamon, 1987); 'it is marginal and peripheral when compared to the fundamental rules of society' (Herman, 1984).

Indeed, the obsession with the organizational dimension of the social economy prevents one from grasping the institutional dimension of collective action. Those taking part in these actions are generating principles to legitimize an action which originated in a feeling of institutional deficiency and ended up in the defence of the common goods created in the process. Thus these actions are concerned with full-fledged institutional framing. In fact, the institutional dimension goes beyond the organization entrusted with supervising the process of production, it is related to the legitimacy claimed by collective action itself and to the deals which the social actors agreed to strike to devise the 'rules of the game' which will regulate their relations (Bélanger and Lévesque, 1990). A number of associations frame projects aiming at institutional change, which turns them into intermediaries between their own members and official institutions. Their public sphere dimension inside the civil societies (Evers, 1993) is for this reason as peculiar as their socioeconomic dimension.

CIVIL AND SOLIDARITY-BASED ECONOMY: THE REBIRTH OF A LONG-FORGOTTEN OUTLOOK

It is first and foremost this political dimension of 'another economy' (Lévesque *et al.*, 1989) which, from the 1960s on, has been displayed in a number of initiatives trying to rearticulate the reciprocal and redistributive aspects of solidarity.

From the early 1960s, the upheavals which took place in the ways that people lived brought aspects of social behaviour into public debate which were previously intangible or had been ruled by tradition (Giddens, 1994, p.120). The inability of wage earners and consumers to make themselves heard, in the realm of labour as well as in the realm of consumption, was subjected to the same kind of criticism to which the process of standardization of demand, through the increasing supply of mass-produced goods and standardized services, had previously laid itself open.

The focus shifted towards the demand for better quality of life, towards the demand for 'qualitative', rather than 'quantitative', growth. In a word, 'way-of-life' politics should replace 'standard-of-living' politics (Roustang, 1987), so as to take into account the need for everyone to play a part in social life, for the environment to be protected, for the relationships between genders and generations to be altered. This movement towards autonomous reflection became evident in the shape of new social movements such as feminism or ecology. At the same time, widespread concerns were expressed about the government's doubtful ability to provide a remedy for the market's deficiencies. Customers began to castigate the bureaucratic and centralizing leanings of redistributive institutions, perceiving that the inability to reform generated inertia, gridlock and cronyism; worse still, that the failure to take individual differences into account explained the resilience of powerful inequalities beneath the veil of egalitarianism.

Some of the new initiatives linked economic concern with a longing for social change. 'Self-governed' or 'alternative' companies sought to experiment with 'democracy through organization' (Sainsaulieu *et al.*, 1983) and pointed towards self-management. New modes of intellectual undertakings, where dedication to one's work was fostered by militant commitment, provided a good example of this; as Marchat puts it (2001), these actors from the 1960s and 1970s 'usher in the creation of collectively-managed experiments where social issues can be addressed, their members being willing to face the usual practice of expertise with a "critical" conception'. The 1970s, characterized by a renewed rush towards associations, ended up with the emergence of 'shops' for law, management and housing open to those consumers who were excluded by the commercial services, and the inauguration of several consultancy firms which used the legal devices of the social economy, while claiming above all democratic and egalitarian rules of organization. This phenomenon can be considered as a response to the issue of unemployment faced by a number of young graduates, but also as a yearning for an alternative professional pattern. The trend was similar among those customers who undertook to devise alternatives to the services delivered hitherto, for instance parents who began to establish child care facilities by themselves.

That many of these organizations finally collapsed under the weight of ideological strife and economic pressures cannot be denied; nevertheless, their original spirit has been revived within other frameworks and by other social groups. This background has had a decisive influence throughout the 1980s. It demonstrates that the rebirth of a civil and solidarity-based economy cannot be explained by unemployment. Employment problems became more and more important in the 1980s and 1990s, but the return of a civil and solidarity-based economy perspective originated earlier. It was correlated with three other contemporary phenomena: the development of the tertiary sector within productive activities, leading to the emergence of related services such as health and social action, personal and domestic; sociodemographic trends, such as the general ageing of the population, the diversification of family structures and the growth in women's activity; and the growing inequalities generated by neoliberal globalization.

Ever since the 1980s, civil and solidarity-based initiatives have been local and have concentrated on creating new services or adjusting existing ones ranging from those that relate to everyday life to the improvement of the cultural environment, and integrating disadvantaged populations and territories within the general economic framework (Jouen, 2000; Gardin and Laville, 1997). They are extending their reach on the global stage, with attempts to forge new bonds between southern producers and northern consumers, particularly through fair trade.

The social economy has emphasized the great diversity in the various patterns of ownership, which received a new relevance with the growing unease felt by public opinion in the face of the exorbitant influence wielded by shareholders inside companies. However, the changes experienced within the social economy have proved the insufficiencies of mere 'not-for-profit' statuses, and the need to mobilize the diversity of economic principles as well as the benefits of the various patterns of ownership. The civil and solidarity-based economy perspective emphasizes the issues of hybridization between economic principles and participatory democracy. It is a reminder of the inadequacy of mere statutory specificity: the integration within the general framework of the market economy tends to generate isomorphisms, which can be fended off only through the combination of several economic principles (the market, but redistribution and reciprocity as well). In other words, the solidarity dimension cannot last unless it is rooted in voluntary commitment, which is itself based upon reciprocal relationships between citizenship and the establishment of adequate public regulation. Two questions in particular are raised by the civil and solidarity-based economy perspective. How best to ensure participatory democracy within non-capitalist legal entities? What kind of public regulation is most likely to favour a pattern of sustainable development, including the social as well as the environmental questions, and to espouse civic claims in contemporary societies both at the local and international levels?

History has isolated social economy from social movements. The solidarity-based economy perspective and the current circumstances are making it easier for a dialogue to take place, particularly with anti-globalization movements eager to combine fresh criticism with practical propositions for a different kind of globalization (Ortiz and Muñoz, 1998; Passet, 1996). Certain events show that this dialogue is being renewed, for the first time in its history. The international anti-globalization movement, Attac, brought the issue to the fore in its summer university, in 2001. Another example is provided by the social movement of the jobless, which framed a national project for the development of a civil and solidarity-based economy. Lastly, the trade unions have also shown a recent interest: the Confédération française du travail (CFDT) bore witness to a shifting of attention towards new forms of solidarity (Joubert *et al.*, 1998); the Confédération générale du travail (CGT) has moved in the same direction (Le Duigou, 2001).

This change is paralleled by emerging governmental recognition, evidence of which was displayed in 2000 by the regional consultations on a social and solidarity-based economy (Lipietz, 2001) and the celebrations greeting the centenary of the Act of 1901. To this must be added the creation of a state secretary for the civil and solidarity-based economy who, among other things, held a European meeting between various networks of the civil and solidarity-based economy and social economy. This recognition remains fragile at the national level, as shown by the abolition of the position of state secretary in 2002, but it is also progressing at the local level with a few hundred delegates to the solidarity-based economy in the local authorities elected in 2001.

The future will probably depend heavily on the ability to increase cooperation between the institutionalized social economy and the initiatives influenced by the solidarity-based economy perspective, together with a capacity to improve relations between social movements and public bodies.

CONCLUSION

Overall, the initiatives which have been taking place for the last quarter of a century are evidence of the rebirth of nineteenth century-style associations, with their insistence on economic action through solidarity. Not limited to social economy organizations, the civil and solidarity-based economy can be broadly defined as a perspective centred on all the activities contributing to the democratization of the economy and arising from a public engagement in civil society. Contrary to the impression conveyed by the use of the word 'solidarity' to define certain charitable actions, the civil and solidarity-based economy has nothing to do with the yearning for deregulation which aims at ditching state intervention in favour of charity. It originates in collective actions aimed at implementing international and local regulations, together with national regulations, or filling vacuums they may have left. It does not mean a switch from a redistributive form of solidarity to a more reciprocal one, but rather mixing the reciprocal and redistributive dimensions of solidarity, in order to reinforce the ability of society to resist social atomization, which is itself increased by the growing monetarization and commercialization of everyday life (Perret, 1999).

Ultimately, the civil and solidarity-based economy arises from actions taken by individuals such as customers, workers, volunteers, producers and consumers, through the setting up of places of exchange and dialogue which one could call 'proximity public spheres' (Eme and Laville, 1994). These actions are consolidated through an appropriate combination of resources (market resources stemming from the proceeds of a sale, non-market resources stemming from redistribution, non-monetary resources stemming from voluntary contributions). This established fact seems to promote hybridization as a general means of self-perpetuation.

The French approach to the third sector is generally considered to be the social economic approach. But beyond this attempt to gather different organizations under the same umbrella, the French experience of the last 30 years has been marked by the rise of a civil and solidarity-based economy perspective, reinterpreting some of the debates on the origin of social economy. According to this perspective, no legitimacy will ever be retained by the social economy unless the question of the political nature of the economy is raised once more. The aim must be to switch from the dominant conception of a market society to the conception of a plural economy (Passet, 1996; Aznar *et al.*, 1997; OECD, 1996), which means an economy extending beyond the realm of the market, to incorporate other economic poles. In an environment shaped by the rebirth of the liberal utopia of a market society (Rosanvallon, 1989), the accent put on the pluralist dimension of economy has become a key-point for both public bodies and civil society actors wishing to promote balanced relations between economics and politics.

NOTE

1. To recount this history from such a perspective is not to deny to other traditions their specific contributions. Obviously, French associationism did not invent or experiment alone with the project of a civil and solidarity-based economy. But historians seem to have failed to see the central importance of this tradition of cooperative socialism so closely bound up with the democratic republican movement (Moss, 1980; Sewell, 1983; Chanial, 2001).

REFERENCES

Aznar, G., A. Caillé, J.L. Laville, J. Robin and R. Sue (1997), *Vers une économie plurielle*, Paris: Syros, Alternatives économiques.
Bélanger, P.R. and B. Lévesque (1990), *La théorie de la régulation, du rapport salarial au rapport de consommation*, Montreal: Université du Québec à Montréal.
Bidet, E. (2000), 'Economie sociale, nouvelle économie sociale et sociologie économique', in M. Lallement and J.L. Laville (coord.), *Qu'est-ce que le tiers secteur? Associations, économie solidaire, économie sociale*, special issue of *Sociologie du Travail*, 4, Paris, 587–99.
Bidet, E. (2001), 'Economie sociale et tiers-secteur en Corée du Sud', thesis, Université Paris X – Nanterre.
Boulding, K. (1973), *La economia del amor y del temor*, Madrid: Alianza Editorial.
Bourgeois, L. (1992), *Solidarité*, Paris: Colin.

Caillé, A. (1993), *La dimension des clercs. La crise des sciences sociales et l'oubli du politique*, Paris: La Découverte.

Castel, R. (1995), *Les métamorphoses de la question sociale*, Paris: Fayard.

Cefaï, D. and P. Chanial (2000), 'Politiques de l'association. Une généalogie de l'associationnisme civique en France', *La revue du GERFA*, 1, 'L'économie solidaire', 203–24.

Chanial, P. (2001), *Justice, don et association. La délicate essence de la démocratie*, Paris: La Découverte/MAUSS.

Demoustier, D. (1984), *Les coopératives de production*, Paris: La Découverte.

Di Maggio, P.J. and W.W. Powell (1983), 'The Iron Cage Revisited: Institutional Isomorphism and Collective Rationality in Organizational Fields', *American Sociological Review*, 48 (April), 147–60.

Eme, B. and J.L. Laville (1994), *Cohésion sociale et emploi*, Paris: Desclée de Brouwer.

Esping-Andersen, G. (1990), *The three worlds of welfare capitalism*, Cambridge, MA: Harvard University Press.

Evers, A. (1993), 'The welfare mix approach. Understanding the pluralism of welfare systems', in A. Evers and I. Svetlik (eds), *Balancing Pluralism. New Welfare Mixes in Care for the Elderly*, European Center Vienna and Aldershot: Avebury, pp.3–31.

Fauquet, G. (1965), *Œuvres complètes*, Paris: Editions de l'Institut des études coopératives (1st edn 1935).

Gardin, L. and J.L. Laville (1997), *Les initiatives locales en Europe. Bilan économique et social*, Paris: LSCI, CNRS.

Gauchet, M. (1991), 'La société d'insécurité', in J. Donzelot (ed.), *Face à l'exclusion*, Paris: Editions Esprit.

Giddens, A. (1994), *Beyond left and right. The future of radical politics*, Cambridge: Polity Press.

Gossez, R. (1967), 'Les ouvriers de Paris. L'organisation 1848–1851', Bibliothèque de la Révolution de 1848, vol. 24, La Roche-sur-Yon.

Gueslin, A. (1989), *L'invention de l'économie sociale*, Paris: Economica.

Herman, R.D. (1984), *Why is there a third sector? Bringing politics back in school of business and public affairs*, Kansas City: University of Missouri.

Jeantet, T. (1999), *L'économie sociale européenne*, Paris: Ciem.

Joubert, F., B. Quintreau and J. Renaud (1998), 'Syndicalisme et nouvelles solidarités', *La Revue de la CFDT*, 11 (June–July), 32–7.

Jouen, M. (2000), *Diversité européenne: mode d'emploi*, Paris: Descartes & Cie.

Lafore, R. (1992), 'Droit d'usage, droit des usagers: une problématique à dépasser', in M. Chauviere and J.T. Godbout (eds), *Les usagers entre marché et citoyenneté*, Paris: L'Harmattan, pp.257–74.

Laville, J.L. (1994), *Collectifs et coopératives de travail en Europe – éléments pour un bilan 1970–1990*, Paris: LSCI, CNRS.

Laville, J.L. (1999a), *Une troisième voie pour le travail*, Paris: Desclée de Brouwer.

Laville, J.L. (1999b), *The future of work. The debate in France, the Welfare Society in the 21st century*, Oslo: Institute for Applied Social Research.

Laville, J.L. (2000), 'Le tiers secteur, un objet d'étude pour la sociologie économique', in M. Lallement and J.L. Laville (coord.), *Qu'est-ce que le tiers secteur? Associations, économie solidaire, économie sociale*, special issue of *Sociologie du Travail*, 4, 531–50.

Le Duigou, J.C. (2001), 'Pour une possible convergence entre le syndicalisme et l'économie sociale et solidaire', in C. Fourel (ed.), *La nouvelle économie sociale*, Paris: Syros-Alternatives Economiques, pp.79–95.

Leroux, P. (1997), *A la source perdue du socialisme français*, anthology collected and presented by B. Viard, Paris: Desclée de Brouwer.

Lévesque, B., A. Joyal and O. Chouinard (1989), *L'autre économie: une économie alternative?*, Quebec: Presses Universitaires du Québec.

Lipietz, A. (2001), *Pour le tiers secteur – l'économie sociale et solidaire: pourquoi, comment?*, Paris: La Découverte/La Documentation Française.

Marchat, J.F. (2001), *Engagement(s) et intervention au CRIDA: recherche et espace public démocratique*, Paris: LSCI–CNRS.

Mauss, M. (1989), 'Essai sur le don', *Sociologie et anthropologie*, Paris: Presses Universitaires de France, pp.145–279.

Meister, A. (1974), *La participation dans les associations*, Paris: Editions Ouvrières.

Moss, B.H. (1980), *The origins of the French labor movement, 1830–1914*, Los Angeles: University of California Press.

OECD (1996), *Reconciling economy and society. Towards a plural economy*, Paris: OECD.

Ortiz, H. and I. Muñoz (eds) (1998), *Globalización de la solidaridad. Un reto para todos*, Lima: Grupo Internacional Economía Solidaria–Centro de Estudios y Publicaciones.

Passet, R. (1996), *L'économique et le vivant*, Paris: Economica.

Perret, B. (1999), *Les nouvelles frontières de l'argent*, Paris: Le Seuil.

Perroux, F. (1960), *Economie et société, contrainte – échange – don*, Paris: Presses Universitaires de France.

Polanyi, K. (1944), *The Great Transformation*, New York: Rinehart & Company.

Proudhon, P.J. (1848), 'Programme révolutionnaire', *Le Représentant du Peuple*, May/June.

Razeto Migliaro, L. (1988), *Economia de solidaridad y mercado democratico. Libro tercero. Fundamentos de una teoria economica compensiva*, Programa de Economia del Trabajo, Santiago de Chile.

Rosanvallon, P. (1989), *Le libéralisme économique: histoire de l'idée de marché*, Paris: Le Seuil.

Roustang, G. (1987), *L'emploi: un choix de société*, Paris: Syros.

Sainsaulieu, R., P.E. Tixier and M.O. Marty (1983), *La démocratie en organisation*, Paris: Librairie des Méridiens.

Salamon, L.M. (1987), 'Partners in public service: The scope and theory of government–nonprofit relations', in W.W. Powell (ed.), *The nonprofit sector: A research handbook*, New Haven: Yale University Press, pp.99–117.

Sewell, W.H. (1983), *Gens de métier, gens de révolution*, Paris: Aubier.

Vienney, C. (1981–2), *Socio-économie des organisations coopératives*, 2 vols, Paris: Ciem.

Vivet, D. and B. Thiry (2000), 'Champ de l'étude, importance quantitative et acceptions nationales', *Les entreprises et organisations du troisième système. Un enjeu stratégique pour l'emploi*, action pilote 'Troisième système et emploi' de la Commission Européenne, Liège: CIRIEC, pp.11–32.

5. From institutional fixation to entrepreneurial mobility? The German third sector and its contemporary challenges

Ingo Bode and Adalbert Evers

The introduction of the notion of the 'third sector' into economic and social sciences during the last two decades has without a doubt proved to be a success story, becoming a catchword for a broad area of theory and research. Analytically it does not provide many insights into the economic, sociopolitical and cultural logic shaping the various fields in which non-profit organizations are engaged. However, this notion symbolizes a research agenda directed towards ideas that have been ignored for a long time. Therefore it has a pragmatic quality which makes it useful for this chapter.

On a more theoretical level, understanding these fields as an 'intermediary sphere' of modern society has some advantages over conceiving them as a 'third sector'. The organizations operating in this sector are rooted in civic action, but in their everyday existence we find an intertwining and mutual balance of rationales coming from all sectors of society. Each of these rationales is dominant in the basic institutions of the other sectors, whereas in the third sector they interact in various ways. Thus third sector organizations (TSOs) are linked to the sphere of politics by their attempt to spell out versions of a public good. Correspondingly, they make use of state-derived resources. Moreover, there are influences from the market side: many TSOs experience a need to compete, to try to gain economic autonomy (for example by the means of a surplus) and are driven by a kind of entrepreneurial spirit. Finally, TSOs are bound to the community. They are places in which 'social capital' is processed, with trust, voluntary commitment and social support being important ingredients of organizational action. Therefore, if the third sector is an 'intermediate sphere', TSOs can be seen as 'hybrid' organizations (Evers, 2001; Evers et al., 2002).

To see TSOs as belonging to an intermediary sphere allows for conceiving transitions between these organizations and private firms as well as between TSOs and state-run public goods and services. Moreover, it allows an understanding of the extremely varied nature of TSOs. Within the sector, there are not only differences between small local organizations and big national or international organizations: TSOs can also be differentiated according to what they produce and which services they offer. Some of them are engaged in the provision of tangible services, whereas others solely (or mainly) contribute to shaping public opinion. While both types have values relating to the organization of modern society, whether these values are given material expression or not is important. Furthermore, those organizations which are economically active may be concerned with direct income redistribution, giving to the needy what they collected from the wealthy, as do associations based on altruism, solidarity and charity, or they may constitute organizations such as cooperatives or mutuals which see themselves as struggling for a certain economic organization of society, by creating reformatory concepts of a 'social economy' beyond market enterprises and the logic of bureaucratic redistribution. Including the latter in the third sector diverges from the debate in the United States and the so-called 'Johns Hopkins project' (Salamon and Anheier, 1996).

Another internal differentiation to be respected is that between organizations engaged in economic activities (in a broad sense) and civil society organizations such as non-governmental organizations (NGOs) that focus almost exclusively on advocacy, lobbying and public opinion building. From a social science perspective, it is obviously difficult to make sense of such a varied field, comprising, as it does, things such as choral singing and housing production, trade unionism, advocacy for environmental concerns and membership of mutuals.

In the following we will therefore leave aside organizations which are primarily interest or community groups and limit our analysis to those organizations whose central purpose is to produce goods or to supply tangible services. The analytical focus is narrowed further, insofar as matters of social welfare will be the major point of reference whereas broad categories of TSOs, such as environmental organizations, are largely left aside. Keeping this analytical restriction in mind, the chapter will retrace recent evolutions in the German third sector. It will be argued that the organizations that dominated the third sector in postwar Germany have entered a period of deep political and sociocultural change, the latter in some ways reminiscent of the transformations experienced by the early pioneers of the German third sector.

We start by presenting a broad historical background to the third sector as we find it in modern Germany. This considers those parts of the sector which over the course of time have become marginalized (the cooperatives or mutual health insurance companies) as well as the process by which traditional welfare associations became a central pillar of the sector. A second section will elaborate on the ways in which this pillar is called into question today. More concretely, it will show that the whole sector has entered an age of insecurity, in which political and cultural evolution creates a climate of continuous change in the environment of TSOs, which forces them to reinvent themselves through processes which are both creative and destructive. In short, after a loop period of institutional fixation, entrepreneurial mobility has become a key to successful organizational development in the German third sector.

THE HISTORICAL BACKGROUND

The Different Elements of the Third Sector in the Formation of a Civil Society

The right to associate with others is a basic element of modern liberal thought, ensuring the establishment of organizational forms alongside the creation of a civil society. Descriptions of this historical process are abundant.[1] Usually they stress the influence of the churches and the labour movement (both very important in Germany) or the role of the associations voluntarily providing welfare for their members or with an eye to the needs of others (marginal groups). In the case of Germany, one historical element is of particular importance: the more the aims of these civic founders questioned the existing imperial order, the more difficult it was to create what was, in abstract terms, guaranteed by the right to associate freely. Hence these actors searched for roundabout ways to serve their aims. As far as the workers' movement is concerned, for example, involvement in the self-administration of health insurance schemes helped the movement to survive when trade union associations were forbidden. In the days when civil society was in the making, working men's associations were at once trade unions, lobbies vis-à-vis the public authorities, mutuals and service-providing welfare associations.

It took a long time for it to become possible to discern basic elements of what we call nowadays a third sector. There were distinctions to be made between organizations with a material purpose aimed at the delivery of services and others, which were more concerned with issues such as advocacy and influencing public opinion, although obviously, there was and is no clear line to be drawn here. The big welfare associations, backed by the churches, are mainly composed of a conglomeration of service-providing local and regional organizations, but at the same time they also operate as advocacy organizations and lobbies.

Apart from these two groups, there was another important element of the German version of a third sector: the mutual insurance companies (especially health mutuals) which had developed from free self-help associations into para-state organizations by the end of the nineteenth century. The German system of social security, built on insurance, was public, but not state-owned, heavily state-regulated but in many aspects decentralized and self-administered.

Therefore it can be seen as a part of association forming in civil society rather than as a part of welfare state institutions. This holds true in particular for the thousands of mutuals created alongside professions and the upcoming worker movements. Bismarckian law allowed them to persist. It did not prescribe joint funding and administration with the employers. For a long time, the government faced considerable difficulties in limiting the activity of these organizations to administration of insurance funds, and preventing them from serving as agencies with broader concerns, including discussion of social politics.

Among the organizations concerned with material goods and services another differentiation must be made. While some were setting up alternative economic operations within a group, others addressed social needs by giving a helping hand to other groups, motivated by solidarity or charity. Even though there is no clear-cut separation to be made here, the difference between these two types soon became institutionalized in Germany. The churches and bourgeois groups created associations for social help which, later on in the Weimar Republic, united under national umbrella organizations such as the church-linked 'Caritas' and 'Diakonie'. In contrast, the workers' movement and the farmers envisaged 'bottom-up' reforms to the economy. This vision crystallized in cooperatives serving their members, especially in the area of consumer goods and housing, but also in product marketing (in farming), and finally through spin-off processes by the institutionalization of cooperative banks. It should be noted that it was not until late in the 1920s that the German workers' movement (the country's major social–democratic current) created its own welfare association, the Workers Welfare Association. Until then, the predominant option had been to create municipal services in order to substitute state-based rights for conservative clientelism and dependency on traditional charity.

In a way one might say that the sub-sector of associations with social and charity aims in health and welfare was dominated by churches and bourgeois currents, while the workers' movements – and therein the social democrats – dominated the sub-sector of cooperatives and mutual insurance companies. Originally many housing cooperatives, and especially the broad rural movement of the Raiffeisen cooperatives, were carried socially by the 'lower' and politically by the 'upper' classes.

Maintaining some Impact but Losing its Meaning: the Social Economy Tradition and its Fate

In the short period of the Weimar Republic there was a clear increase in both basic elements of the goods and services-producing part of the third sector: the social economy on the one hand, and associations for welfare and charity on the other. The latter were able to formalize their role as privileged partners of the respective governments when it came to the establishment of social services funded by insurance and public budgets.[2] The development of the social economy was somehow different. Two important pillars of this structure will be discussed here: cooperatives and mutual health insurance associations.

Cooperatives underwent drastic expansion in the early twentieth century. First, there was the middle-class cooperative movement: small craftsmen, farmers, shop owners as well as housing cooperatives for both middle classes and some better off groups among the working class. The cooperatives for credit, purchasing and marketing proved to be adept vehicles for improving the economic position of the respective agents in the markets. Their role within the market economy was to provide an institutional means of improving the social and economic situation for members of the cooperatives who considered themselves disadvantaged, and to allow them to take part in the market economy on equal footing with others. This movement proved very successful. It expanded under the Weimar Republic and survived during the Third Reich.[3] This specific part of the cooperative movement managed to recover quite well after the end of Fascism because it was in line with the conservative and pro-market orientation shaping the climate in Germany through to the end of the 1960s. Today a clear majority of all craftsmen and merchants and the vast majority of farmers are still shareholders either in the 'Volksbank' or in the 'Raiffeisenbank' (banking cooperatives). Most grain and milk is also marketed through cooperatives. Such cooperatives are market actors. However, the specific cooperative element made a difference. Without cooperative organization the market position of small economic actors in Germany would be much weaker in the big competitive markets of which they are part.

Obviously, the issue of forming cooperatives was understood in much wider and more radical terms by a second strand of the cooperative movement which was dominated by the social–democratic groupings of cultural associations, trade unions and the party itself. Alongside the powerful consumer cooperatives which had about 4 million members in 1930, the housing cooperatives were the chief domain of this strand in the 1920s. Here the cooperatives made cost reductions possible by increasing standardization and exploiting technological progress. By uniting with the progressive stream of functionalism in architecture they provided one of the very rare examples of working-class economic institutions that were able to go ahead in defining progressive standards of modernity. The cooperative movement attracted support from many municipalities who wished to widen the sector of 'Gemeinwirtschaft' (economy for the public good), which is made up of both municipality-owned and cooperative organizations. It also drew support from the trade unions in creating a powerful working-class 'self-serving economy'

(Eigenwirtschaft). Fascism was detrimental for this strand of the cooperative movement and the climate in the new Federal Republic of Germany (FRG) was unfavourable (for this strand of the cooperative movement and its history, see Novy, 1985).

Despite the support network of linkages, agreements and cultures that had enabled this distinct part of the cooperative movement to grow and shape the orientation of its associates, it was destroyed by the Fascist regime, which passed laws banning this and other workers' organizations.

Later on, in the FRG the reorganized cooperative movement, as a part of the broader grouping of social–democratic organizations, could not rely on the supportive environment that it found during the Weimar Republic. In the eyes of the Social Democrats, economic and welfare reform was a task for the state. In a new consumerist culture, the meaning of welfare changed. Deprived of their former social and moral resources, most of the surviving cooperatives, especially in the housing sector, were big and bureaucratic and riven by corruption and scandals (see Weinert, 1994). The most famous of these scandals, concerning the trade union-owned housing company 'Neue Heimat', meant the end of 'Gemeinwirtschaft' and 'Genossenschaften' (cooperatives) as a distinct part of social democratic reform concepts.

Today, cooperatives have largely died out as agents for social reform, for socially oriented products and services and as pioneers for new technological and cultural orientations. Their concerns became normalized as a special part of the market economy. Furthermore, until recently, economic reasoning did not give much thought to the social embeddedness of economic interaction. For decades, therefore, the cooperative idea was considered irrelevant within economic thinking and, accordingly, no emphasis was given to the cooperative idea by the social policy community. Obviously, this has altogether strengthened the current notion in Germany that economy is equivalent to market economy (to be supported and/or limited by state regulation and the economy of public enterprises and budgeting). What is understood as constituting the third sector – social and welfare associations – is seen as an arrangement without any special economics of its own. This again fosters the view, characteristic of current ways of arguing, that economy or 'economic thinking' has to be injected here.[4]

Another important branch of social economy was mutual health insurance.[5] At the end of the nineteenth century, the economic strength of these organizations grew considerably. Seemingly, their special character was to a large extent absorbed when the welfare state health insurance became a quasi-element of the public sector (Tennstedt, 1976; Tauchnitz, 1999). Before Bismarck made it binding for workers and employers to contribute to health insurance, various different insurances had developed and taken shape, most of them on a solidarity basis, following a corporatist model like, for example, an insurance association for technicians, based on factory or branch member-ship. The welfare reform of 1883 gave these organizations a public status and added a further type of mutual association that was bound to a local commu-nity/municipality. The new insurances became part of a state-regulated, compulsory system, covering all workers and employees with low or middle incomes. The state set up a closely defined catalogue of medical services for which the different insurances had to pay. All mutuals were obliged to provide the same level of financial guarantees and the same scope of services for which refunding can be claimed.

However, the former pluralism survived. Today, there are still about 350 health insurance companies under social law, with different contribution rates and administrative structures.[6] Moreover, the mutuals are still governed by a board representing their personal members. In many of them, these represen-tatives were delegated by interest organizations, for example, employer asso-ciations and trade unions. The trade unions in particular were eager to use the new institutions as a means to promote public health initiatives and as a plat-form for social policy ideas. Thus mutual health insurance companies have become a strong symbol of the corporatist German welfare state (see Bode, 2003a). They are major forces of civil society that collaborate with the state without entering its bureaucratic structures. With this organizational underpin-ning, mutuals were *fixated to institutions*. They served as a technical tool for implementing public policies, while the collective actors involved in their administration were empowered to negotiate these policies. Seen in this light, the German health insurance companies have remained at the intersection between the welfare state and the third sector.

Welfare Associations and the Rise of a Corporatist Model of Social Service Provision

As already mentioned, the only part of the traditional social economy which has maintained a considerable degree of autonomy as a third sector branch comprised voluntary welfare associations (the so-called 'Wohlfahrts-verbände'). Thanks to their special legal status, these associations have been able to re-establish themselves within the institutional framework of postwar Germany up to the present day. Their 'productive' area consists of various local agencies and non-profit enterprises, both of which are autonomous with respect to questions of administration and programming. Moreover, a close network with coordinating and lobbying functions exists at the regional as well as at the national level in the form of the so-called head unions ('Spitzenverbände'). Thus, during the twentieth century, welfare associations developed into nationwide entities. Today there are six nationally organized welfare federations; two are linked to the churches, one to the Social

Democratic Party, one is not aligned and the remaining two are aligned with the Red Cross and a small Jewish agency (see Boeßenecker, 1998).

In 1996, more than a million people (about 3 per cent of all employed people) were employed in such voluntary welfare organizations and enterprises. In addition, official statistics estimate the number of volunteers working in these associations to be about 2.5 to 3 million. The scope of activities of welfare associations is wide and diverse: they are responsible for nearly two-thirds of all homes for the elderly and people with disabilities and account for about 50 per cent of all services in the field of youth assistance as well as about 40 per cent of all hospitals. The costs of most services provided by these organizations are refunded by the state, by the municipalities or by one of the social insurance schemes. Income from contracts with state authorities and reimbursements for services from social insurance schemes make up about 80 per cent of their total income, additional public grants comprise another 10 per cent (data for 1996, see BAGfW, 1997). In this branch, then, the state has taken over an important part of the economic responsibility without taking over the service provision. As a consequence, major non-profit organizations have become 'welfare specialists' in Germany.

The demand for economic accountability within welfare associations has been low. Rather, they have received a licence to mobilize public resources in order to meet needs they have identified themselves. They were part of what one might call a two-tiered welfare corporatism (see Seibel, 1992; Zimmer, 1999; Bode, 2003a): until today, a huge share of their resources came from a corporatist insurance system and the terms of financing, cooperation and service provisions were negotiated between the state and the associations at both the local and regional levels, thus constituting a second corporatist tier.

Until now public regulation was based on two elements, the so-called 'subsidiarity principle' and a 'for public good assumption' (see Daum, 1998). Not only was this latter aspect of the corporatist partnership at the core of the political exchange between the state and its intermediary partners, but it also gave legitimacy to the specific fiscal treatment (grants through tax exemptions) of welfare associations ('Gemeinnützigkeitsrecht'). So far, welfare associations are supposed to provide for universal services (as far as possible), without being accountable. Through the 'subsidiarity principle' they achieved a monopoly on the majority of social services.

Even though things are beginning to change now, it remains a peculiarity of the traditional German welfare system that the responsibility for running social services is preferably handed over to a non-state and non-profit organization (see Bönker and Wollmann, 1996, pp.445ff). While for many areas of welfare, such as advice for families and assistance for young people with special difficulties or, more recently, the availability of a place in a day care facility for children between three and six years of age ('Kindergarten'), the municipalities have a firm responsibility to guarantee basic supply, they very often delegate these tasks to TSOs. For instance, social law stipulates that municipalities have to establish a youth assistance plan in cooperation with local non-profit providers. As a consequence, the established local TSOs have been given considerable influence over the design of social services for young people. Importantly, local social assistance offices have to pay for people in need of services for which no claims on insurance refunds can be made (for example concerning health services for people who depend on social assistance for their daily living and who are not insured). Thus considerable financial securities are given to the third sector providers of such services (for the history of state–third sector relations in the fields of child and elderly care see in more detail Evers and Sachße, 2003).

Despite the fact that this welfare culture is marked by a tradition of strong public 'tutelage', the state has not, until today, done away with the social bases of the welfare associations. Within their various agencies, particular moral and professional rationales have developed that remain different from the 'philosophy' of statutory welfare bureaucracies in many respects. Moreover, the associations maintain their connections with their original constituency, evidence of which is the considerable amount of voluntary contributions that they receive. This supplementary funding consists of church subsidies and private donations (which make up for about 5 per cent of the total budget of the welfare associations) and, although the total is decreasing, this input flow persists today. The material weight of voluntary work is also still of crucial importance. Estimates say that it doubles the financial impact of donations.

Welfare associations have remained embedded politically as well. At the regional and local levels, they form solid alliances with public authorities and other welfare associations, but also with political parties. Strong cultural roots guarantee this embeddedness, especially in the Catholic Church and the workers' movement. Again, what occurred was an *institutional fixation*. The political system has conferred considerable responsibility upon non-statutory agents with which it is tightly coupled, if not in a state of harmony. It is worth noting that the public–private partnership has never worked as a 'top-down' process but has left much room for influences from the associational 'welfare specialists'. By the same token, the state has always acted as a driving force in the universalization of services that had previously been scattered and unevenly spread owing to the fact that the associations were solely responsible for service provision. However, in the long history of postwar Germany, the sociopolitical embeddedness of the welfare organizations as described above has continually weakened. The links with the public authorities have turned out to be much more indirect, as an informal relationship between stakeholder hierarchies on the one hand and political actors (governments and ministries) on the other. Welfare services have increasingly employed salaried professionals, who frequently distanced themselves from former religious or ideological relationships. During the 1970s in particular, the welfare associations considerably widened both their activities and their organizational resources (staff and infrastructure). During this period, they enjoyed a 'golden age' in which their institutional standing was taken for granted.

NEW CHALLENGES AND WELFARE REMIX

The Neoliberal Challenge: Managerial Deregulation in Social Welfare

The return of economic liberalism is an international trend which began in the 1980s and has had significant, though varying, impacts on the welfare systems of the western world (Pinch, 1997; Taylor-Gooby, 2001). We do not want to discuss the reasons for this evolution here, but rather to consider its consequences for the German third sector. The corporatist model has generally come under pressure. It was contested by political and economic forces claiming that the welfare system (its material impact and institutional weight, both of which had been growing since the end of World War II) was no longer supportable. These forces opposed the relative autonomy and the bureaucratic structures of the big welfare–state partners, and there was growing pressure on them to economize by means of service contracting, quasi-marketing and managing cuts in public subsidies (see Bönker and Wollmann, 1996; Evers and Strünck, 2002). Yet the neoliberal turn went beyond a mere short-term rationalization of social service supply. Economic deregulation had a second face and the public status of TSOs has been called into question; that is, there is a new focus on the institutional difference between market organizations on the one hand and state-protected TSOs on the other.

Short-term rationalization was promoted by various social policy reforms which have created a serious challenge for TSOs: what had been an asset in the corporatist era became a problem, namely the strong integration of TSOs in the welfare state. The state turned out to be the dominant partner, transforming itself into a kind of 'managerial state'.[7] In fact, new regulations changed the way in which public resources are transferred from public agencies to non-statutory providers or administrators of services. The welfare associations have been faced with a new 'contract culture' that increasingly forces them into task-linked and time-limited arrangements with public bodies, requiring a permanent strategy of 'flexible response' (Bode, 2003b; Evers and Strünck, 2002). As a general tendency, grants have been reduced by local authorities. Moreover, the transfer of public money has become difficult to calculate since, under conditions of financial austerity, budgets can be cut unexpectedly. In short, public funding has become less secure. As in other countries, the 'arm's length grant aid in cozy "partnership" arrangements and direct government provision ... is simply not on offer any more' (6, 1997). Instead, provision of services is increasingly managed by contracts, eliminating most of the organizational slack the non-profit agencies could make use of before.

In the case of youth assistance, for instance, the transfer of public money has become much more selective. In some regions, there are public tenders for particular projects, with contracts based on narrowly calculated input and output benchmarks. Because of shortcomings in municipal budgets, many agencies have had to reduce their facilities. Higher demands on economic accountability, programme evaluation and additional administrative documentation have caused TSOs to change from a value-based mission to an economy-driven management. A further example of reorganization is care for the elderly, in which private firms have been allowed to provide service (Evers, 1998). Even though the sector as a whole has been expanding with the creation of a social care insurance,[8] welfare associations can no longer derive benefit from their service monopoly. As funding is restricted to a list of defined care acts, non-profit providers have been led to focus their activities in areas which are reimbursed by the refunding institutions. Grants from public authorities or subsidies from their own associational network are much less readily available than they were in the past. For additional services, users have to accept private fees. This, however, threatens to compromise their non-profit status.

This development mirrors a second stream of change in which many social policy actors are inclined to take new partners on board, be they commercial or third sector providers, which are independent of the big welfare associations' lobbies. Thus the traditional subsidiarity principle is modified in so far as the exclusive responsibility of welfare associations is no longer taken for granted. Furthermore, the rise of a new pluralism of providers, which is in fact a loosening of the institutional fixation in the field of social services, has been accompanied by an attack on the non-profit status of service providers themselves. At the national level, this became an issue in 1994, when the care insurance was introduced and private providers were accepted as contract partners with 'equal rights'. At the European Union level, the public status of the welfare associations is contested as well, even though final decisions have not been made. There are strong forces opposing any kind of 'public good' status as is given to social service suppliers by current German legislation.[9] Rather, private and non-profit providers will be given the same status, allowing only for two kinds of service agents acknowledged by law: the state and other organizations, be they for-profit or not-for-profit. Thus the role of TSOs to combine service provision with the raising of social capital, whether organized political advocacy, volunteer participation or professional engagement, seems no longer to be acknowledged.

The neoliberal turn affects another organizational pillar of welfare corporatism in Germany as well, the *mutual health insurance associations*. First of all, having a semi-public, semi-private status, the health insurances do not fit the above-mentioned two-sector logic defended by major forces of the European Union administration. As a result, there is considerable juridical insecurity in this field. Second, national policy reform has led to deregulation of the system (see Busse *et al*., 2000), although the impact of this deregulation was somehow different from what happened to the voluntary welfare organizations. The mutual health insurance associations retained part of their economic autonomy. They now compete for new members on a free market, offer new services to their clientele and negotiate contracts with medical service providers. At the same time, those social–professional ties which had been at the origin of the mutualist movement are definitely lost. There is no longer a special link, for example, between an occupation/profession and a mutual health insurance association. As a result, what had in the past provided for some sociocultural embeddedness of the health mutuals has completely disappeared.

Of course the economic deregulation of this field had its limits. There is still a range of rules providing for solidarity between all members of the health mutuals.[10] Besides that, they are invited today by social policy to reactivate their public health mission, for example by developing new kinds of health care coordination in favour of the chronically ill (Bode, 2000).[11] Nonetheless, examining the new economic strategies of the German mutuals in the health sector, it becomes evident that selecting risks according to their relative cost is quite profitable for them. There is empirical evidence that many of them have been busy remodelling the structure of the insured risks (Daubenbüchel, 2001). They attract young people through special service offers, deter those who are believed to consume too much, and build up new sub-organizations concentrating good risks, thus reducing contribution rates (this had been possible for company-related mutuals until 2000). The overall goal is to offer attractive insurance conditions, but to reserve them as far as possible for members that represent 'good risks'.

The Other Side of the Story: Sociocultural Challenges and Deregulation from Below

At first sight, neoliberalism seems to be the decisive force behind institutional change in the third sector. What is perceived less frequently in this context, however, is that the neoliberal agenda went along with sociocultural challenges. These challenges resulted from a legitimacy crisis in the welfare model of postwar Germany (see Mayer and Roth, 1995; Offe, 1996, pp.147ff; Anheier and Seibel, 2001, pp.4f) in which major structures of the welfare system have been called into question. Underlying this development is a breakdown of state-centred, universalistic approaches to social welfare and the appearance of new micro solidarities, together with an emphasis on autonomy rights. Responding to these challenges, a deregulation 'from below' took place. New social movements contested the 'old' institutions and the way they offered their services. Importantly, whereas the 'old' third sector taking shape during the first decades of the twentieth century had been based on collectivist ideas in one way or another, the new initiatives followed a more individualistic approach. The rise of this individualistic culture of welfare, mainly among the well-educated academic middle classes, proved to be a second driving force for the erosion of the corporatist model.

From the 1970s on, the traditional welfare associations were confronted by serious problems. The flow of private input into these associations was slowly eroding. An increasing number of people left the big churches which, as a consequence, lost financial support that originated in donations and, above all, from church tax. In addition to that, the 'old' model of lifelong and humble volunteering did not attract as many (young) people as before. At the same time, the traditional welfare associations faced practical competition from the grassroots level. New initiatives came into being which sought to open new spaces for individual participation and for the role of the individual as a 'co-producer'. A new self-help orientation emerged, combining volunteer commitment with micro democratic forms of service provision. Many initiatives rapidly developed into formal organizations of different kinds, thus making the third sector in Germany more diverse. The new organizations used particular funding techniques, with private contributions and sales becoming an important additional resource of many projects.

One current of the new associational activism has been captured under the label 'self-help groups'.[12] These groups have in common that the majority of cooperating members are lay persons and engage on a voluntary basis.[13] Paid work and the professional element are throughout of minor importance. The most frequent topics these organizations deal with are health problems (such as disabilities or chronic diseases); next to these, psychosocial and social topics are important. Groups concerned with these topics reflect a growing scepticism among citizens towards the professional sociomedical system.

It is worth noting that health policy became aware of this evolution and began to support these organizations. Since the year 2000 health mutuals are forced by law to give some funds to them.

Another interesting element of this movement is child care (Becker and Bode, 2000). The churches and the big welfare associations as service providers have lost their traditional monopoly, together with the public kindergartens. From the 1970s, a growing number of parents opposed to the traditional philosophy of child care and dissatisfied with what they thought to be an authoritarian education joined together in associations which established and ran child care services on a more or less experimental basis.

These movements gave a fresh impulse to the politics of child care in Germany, even though a lot of the first initiatives were not long-lived. Nonetheless, as a consequence of this movement, associations of (academic, middle-class) parents began to multiply. They established child care services according to their personal needs, which in many cases meant full-time care in order to facilitate the life of working mothers. The juridical system of public control took into account this new welfare pluralism, as it allowed for new forms of non-statutory child care to be funded by public authorities. Numbers of these parental associations have joined already existing welfare federations (primarily the DPWV) because the technical support of the latter made their life much easier. Nonetheless, they have remained quite independent.

These examples show that the deregulation of the German welfare system and the new role TSOs began to play within the welfare mix have been paralleled or even underpinned by movements striving for individual or micro group autonomy and being less concerned with the fact that a system of patchy services is far from universal coverage. Importantly, as will be shown below, the cultural turn within the non-profit field had a considerable impact on the self-perception of third sector actors. Both economic and cultural liberalism were accompanied by the rise of entrepreneurial thinking in the third sector, with equivocal consequences concerning the quality and the structure of social welfare.

Entrepreneurial Mobility and its Different Meanings

The challenges described above have demanded a change from the type of bureaucratic behaviour, supported in part by a professional culture, which was strong in the preceding decades. This points toward a strengthening of entrepreneurial mobility. We have chosen this term consciously, because on the one hand it indicates that nowadays TSOs are generally shaped by issues of 'risk taking', 'managing an organization' and 'searching for best practices'. On the other hand, the term 'entrepreneurial' indicates that, owing to a changing environment, there has been a shift towards a greater recognition of the impact of market values which stress mobility in terms of rapid and broad adaptation to external economic constraints.

The way of dealing with the general entrepreneurial challenge of steering one's boat in a changing environment depends on the history of the respective organization, the status of the service task and the context in which the organization is placed. In order to give a rough idea of the variety of entrepreneurial orientation, three different versions are presented below.[14]

Entrepreneurship as a component of 'normalizing' welfare business

There are sectors where commercial actors are strong and/or the respective tasks rather standardized, routine and well established, for example nursing homes, hospitals, occupational training and health insurance. With an eye on such regulated market sectors, the big welfare associations have increasingly begun to create business agencies which are only indirectly linked to the welfare associations themselves ('Ausgründungen'). While they can basically be managed like an ordinary business,[15] they benefit from reduced taxation, as organizations 'for the public good'. This kind of agency, and its 'embeddedness' in the relational structure of the respective market, offers an advantage for organizations under the umbrella of a big welfare association which can also provide additional backing, through consultancy and so on. In Germany, the area of care provision has been an often quoted example of the build-up of a competitive market with a growing inflow of private capital. One can imagine that more service areas will become subject to open subscriptions at the European level, with non-profit providers being just another competitor.

Becoming a social entrepreneur

As has been said, a lot of organizations have developed services out of local concern or because of the special concerns of a group, for example people with AIDS, people suffering from disabilities, those who are unemployed or who have special cultural interests. Building solidarity and publicity, creating trust and personal connections, and providing social support are of utmost importance here. Furthermore, active networking is required. This means, at least when starting up, applying for institutional support by public authorities, campaigning for social goals and making oneself known to a wider public. These are important prerequisites for gaining access to sponsors and, in the longer term, for receiving acknowledgment as a standard service provider. The social entrepreneurs involved must strive for a public-oriented type of 'high profile strategy' in matters of social concern. Here, the entrepreneurial orientation is supposed to be far removed from simple (commercial) rent seeking. If there is a surplus it will most probably be used for risk management and reinvestment. What is most important is 'local embeddedness': the respective organizations must know the key actors and earn their trust. The 'social enterprises' (Evers, 2001) that correspond to this type of social entrepreneurship forge links with the goals and resources of the public authorities, managerial and market oriented components and the use of the various forms of social capital that stem from networking and local embeddedness.

Linking different types of entrepreneurship

This third strategy is found in organizational contexts linked to different markets or different rationales. We can find this mixture in welfare associations. As mentioned above, they are organized at a local, federal and central level, with a high diversity of management styles and 'market' involvements. This entails the possibility of internal mechanisms of risk sharing or of cross-subsidies.[16] In a forward-looking entrepreneurial perspective, the association of different organizations in different fields can be used to maintain market share in one field while simultaneously creating new options elsewhere. This can mean an umbrella organization supporting different styles of entrepreneurial action in different service sectors and political environments. Thus a managerial style in the hospital business can go along with a soft community building-oriented style of action in a local centre for neighbourhood redevelopment under the roof of one and the same welfare association.

CONCLUSIONS: WILL A THIRD SECTOR PERSIST?

Interestingly, some of the tendencies depicted above for the core of the German third sector recall the history of the cooperatives. In the near future, the umbrella organizations of the welfare associations may play the same role as peak structures in the cooperative sector do today: that is, serving as a link between social service organizations and the world of social insurances and other purchasers and regulators (public authorities). Thus they would be different from ordinary business only in so far as they make clever use of their specific networking facilities. They would bring into a competitive market not just single TSOs but organizations which are backed by a quite powerful infra-structure. This could make them altogether different, not by constituting a sector that is different *from* the market sector, but as being different organizations *within* a broad and diverse market sphere. And the concept of entrepreneurship would then not only relate to risk taking and innovating but also to 'minding one's own business'.

To the degree one conceives organizations as different from other market actors to the extent that they are '*social* entrepreneurs', forecasts concerning the future impact of the third sector will, however, be more optimistic. Today the common-good orientation matters and, in addition to sales and state support, the use and mobilization of social capital is supposed to remain a central element of the constituencies, goals and resources of non-profit organizations. However, in order to make the most of these in the future, four critical issues need to be considered.

First is *the service culture*. The more one imagines services as a highly standardized product, like computer-monitored medical treatments or coast-to-coast chains for nursing care and homes for the elderly in the USA, the more service delivery will be national or on a European scale. Local self-made services may then have a decreasing role, and the active participation of civil society will be limited to its ability to raise public awareness of particular issues and to make consumer criticism heard through the media, though no longer through social cooperation. Only if services are able to allow for differences in standards and processes, and if they are to a large degree in tune with special local circumstances, might they be seen as something to be co-produced by the users and the local public. In these circumstances the need for a 'local' economy of services, which may entail varying proportions of public, private and third sector ownership, may be retained. However, the question remains open to what degree a specific type of service concept really includes a specific institutional solution. While many services could be thought to be run by for-profit providers, it is, for example, still hard to imagine a commercial company striving for a community-oriented hospital.

Second is *the structuring of service tasks*. While there are well-established areas of services on the way to becoming routine for a consumerist culture, there are others which are very uneven and multifaceted. For instance, urban renewal is a task that calls for multiple interactions between the market, TSOs and public authorities. Here the notion of the common good (the living and working conditions in a city area) is a really complex one, and it cannot be simply broken down into the mere problem of defining the right manner of public financing for giving broad access to basically uncontroversial types of services. Will there be special opportunities for TSOs to play an influential part in such a partnership?

The third critical issue is *the role of civic and moral commitment*. So far, social practices in the third sector have been shaped by the specific civic and moral commitments of volunteers and professional actors. Volunteering was supposed to be long-term and reliable, and the 'social economy manager' assumed to be motivated by non-economic ends. Both of these underpinnings of the third sector are under strain today. Volunteering has become more volatile and less sustainable, and the growing economic competition within the third sector tends to weaken the dominance of moral values as a guideline for social management and political work. Given this development, will civic and moral commitment continue to be a driving force for action in the sector?

A final critical issue is *the strategy of public authorities*. There is a strong tendency to perceive the role of governments and public authorities largely as regulation, quality control and funding of services that they should no longer carry out themselves, but that should be provided by 'private' organizations in the present circumstances. TSOs *can* offer such services, just like commercial suppliers, yet, in principle, they are not needed. The need for TSOs can only be argued on the grounds of their special contributions: for example, identification of new demands and services in sectors and areas which are not (yet) of interest to public authorities or market actors. Another special 'raison d'être' of TSOs might be that, by fashioning their specific version of a public service, they may contribute to the political process by which the nature of public goods is defined. Such a competitive process, shaped partly by policy networks which link actors from different sectors of the civil society, the state and the market, would avoid leaving the definition of social welfare entirely to the market and consumers on the one hand and to public authorities on the other. At present, however, it seems that public policies in Germany use TSOs very pragmatically (simply because they are there), without giving them a particular place as a special part of the architecture of welfare and governance.

NOTES

1. In this chapter, we confine ourselves to a short outline of the historical path the German third sector followed during the nineteenth and twentieth centuries. Details are provided by Anheier and Seibel (2001).
2. Of course there has always been a small amount of economic input from the welfare associations themselves as well.
3. Those organizations which were more conformist in political terms had few problems surviving the changes administered during that period. These changes consisted of centralizing and unifying the very differentiated and localized field of cooperatives and putting them under the command of the Nazi state.
4. This is precisely the message of the 'new managerialism' (see Clarke and Newman, 1997; Young, 1998; Wex, 2003).
5. Known in Britain as 'friendly societies' and in France as 'mutuelles'.
6. In addition, another branch of the insurance system exists which also has its roots in the social economy: that is, free mutuals who offer insurances to association members (but only for additional services or people with high income who need not enter the legal system). These, however, are very close to private insurances today (see Greisler, 1997).
7. To use an expression of Clarke and Newman (1997), who employ it to depict the configuration in Great Britain.
8. The long-term care insurance funds operate under the organizational 'roof' of the various health insurers, so that every health insurance company has a care insurance branch as well. Services provided to their members by social service are paid for by organizations they have an agreement with. These might be commercial and not-for-profit agencies running a hospital, a care service centre or a nursing home. The services are rendered according to a catalogue of what can be refunded by the care insurance.
9. For discussion on this, see Lange (2001). Note that there is also a European jurisdiction causing piecemeal changes of fiscal regulation in this direction.
10. Indeed, strong market regulation has persisted. The field is limited to non-profit insurers funding service providers according to a national reimbursement scheme. These insurers must accept all those who want to join them. Moreover, by a system of enforced cross-subsidizing, those funds with a high share of 'good risks' support their competitors with 'bad risks'. Nonetheless, after cross-subsidies, the risk structure of the health care funds is still not the same.
11. Some mutual health care providers have set up new concepts of quality management. For instance, their agents contact members in order to introduce a sort of case management with the purpose of improving the course of medical treatments. Sickness funds try to establish provision networks, with general practitioners as gatekeepers who supervise the whole range of diagnostics and treatments that may occur during the course of medical treatments. The idea is to raise efficiency by avoiding unnecessary medical interventions, caused by private doctors (the specialists in particular) as well as by hospitals. Frequently, fund managers choose special risk populations to be guided by fund employees or medical experts.

Furthermore, patients are taken into special disease management programmes or given advice on where to go and how to participate in the process of medical treatment (see Niedermeier, 2001).

12. An estimate in a ministry study (Bundesministerium für Familie, Senioren, Frauen und Jugend, 1997) is that in 1997 there were about 70 000 self-help groups and initiatives, with about 2.65 million people involved, for themselves and for others. Note that in Germany it is common practice to include quite different forms of collective action under this label (see Thiel, 1998). There are at least two sub-sectors: (a) smaller self-help groups which are semi-informal and mainly exist in order to give emotional mutual support to their immediate members; (b) outside-oriented groups which provide services to non-members as well (for example an association which brings together parents of children with cancer) and where problems of general and broader interest also play a role.

13. About one-third of all local groups are members of an umbrella organization at the regional or central level (for example, a national association of the blind) and another third are members of a welfare association, mainly in the non-traditional 'Deutscher Paritätischer Wohlfahrtsverband' (DPWV).

14. Note that we present ideal types, in a way illustrated by real types, and that real strategies are quite diverse in all parts of the German third sector today.

15. Since it frequently offers 'organizational promises' – human care, continuing therapy, need-oriented consultancy and so on – rather than ordinary goods, the 'social market' is different from other markets. Hence non-profit providers may have an advantage over commercial firms, as Hansman's theory of the non-profit sector predicts (Hansman, 1986).

16. To give but one example, under the roof of a local organization for the employment and training of jobless people, enterprises which make a surplus (for example a flourishing company initially built up with the help of public employment schemes) and weak new organizations which still make a loss (for example organizations dealing with marginalized young people) may operate side by side. There can be redistribution mechanisms between the two, and they can take place for both good and bad reasons. In the positive case this can be seen as interorganizational solidarity; in the negative case it can be a mere case of 'voluntary failure' where different resources of the local umbrella organizations are matched simply in order to maintain badly managed branches (which, for example, cannot be abandoned for sheer political reasons).

REFERENCES

6, Perri (1997), 'The New Politics of Welfare Contracting', in P. 6 and J. Kendall (eds), *The Contract Culture in Public Services. Studies from Britain, Europe and the USA*, Aldershot: Ashgate, pp.181–92.

Anheier, H.K. and W. Seibel (2001), *The Nonprofit Sector in Germany. Between State, Economy and Society*, Manchester: Manchester University Press.

Aschhoff, G. and E. Henningsen (1996), *The German Cooperative System. Its History, Structure and Strength*, Frankfurt/Main: Fritz Knapp Verlag.

BAGfW (Bundesarbeitsgemeinschaft der Freien Wohlfahrtspflege e.V.) (1997), *Gesamtstatistik der Einrichtungen der Freien Wohlfahrtpflege 1996*, Bonn.

Becker, A. and I. Bode (2000), 'Nonprofits for the Youngest. The Social Economy of Childcare Services in the German Third Sector and its Evolution', ISTR Dublin Conference Papers (http:// www.jhu.edu/(istr).

Bode, I. (2000), 'De la solidarité au marché. En France et en Allemagne, nouveaux défis pour les organismes d'assurance maladie à but non lucratif', *Revue Internationale de l'Economie Sociale* (Revue des Études Coopératives, Mutualistes et Associatives), 79 (278), 67–79.

Bode, I. (2003a), 'The Welfare State in Germany', in Christian Aspalter (ed.), *Welfare Capitalism Around the World*, Hongkong and Taipeh: Casa Verde Publishing.

Bode, I. (2003b), 'Flexible Response in Changing Environments. The German Third Sector in Transition', *Nonprofit and Voluntary Sector Quarterly*, 33 (2).

Bönker, F. and H. Wollmann (1996), 'Incrementalism and Reform Waves: The Case of Social Service Reform in the Federal Republic of Germany', *Journal of European Public Policy*, 3 (3), 441–60.

Boeßenecker, K.-H. (1998), *Spitzenverbände der Wohlfahrtspflege in der BRD. Eine Einführung in Organisationsstruktur und Handlungsfelder*, 2nd edn, Münster: Votum.

Bundesministerium für Familie, Senioren, Frauen und Jugend (Ministry of Family Affairs) (ed.) (1997), *Selbsthilfe und Selbsthilfeunterstützung in der Bundesrepublik Deutschland*, Stuttgart: Verlag W. Kohlhammer.

Busse, R., N. Goodwin and E. Mossialos (2000), *The German Health Care System*, Aldershot: Ashgate.

Clarke, J. and J. Newman (1997), *The Managerial State. Power, Politics and Ideology in the Remaking of Social Welfare*, London: Sage.

Daubenbüchel, R. (2001), 'Die Krankenkassen im Spannungsfeld zwischen Wettbewerb und staatlicher Aufsicht', in A. Alexander and T. Rath (eds), *Krankenkassen im Wandel. Organisationsentwicklung als Herausforderung*, Wiesbaden: Gabler, pp.77–87.

Daum, R. (1998), 'Zur Situation der Vereine in Deutschland. Materialien für eine europäische Studie über das Vereinswesen am Beispiel der Freien Wohlfahrtspflege', special number of *Zeitschrift für öffentliche und gemeinwirtschaftliche Unternehmen*, 23.

Evers, A. (1998), 'The New Long-Term Care Insurance Program in Germany', *Journal of Ageing & Social Policy*, 18 (1), 77–98.

Evers, A. (2001), 'The Significance of Social Capital in the Multiple Goal and Resource Structure of Social Enterprises', in C. Borzaga and J. Defourny (eds), *The Emergence of Social Enterprise*, London: Routledge, pp.298–311.

Evers, A. and C. Sachße (2003), 'Social Care Services for Children and Older People in Germany: Distinct and Separate Histories', in A. Anttonen, J. Baldock and J. Sipilä (eds), *The Young, the Old and the State: Social Care Systems in Five Industrial Nations*, Cheltenham, UK and Northampton, MA, USA: Edward Elgar, pp.55–80.

Evers, A. and C. Strünck (2002), 'Answers Without Questions? The Changing Contract Culture in Germany and the Future of a Mixed Welfare System', in U. Ascoli and C. Ranci (eds), *Dilemmas of the Welfare Mix. The Privatisation of Social Care in Europe*, New York: Plenum, pp.165–96.

Evers, A., U. Rauch and U. Stitz (2002), *Von öffentlichen Einrichtungen zu sozialen Unternehmen. Hybride Organisationsformen im Bereich sozialer Dienstleistungen*, Berlin: Sigma Verlag.

Greisler, P. (1997), 'System- und Selbstverständnis des Versicherungsvereins auf Gegenseitigkeit. eine europäische Herausforderung', in R.H. Jung, H.M. Schäfer and F.W. Seibel (eds), *Économie Sociale: Fakten und Standpunkte zu einem solidarwirtschaftlichen Konzept*, Frankfurt: IKO Verlag, pp.128–49.

Hansman, H.B. (1986), 'The Role of Nonprofit Enterprise', in Susan Rose-Ackerman (ed.), *The Economics of Nonprofit Institutions. Studies in structure and policy*, New York: Oxford University Press, pp.57–84.

Lange, C. (2001), *Freie Wohlfahrtspflege und europäische Integration. Zwischen Marktangleichung und sozialer Verantwortung*, Frankfurt: Eigenverlag des DVfÖPF.

Mayer, M. and R. Roth (1995), 'New Social Movements and the Transformation to Post-Fordist Society', in M. Darnowski, B. Epstein and R. Flacks (eds), *Cultural Politics and Social Movements*, Philadelphia: Temple University Press, pp.299–319.

Niedermeier, R. (2001), *Von der Krankheitsverwaltung zur Gesundheitsgestaltung? Organisationale Lernprozesse in der Gesetzlichen Krankenversicherung*, Bremerhaven: Wirtschaftsverlag NW.

Novy, K. (1985), 'Vorwärts immer, rückwärts nimmer: Historische Anmerkungen zu einem aktuellen Problem', in H. Bierbaum and M. Riege (eds), *Die neue Genossenschaftsbewegung. Initiativen in der BRD und in Westeuropa*, Hamburg: VSA, pp.124–41

Offe, C. (1996), *Modernity and the State. East, West*, Cambridge: Polity Press.

Pinch, S.P. (1997), *Worlds of Welfare. Understanding the Changing Geographies for Social Welfare Provision*, London: Routledge.

Salamon, L.M. and H.K. Anheier (1996), *The Emerging Nonprofit Sector – An Overview*, Manchester and New York: Manchester University Press .

Seibel, W. (1992), 'Government–Nonprofit Relationship: Styles and Linkage Patterns in France and Germany', in S. Kuhnle and P. Selle (eds), *Government and Voluntary Organizations. A Relational Perspective*, Aldershot: Avebury, pp.53–70.

Tauchnitz, T. (1999), *Krankenkassen – Fluch oder Segen? Organisationsgeschichte des deutschen Krankenkassenwesens im 'langen' 19. Jahrhundert*, Opladen: Leske & Budrich.

Taylor-Gooby, P. (ed.) (2001), *Welfare States Under Pressure*, London: Routledge.

Tennstedt, F. (1976), 'Sozialgeschichte der Sozialversicherung', in M. Blohmke, C.V. Ferber, K.P. Kisker and H. Schäfer (eds), *Handbuch der Sozialmedizin*, Stuttgart: Enke, pp.385–492.

Thiel, W. (1998), 'Selbsthilfe als Fremdhilfe. Über Struktur und Bedeutung der Arbeit von Selbsthilfegruppen', in R. Strachwitz (ed.), *Dritter Sektor – Dritte Kraft. Versuch einer Standortbestimmung*, Düsseldorf: Raabe, pp.327–47.

Weinert, R. (1994), *Das Ende der Gemeinwirtschaft. Gewerkschaften und gemeinwirtschaftliche Unternehmen im Nachkriegsdeutschland*, Frankfurt/New York: Campus.

Wex, T. (2003), 'Die Strategie erwerbswirtschaftlicher Ökonomisierung. Eine Kritik und ein Plädoyer für eine genuine Nonprofit-Ökonomik', forthcoming in Arbeitskreis Nonprofit-Organisationen (ed.), *Mission impossible? Strategie im Dritten Sektor*, Frankfurt: Eigenverlag des DVÖPF.

Young, D.R. (1998), 'Commercialism in Nonprofit Social Service Associations. Its Character, Significance, and Rationale', in B.A. Weisbrod (ed.), *To Profit or Not to Profit. The Commercial Transformation of the Nonprofit Sector*, New York: Cambridge University Press.

Zimmer, A. (1999), 'Corporatism Revisited – The Legacy of History and the German Nonprofit-Sector', *Voluntas*, 10 (1), 37–49.

6. The welfare mix in the United Kingdom

Marilyn Taylor

INTRODUCTION

Until relatively recently, the commonly used terms used to describe the 'third sector' in the UK have been 'voluntary action', the 'voluntary sector' and 'charity'.[1] The language of a 'non-profit' or 'not-for profit' sector has become more familiar with the introduction of market approaches to welfare. But most official documents continue to refer to the voluntary sector (Commission on the Future of the Voluntary Sector, 1996; Home Office, 1998; HM Treasury, 2002).

Nonetheless, while it has the advantage of familiarity, this is a term which is getting harder and harder to sustain. Firstly, some dispute the whole concept of a separate sector. The boundaries between this and other sectors seem to be increasingly blurred, first with the onset of privatization and more recently with the New Labour government's emphasis on partnership. Secondly, distinctions are increasingly being made within the sector, especially between the larger professionalized organizations, often providing services on contract to government, and organizations which are seen to be closer to their associational roots and embedded more closely in the local or interest communities they serve. The third problem with the term 'voluntary sector' is that, as a recent government report argues (Cabinet Office, 2002, p.14), it fails to encompass the diversity of the organizations within it:

> as the sector becomes more and more entrepreneurial, the term only really captures one element of their activity. It is even harder to see how the term has any relevance to the co-operatives and social enterprises, which often have no voluntary input.

This report argues that many charities might more appropriately be described as social enterprises, especially those who generate their own income rather than relying on grant aid and donations.

When New Labour first came to power in the UK in 1997, it embraced the idea of a 'third way' in public policy which would chart a course between the extremes of state-dominated welfare and the market. This 'third way' not only drew attention to the role that voluntary and community organizations could play, it also revived interest in mutuals (Leadbeater and Christie, 1999), which are an important part of the British tradition but sometimes neglected in the analysis and promotion of third sector issues (Davis Smith, 1995). The concept of 'civil society' as a distinct sphere outside the market and the state is another idea that is also gathering momentum in the UK, although this language is not as widely used as in developing countries, Central and Eastern Europe or, indeed, the United States.

This chapter begins by considering some of the definitional issues that have beset the UK third sector in recent years. It then tracks the historical development of some of the main strands within this territory, particularly in relation to its boundaries with the state. The chapter ends by considering the current challenges that face organizations within this sector and assessing what a 'welfare mix' analysis offers to understanding and addressing these challenges.

DEFINING THE SECTOR

The first, and still one of the most common ways of defining the third sector is through a legal definition – that of charitable status – although, as Kendall and Knapp (1996) remind us, there is no legal definition of voluntary organizations as such and not all voluntary organizations are charitable. Charitable status is still defined by the 1601 Statute of Charitable Uses and applies to four uses: the relief of poverty, the advancement of education, the advancement of religion and other purposes beneficial to the community. But, as Chesterman (1979, pp.174–88) points out, a number of organizations carrying out these purposes are expressly excluded from charitable status, because they engage in political activity or because the trustees of a charitable organization cannot benefit personally from its services or the distribution of its profits. This 'non-distribution constraint' generally rules out mutuals and other social enterprises where members benefit materially. It can also create registration problems for some self-help organizations and other organizations who wish service users to be a majority on the board.

Charitability is a legal status which brings with it, inter alia, tax and reputational benefits as well as protecting donations. But it is not a form of incorporation and does not give charities the legal personality they need to mobilize resources and manage assets. Many self-help organizations and small charities without staff and assets remain as unincorporated associations. But those who need to incorporate usually take the form of companies limited by guarantee, a form which gives them legal personality while limiting the financial liability of trustees. However, the company 'brand' is associated with profit making

and not designed for the particular needs of charities. The legal form traditionally used by mutuals in the UK is the Industrial and Provident Society,
although this has become outdated and inflexible.

Growing calls for a review of charity law (see, for example, the 1996
Commission on the Future of the Voluntary Sector) have recently been heeded
in a review by government (Cabinet Office, 2002), which proposes to extend
the previous four heads to ten, to create new legal forms which serve the needs
of third sector organizations, to improve accountability without introducing
excessive regulation and to reform the regulation of Industrial and Provident
Societies. We will return to these proposals towards the end of the chapter.

For those who wish to measure the size of the voluntary sector and give an
account of its contribution to the UK welfare mix, charitable status is a necessary but not sufficient definition. Kendall and Knapp (1996) included most
charitable bodies in their work on the sector, but also housing associations,
self-help groups, trade unions and professional associations, and recreational
organizations, as well as many community businesses. However, they distinguished between a 'broad' and a 'narrow' voluntary sector, the latter excluding recreational organizations, independent and voluntary-aided schools,
higher education, and trade unions and professional associations, on the
grounds that the latter would not feature in most people's understanding of the
'voluntary sector' in the UK. In 1995, the expenditure of the broad voluntary
sector was estimated as 6.6 per cent of gross domestic product (GDP), that of
the narrow voluntary sector as 2.2 per cent.

However, Perri 6 and Diana Leat (1997) argue that the concept of a 'voluntary sector' is relatively new in the UK; they remind us that the National
Council for Voluntary Organisations, the main generalist umbrella body for
voluntary organizations, only took this name in 1981 (it was formerly known
as the National Council for Social Service). They are critical, with others, of
the implicit assumption in the definition and promotion of a 'voluntary sector'
that this is a discrete sector which contributes particular characteristics to the
welfare mix (flexibility, closeness to the customer and so on). Indeed, a growing number of critics argue that the larger organizations in the voluntary sector
can lay less and less claim to these attributes, as they become more professionalized, less associational and more like their statutory and commercial
counterparts (see, for example, Knight, 1993). It is possible to argue that organizations with annual turnovers in the millions of pounds which pay high
salaries to professional staff and compete in the marketplace for donations
cannot really be defined as either 'voluntary' or 'non-profit'.

This critique is reflected in the increasingly common use of the phrase
'voluntary and community sector' to describe the sector in the UK.[2] This
distinction has been promoted by a Community Sector Coalition, set up to
ensure that the interests of smaller, more associational organizations are not

crowded out by those of larger, more professionalized and formally organized 'non-profit' organizations. There is also a growing tendency in government and elsewhere to make additional reference to faith organizations.

There are problems inherent in defining more and more distinct *sectors* within the voluntary sector, however. It is possible to argue that this distinction may neither reflect the true diversity within the sector nor further the common interests of the range of activity that lies outside the state and private business. 6 and Leat (1997), therefore, contrast the 'invention' of a sector with a looser, earlier definition of voluntary action as a 'style' or 'principle'. Finlayson (1994, p.8) defines voluntarism as 'activity which springs from individual initiative and choice, is expressed and supported, at least in some measure, by the efforts of those who take part in it, and retains some degree of identity and independence'. Such an approach can encompass several traditions within the UK voluntary sector: self-help, self-improvement, charity, philanthropy (Harrison, 1987) and indeed social enterprise.

THE THIRD SECTOR IN THE UK WELFARE MIX

Esping Andersen (1990) has described the UK as operating a liberal welfare regime in common with Australia, the USA and Canada. The liberal regime he described was dominated by the logic of the market, operating income support on a 'less eligibility' model and encouraging private forms of welfare. Although Esping Andersen did not factor the voluntary sector into this model, Lester Salamon and Helmut Anheier have applied his model in their cross-national study of the non-profit sector and come to a similar conclusion, with the UK grouped alongside the USA as a regime with low government expenditure on welfare and a high level of voluntary activity, a regime where the restriction of the state has provided the non-profit sector with room to grow (Salamon and Anheier, 1998).

In fact, this classification of the UK overlooks a number of features. The first is that, while the liberal philosophy has been apparent throughout British history, other currents have tempered and, at times, overlain it. Bagguley (1994) claims that the UK forces Esping Andersen to the very limits of his model and argues instead for a classification that acknowledges the overlapping historical traditions that go to make up current patterns of welfare in the UK.

What are these overlapping traditions? Looking at the welfare mix in the UK, it is possible to outline a progression, which starts with the unravelling of the close relationship between Church and state in medieval times and moves through the development of the individual liberal conscience in the eighteenth century and the era of *laissez faire* in the nineteenth to the gradual entry of the state in the twentieth and the introduction of a fairly comprehensive welfare state. But, in the latter half of the twentieth century, this settlement itself began to unravel, with a rapid move towards the use of market mechanisms in welfare, an emphasis on individual and family responsibility, and a tight reining in of the welfare benefits budget in order to 'encourage' people onto the labour market wherever possible. This clearly matches the liberal regime. Elements of this settlement have continued into the twenty-first century. Nonetheless, the inter-relationship between state and third sector is acknowledged in current policy, which suggests a regime that stands somewhere between the UK's European neighbours and its American cousins. This is reinforced by the evidence from social attitudes surveys that the British public remains wedded to the idea that the state should take the primary responsibility for welfare, especially in health and education. Their attitude to income maintenance, which is central to Esping Andersen's analysis, is more ambivalent.

The Separation of State and Charity

The history of the UK voluntary sector, as in any other country, reflects the accommodation between religion, commerce and the state. Prior to the Reformation in the sixteenth century, the Catholic Church was the dominant institution for meeting social need and exercising social control in the UK, interwoven with the support mechanisms of the informal sector and the feudal system and supplemented by the activities of the guilds in the towns. The Reformation overturned this accommodation and the Church of England continued to dominate social life and civil society well into the eighteenth century as the institutionalized religion of the governing elite. The view of the state was that its role should be minimal and regulatory, unlike most other contemporary European societies, with the landed elites able to use their property as they wished without 'interference' from the machinery of a feudal state (Perkin, 1989, p.5).

Thus the 1601 Statute of Charitable Uses enshrined a division of labour between state and charity whereby local elites were expected to attend to the welfare of their local population, but the assumption was that this could be done voluntarily, keeping taxation to a minimum. The local state would have a residual role, controlling the employable poor, first by providing relief but, as time went on, through the deterrent of the workhouse and the Poor Law.

The administrative organization of the established Church and its close links with the localities in which it operated gave it the capacity to act as 'moral policeman' through the ecclesiastical courts, to run schools, administer local endowed charities, pioneer social insurance schemes and 'shoulder almost alone the burden of providing education for the poor' (Brown, 1991, pp.100–101). But the eighteenth century also saw the rise of a more 'organized' and generalized form of philanthropy, which Owen refers to as 'associative philanthropy', parallel, he suggests, to the growth of joint stock companies (1964, p.3):

> As the century progressed and it became increasingly 'out of the question for the philanthropist, however well disposed, to seek out for himself the causes of greatest need and to become familiar with them' (Owen, 1964, p.92), a range of other societies and associations were formed to act as intermediaries between donors and beneficiaries. These societies were based on subscription, with subscribers often having the power to exercise patronage by recommending beneficiaries, a sure route to the social prestige which has always been one motivating factor within philanthropy. (Kendall and Knapp, 1996, p.35)

Many authors have documented how philanthropy flourished during the nineteenth century (Davis Smith, 1995; Kendall and Knapp, 1996). In a spirit of moral entrepreneurialism, different religious groups vied for the souls of the poor in what Prochaska (1988, p.24) describes as a 'competition for sinners and distress'. Each sect had its full complement of organizations, particularly in education and youth development (Owen, 1964, p.94; Cahill and Jowett, 1980, p.364). Alarmed by indiscriminate alms giving, a national Charity Organisation Society was set up in 1869 to bring a more rational, coordinated and 'scientific' approach to philanthropy (Lewis, 1995). It defended vigorously the notion of 'mutually exclusive spheres' as a framework for the relief of poverty, casting the state in a residual and deterrent role in the spirit of the 1601 statute.

The belief that local philanthropy was the appropriate way to deliver welfare and control domestic society was to continue well into the early twentieth century, even though the influence of organized religion declined. Compared with other European countries, Britain did not in the nineteenth century develop a strong bureaucratic structure at central government level with strong interests of its own. Conversely, it had a strong tradition of freedom of association that was only breached for the briefest period (some 20 years) at the turn of the eighteenth century. As Thane puts it (1982, p.1), the 'central assumption' of the period from 1750 to 1914 was that central government's role was merely 'to provide a firmly established and clearly understood framework within which society could largely run itself', through groups of self-governing citizens, either through the various institutions of local government or through voluntary associations.

The Growth of Mutualism

It is important to recognize that philanthropy was but one element of voluntarism throughout this period. Mutuality had an equally strong tradition.

Indeed, Antony Black (1984, pp.178–9) argues that the history of ideas often ignores the values of 'fraternity, friendship and mutual aid' which characterize working class life, because they are outside the experience of the 'classes that provided the philosophers'. The traditions of equality among members, self-government by general consent and universal participation in elections had their origins in the medieval guild system and were taken over by working class organizations in later centuries, providing the base not only for the development of mutuality over the centuries but also of the structures of local government (ibid., p.11).

Black suggests (ibid., p.172) that the relatively early demise of the guild system in comparison with central Europe, along with an almost unbroken tradition of freedom of association, explains the precocious development of trade unions and friendly societies in the UK and their centrality in working class organization (ibid.). Black found evidence of 'quasi-trade unions' in the seventeenth century, while in the eighteenth century corresponding societies were formed to take up the battle for the franchise and to cut the link that had been formed between property and political rights. Meanwhile the growth of friendly societies from the seventeenth century onwards provided a thread of continuity between the craftsmen's guilds of earlier centuries and the modern trade union movement, as a means of pooling risk, of insuring against unemployment and ill health and of saving. Equally strong was the growth of the cooperative movement, led by consumer cooperatives, which sought to ensure the availability of healthy and affordable food for the working classes. This movement asserted a new form of membership of society which was not confined to the upper or aspiring middle classes and which offered an alternative to the emergent private capitalism: 'The project was for such forms of association to become the norm, to set the rules of economy and society; to define in action a common-wealth, a state of the unions, free association, a new moral world' (Yeo, 2001, p.10).

Mutualism flowered through a host of working class organizations – building societies, consumer and producer cooperatives, friendly societies, housing associations, burial societies, trades unions and so on – and became an increasingly important part of working class culture in the late eighteenth and the nineteenth century. Its power base was in the north, away from and in opposition to London, the established Church and central government. Its organizing principles and values owed much to non-conformist religious dissent – particularly the Methodist revival – and, along with Methodism, mutuality proved to be critical in shaping a coherent working-class identity (Black, 1984; Harrison, 1987, p.9).

Mutuals provided the opportunity to pool economic risk, through insurance and through ownership of the means of production and distribution. They also provided opportunities for social and political interaction, generating significant benefits in terms of self-improvement and education. The Rochdale

Equitable Pioneers, set up in 1841 and seen by many as the founders of the cooperative movement, had a library and a newsroom. Adult education became an integral part of working class mutualism, culminating in the formation of the Workers' Education Association in 1903.

Mutuals were given a robust legal framework in the Industrial and Provident Society laws of 1843 and 1862, including limited liability. But the organized mutuality of the nineteenth century had its limitations. Firstly, mutuals were predominantly a resource for the artisan class – the better off working classes – and were supported by the political elite who saw that, in so far as they gave potential revolutionaries a stake in the status quo, they separated the artisan working classes from the really poor. They were also primarily a resource for working males and largely failed to provide for women and children. However, the Women's Cooperative Guild, in seeking to extend the benefits of cooperation into the poorer classes, introduced many women to local government and public life (Kendall and Knapp, 1996).

Secondly, by the mid-nineteenth century, mutualism was already under way to surmount the limits of localism and rather informal styles of organizing. Finlayson (1994) notes that local friendly societies were tending to become affiliated to nationals in order to gain the stability provided by economies of scale, while trade unions were quite centralized by the 1850s. Building societies were less and less likely to be run by members and became more and more commercial – by 1871, mutuality was giving way to profit as borrowers were charged more in order to give more money to investors. Increased life expectancy placed an intolerable burden on friendly societies, while competition for members meant they could not increase their premiums. Worker cooperatives reached their peak in 1880 and were hard hit by the recession of the mid-1880s. Nonetheless, Yeo (2001) argues that, in terms of an independent cultural presence and potential for building a 'different society', cooperatives and mutuals were at their height between 1890 and 1910.

The Entry of the State

By the turn of the century, the balance in the welfare mix was beginning to shift towards the state. Britain had been the first nation to embrace the industrial revolution, but it no longer had this advantage; it was also in between two major wars, the Boer War and the First World War. The nation needed to have a workforce and a military force that could compete on both the economic and the military front and it was becoming increasingly obvious that it did not have them. The insufficiency of voluntary action, both philanthropic and mutual, had become increasingly apparent.

The shift towards the state was gradual: first regulation, then funding, and only finally taking increasing responsibility for delivery, with the pace of change varying in different policy fields. And support for the entry of the state into welfare mainly came from the middle class. The growth of local state bureaucracies during the latter part of the nineteenth century meant that there was a new generation of professionals within the state arguing for expansion (Perkin, 1989). The working classes tended to be more suspicious, still associating the state with the harshness of the Poor Law (Dearlove and Saunders, 1991). While they argued for reforms conducive to full employment, therefore, they opposed the idea of an 'enslaving and bureaucratic state' (Thane, 1982, p.292). However, the growth of the Labour Party from the late nineteenth century opened new channels for organized labour within the system, initially in the municipalities and eventually in national government.

As we have seen, the capacity of mutuality at the local level to meet the health and security needs of the working classes was under severe pressure at the turn of the century. By the early 1900s, even friendly societies were beginning to see the advantages of a state pension, although as a complement to their provision rather than an alternative (Finlayson, 1994). Despite some continued resistance, the entry of the state seemed to offer them a lifeline. Both friendly societies and trade unions were approved as administrators for health insurance in the National Insurance Act of 1911. However, the opposition of the medical profession significantly limited their role. Furthermore, the depression of the 1930s put renewed pressure on their health insurance role and proved fatal to unemployment insurance. Finlayson (1994) reports that the trade unions lost members and many found the insurance burden severe. They increasingly saw their future in negotiation rather than savings (ibid., 1994, p.212).

It was the centralized collecting societies and commercial insurance organizations who were able to survive. By the late 1940s, Yeo reports, friendly societies, building societies, cooperatives, educational associations and clubs and institutes were 'very large organizations indeed, not only in their own right but as regards their market presence in their own produce areas, i.e. insurance, mortgages, retail distribution, adult learning and sociability, as well as the manufacture of some products' (2001, p.21). However, Beveridge in his landmark study, *Voluntary Action*, reported that societies became 'more official and less personal; more of insurance agencies and less of social agencies' (1948, pp.78–9). The working class habit of saving for old age through the mutuals declined and members were largely passive by the end of World War II. As Davis Smith (1995, p.34) argues, the 'real tragedy ... was not the assumption by the state of responsibility in 1911, but the undermining of the spirit of mutuality and members' control which was such a key feature of the early societies'.

The mutual tradition had been a crucial building block for the rise of the Labour Party in Britain, yet some would argue that the rise of the Labour

Party, with its formal access to the political process, probably diverted the political and cultural energies of mutualism into new channels (Yeo, 2001). This was of benefit to the trades unions, once they redefined their role away from insurance and towards the political. However, as the Labour Party and the unions gained in strength, local mutual traditions faltered and the party itself forsook its local cooperative roots for a more centralist/statist ideology (Brenton, 1985). Sidney and Beatrice Webb, key architects of the Labour Party, defined common ownership as state ownership rather than mutual ownership. Against this background, it is perhaps not surprising that, although cooperative and mutual enterprises may still have been at their height in the 1950s in terms of sheer bulk and size, they lost their identity as an alternative political and economic force, or as a common movement for social change (Yeo, 2001).

However, the influence of the cooperative movement should not be under-estimated. It formed its own political party in 1917 to promote the interests of cooperativism and its first member of Parliament (MP) was elected in 1918. Although he and his successors have taken the Labour whip, the Cooperative Party continues to have its own MPs and local councillors (currently 29, according to its website, and 700 local councillors) and some argue that it retains a significant influence (Jim Brown, personal communication) as a party within the Labour Party.

From Welfare State to the Market

The years between 1942 and 1948 saw the surge of legislation that would put the state at the centre of the welfare mix. The third sector, both philanthropic and mutual, was demoted to 'junior partner in the welfare firm' (Owen, 1964). Nonetheless, traditional voluntary organizations demonstrated their resilience over the 1950s and 1960s, maintaining a specialist role in some fields, continuing to provide services in areas which were not seen as a priority by the state, and developing a complementary role in others. Cooperative and mutual enterprises were at their height in terms of sheer size in the 1950s and the durability of the cooperative movement, which had always been dominated by retail societies, is illustrated by the fact that the Cooperative Society was the market leader in retailing in 1968. Yeo suggests, though, that the sense of movement had largely been lost and there was little interaction between different forms of cooperative and mutual enterprise movement.

As dissatisfaction with state welfare grew in the 1960s and 1970s, a new wave of voluntary action developed, drawing on the inspiration of the civil rights movement and other social movements of the 1960s across the world. The very scale of state intervention provoked reaction. A series of campaigns emerged to demand action on poverty, homelessness, peace and the environment. Advice organizations provided a path through the intricacies and often insensitivity of state bureaucracy. And new forms of mutualism emerged as welfare consumers organized for better goods and services: welfare claimants set up their own advice services and take-up campaigns; parents set up pre-school provision for their children; people with chronic illnesses set up self-help groups; disabled people organized themselves to transform a medical model of dependency; black and ethnic minority organizations organized themselves to tackle entrenched racism and fight for their own services and facilities; and public housing tenants organized themselves against poor services and large-scale housing developments which they felt were destroying their communities.

There was also a new impetus for social enterprise, with the formation of the Industrial Common Ownership Movement in 1971 and legislation later in the decade to promote common ownership, housing cooperatives and credit unions. In 1979, the government set up a National Cooperative Development Agency. Meanwhile government schemes to tackle increasing unemployment provided new resources for community activity and acted as a seedbed for new forms of community enterprise, although it was only in Scotland and Wales that these community businesses established any significant presence (Pearce, 1993).

Some of these movements were 'alternative' in character, promoting new anti-capitalist ways of organizing and new forms of politics. But few of the new welfare organizations were looking to take over responsibility from the state. Their aims were to complement state provision and to act as a watchdog to force the state to improve its own policies and provision (Brenton, 1985). Nonetheless, the mainstream voluntary sector was pushing for change. By the end of the 1970s, the National Council for Social Service (soon to become the National Council for Voluntary Organisations) and other influential advocates for the sector were advocating a much more central role for the 'third sector' (Gladstone, 1979; Hadley and Hatch, 1981). In the wake of an independently financed report on the future of voluntary organizations (Wolfenden, 1978), they advocated a 'welfare pluralism' in which the state would continue to provide funding, but the voluntary sector would provide the services.

However, as Nicholas Deakin reports (1995, p.54), the point for patching up state welfare had already been passed – public disillusionment with state welfare was already far advanced. 'Welfare pluralism' was about to be overtaken by a much more radical departure. With the election of a Conservative government in 1979, committed to rolling back the frontiers of state welfare, the stage was set for the advance of the New Right and the welfare market. For a while Labour municipalities in the major urban centres continued to resist the new agenda, providing support for community-based and self-help activities as part of a 'rainbow coalition' of resistance to the market. But by the late

1980s the writing was on the wall for the postwar welfare state, with a wide range of legislation, privatizing some services and introducing internal markets into others. By this time, the commercial sector had already established itself as a significant player in social care and government policies were seeking to shift the burden of finance from the state to private insurance. The Conservative government also wanted to shift responsibility for welfare to another corner of the welfare mix triangle – the family – with a renewed emphasis on personal and family responsibility for caring.

Privatization was to give the service-providing agencies within the third sector a much greater role in the welfare mix. This was particularly true in the fields of social housing and social services, where there was a clear intention to transfer service delivery to the voluntary and commercial sectors. Financial support for voluntary organizations more than doubled in the years from 1979 to 1987 and, after a few hiccups, shot up again in the early 1990s. As local authority housing was sold off and starved of funds, housing associations were groomed to become the major providers of social housing.

But the enthusiasm for these changes within the third sector was mixed. Voluntary organizations were concerned that they would become agents of government rather than partners, with their goals and operating values distorted by government purchasers. This fear was not without precedent. Beveridge was already critical of this tendency in his 1948 review of voluntary action and Owen's 1966 history reports similar concerns. In the welfare market of the 1990s, voluntary organizations also feared that they would be a stalking horse for the commercial sector, preparing the market for its more 'natural' beneficiaries.

Early research suggests that this was an overreaction. Large organizations in particular possess considerable power when negotiating with smaller local authority purchasers and the evidence suggested that there was less distortion than had been anticipated. However, the effects of change were variable and its long-term effects are not yet known. Many organizations feel that they are doing more for less, and successive National Council for Voluntary Organizations (NCVO) surveys suggest that medium-sized organizations can be particularly vulnerable to insecure funding arrangements (Passey *et al.*, 2000). They also suggest that, although there were huge increases in overall government funding of the sector in the early 1990s, these are now levelling out and it remains to be seen how sustainable the role of the sector and particularly the diversity of its contribution will be as the welfare market develops.

However, there have been other trends as a result of the market-based culture of the 1980s and 1990s, with larger charities in particular becoming increasingly entrepreneurial in response to funding pressures, adopting more aggressive approaches to the fund-raising marketplace and developing trading arms to generate earned income, whether from government contracts or from the sales of goods and services. Parallel developments have taken place amongst mutuals. Trade union membership is in decline (along with the membership of many traditional voluntary sector membership organizations). Some, like the housing associations, are losing their identification with the voluntary sector; a growing number of building societies and insurance associations are demutualizing.

At the same time, Yeo (2001) points to a revival and rediscovery of purpose among some older cooperative and mutual enterprises. The Cooperative Bank, founded in 1872, looked to be in terminal decline in 1990, but, to the surprise even of the cooperative movement itself, turned itself around by rebranding itself as the 'ethical bank' and successfully warded off an attempt to take it over and demutualize it in the late 1990s. Meanwhile, new forms of mutuality have begun to attract the attention of a government that is looking both for new ways of delivering welfare services in the twenty-first century and for sustainable solutions to the persistent social exclusion of particular communities in the UK.

Ironically, this has been helped by the market ideology, with its emphasis on consumers. The welfare market has brought new opportunities for service users to influence and even manage their own services. As the 1990s progressed, for example, tenant management organizations were actively encouraged in social housing, and control of schools was devolved to local governing bodies, although in the latter case under strict central government controls. Disability organizations were drawn into the care-planning and policy-making process and some began to develop radical new approaches to service delivery which gave service users more power as co-producers (see, for example, Lindow, 1994). Black and minority ethnic organizations developed services that would be more sensitive to their cultural traditions and needs. It has to be said, however, that these organizations were as critical of traditional voluntary organizations as they were of public authorities, criticizing them for their paternalism and insensitivity to the needs of users and marginalized communities.

There were other new players arriving on the scene. Leadbeater and Christie drew attention in their 1999 study to the growth of the following:

- pre-school play-groups run by parents (18 000 in 1998, providing for 19 per cent of under fives);
- credit unions (665 in 1999) and community loan funds (5);
- the University of the Third Age (with 365 branches);
- housing cooperatives (12 per cent of registered social landlords, with 259 fully mutual cooperatives registered with the Housing Corporation covering some 10 000 homes – cooperative housing is particularly strong in Scotland);

- community foundations (154 grant-making bodies using local donations to fund local activities).

Community development trusts were set up in disadvantaged neighbour-hoods to protect community assets from development or bring them back into use, and to ensure that local assets generated local jobs and wealth. Leadbeater and Christie claimed that there were 139 such organizations in the UK in 1999, built around land, buildings, workspace or the provision of services. They provide further examples of innovative mutual finance and social investment initiatives and cooperative Internet and software firms. They also attest to the health of cooperativism in some parts of the business world, with 544 co-operative or jointly controlled farm businesses, and with 6 per cent of the grocery market and 4 per cent of the total market in the hands of cooperative retailers. The worker cooperative market in the UK is very small compared to some parts of continental Europe, but Leadbeater and Christie suggested that there were 1550 workers' cooperatives in 1999, employing about 15 000 people.

A Third Way?

By 1997, the British public was becoming as disillusioned with the excesses of the market as it had been with the state in 1979. The New Labour govern-ment, which it elected in 1997, was searching for a 'third way' (Blair, 1998; Giddens, 1998) between market and state. Key elements in this search were a commitment to a partnership rather than a contract culture, a commitment to tackle social exclusion, a positive climate for enterprise and the mobilizing of citizens and communities under a banner of rights *and* responsibilities. The 'third way', not surprisingly, offered new opportunities to the 'third sector', which was to enjoy increasing prominence under the new administration. This was underlined by the priority given to establishing a written 'compact' with the voluntary and community sector (Home Office, 1998) and by the increased profile and additional funding given to the former Voluntary and Community Unit in government (renamed as the Active Community Unit). It was further strengthened by the requirement imposed by central government on local public bodies to consult voluntary organizations, communities and service users (as well as other stakeholders) in developing services and in defining a 'best value'[3] framework to which public services should conform. Although the term 'the third way' has fallen into disuse, two key themes remain and are likely to have a particular impact on the welfare mix in the UK. The first is the emphasis on partnership. Previous Conservative administrations had seen the market and the third sector as alternatives to state control. In contrast, the New Labour government saw partnership as its central theme, emphasizing 'go-vernance' rather than 'government'.

Partnership cuts across all policy areas but is a particularly strong theme in the government's commitment to address area-based social exclusion. The government's National Strategy for Neighbourhood Renewal (Social Exclusion Unit, 2000) is committed to finding new ways to revive the economies of the worst affected areas, to revive communities and to improve services. The new strategy is promoting new forms of delivery, which will bring all agencies (public, voluntary and commercial) together at neighbourhood level to find 'joined up' solutions to the problems experienced in these areas. Key features of the strategy are proposals to devolve service budgets to the local level under joint management, with residents as equal partners.

The strategy has also set up new local strategic partnerships at the local authority level. These new multi-agency partnerships have responsibility for developing a neighbourhood renewal strategy, drawing down central government funds to carry it out. They are also expected to work with local authorities to develop broader community strategies for promoting local well-being.

The development of local strategic partnerships and their neighbourhood equivalents (although these are not yet universal) has the potential to create new kinds of institution which cut across the sectors and provide the optimal 'mix' to address the problems of exclusion. These new hybrid institutional forms could transform the relationship between the state, voluntary, community and private sector players, perhaps redrawing the triangle in Figure 1.1 by operating more explicitly in the tension field at the centre of the triangle. But by drawing the institutions commonly associated with the state and the market into the centre ground, such partnerships could equally find themselves in murky territory, unclear about accountability, role and constitution – a point to which we return in the final section of this chapter.

As well as promoting partnership, the search for a 'third way' has also embraced the language of social enterprise and the social economy.[4] This language promises to 'combine the promise of social cohesion and self-organization within a market economy' and 'provide an alternative to both the paternalism of public services and the privatism of the market' (Leadbeater and Christie, 1999, p.10). One of the 18 Policy Action Teams (PATs) set up to develop the National Strategy for Neighbourhood Renewal focused on enterprise and social exclusion and, in its wake, the government is seeking to encourage social enterprises such as credit unions, community businesses, community development trusts and social cooperatives. It points to enterprises already developed in fields such as home care and child care, security, adult education, housing and neighbourhood improvements, local shops, cultural and leisure activities, audio-visual services, new information technologies and waste disposal and recycling activities, with some 1.5 million people estimated as being regularly engaged in local community economic initiatives:

The social economy can be effective at developing services which may be unattractive or inappropriate for the private sector, or cannot be delivered effectively by the public sector. It can also be valuable in engaging local people in economic activities in ways that public agencies have found difficult. The social economy does not simply provide substitutes for real jobs and services where there has been market failure. It also helps develop a stronger sense of community. (HM Treasury 1999, p.14)

Local strategic partnerships and neighbourhood management boards will be looking to redeploy mainstream service budgets in ways which are more responsive to community priorities and needs. But, to fuel the social economy, the government is being urged to look at ways to improve social investment. The PAT report urges 'a change in culture' in the voluntary and social enterprise sector away from grants and towards loans and gives examples of loan and investment funds which have been set up in recent years to support the growth of social enterprise (HM Treasury, 1999). It also calls for the kinds of support available to small business to be extended to the social enterprise sector. This is an agenda to which the government is now beginning to respond.

THE FUTURE OF THE UK THIRD SECTOR

The above account of the development of the third sector in the UK suggests that the concept of a welfare mix is a useful analytical tool, which reflects more faithfully than other models both the necessary diversity within this territory and the interrelationship between different players in society.

First, this model moves us away from any analysis based on the presumed superiority of one sector over another, to an understanding of their interdependence. Secondly, it also discourages the simplistic division of the third 'sector' into two main parts, contrasting the virtues of the smaller community-based organizations with the cooption of the larger charities. Instead it allows a more sophisticated analysis of the variations across organizations in this territory, the different pressures they face and the way they develop over time. Thirdly, the model highlights the contribution made by mutuality and solidarity to the welfare mix, a contribution that has been neglected in some quarters, but one which is now attracting increasing interest. And fourthly, this model draws our attention to the way in which the institutions traditionally associated with the state and market are themselves shifting into the centre ground, with all the tensions that implies. This has a number of implications for policy.

Legal and Institutional Issues

Martin Rein argued in 1989 that 'the future of the welfare state is the invention of institutions that are not public nor private' (Rein, 1989, p.70). Demos, an influential UK think tank, has more recently described Britain as 'the silent revolutionary, inventing new forms of organizations and new ways of running society' (cited in Yeo, 2001, pp.2–3). But until now the constitutional tools to support this innovation have been lacking. This has created a number of problems, especially for mutuals and social enterprises. Firstly, forcing social enterprise and similar activities into inappropriate forms is likely to discourage rather than encourage innovation. Second, there are still restrictions on trading and investment which prevent social enterprises from reaching their potential. Thirdly, the most common form of mutual incorporation, the Industrial and Provident Society, is in urgent need of reform.

These issues have now been grasped in a comprehensive government review whose aims are to modernize charity law and status and to improve the range of legal forms available, as well as developing greater accountability within the bounds of fair and proportionate regulation. In a consultation document published in September 2002, this review (Cabinet Office, 2002) proposes updating and expanding charitable purposes, with a clearer focus on public benefit, but also an emphasis on encouraging entrepreneurialism. The document proposes a new legal form for social enterprises – the Community Interest Company – which would improve access to finance, protect against demutualization and preserve assets and profits solely for social purposes. It also proposes modernizing the law on Industrial and Provident Societies and introducing a new form of incorporation for charities called the Charitable Incorporated Organisation, which would be more appropriate than the current route of 'company limited by guarantee'. Much will depend on how these proposals develop but, as the first major revision of charitable status in 400 years, they could represent a major breakthrough.

Maintaining a Distinctive Approach

The move from government to 'governance' and the increasing prevalence of multi-agency and intersectoral partnerships mean that the tension field at the centre of the triangle in Figure 1.1 is becoming increasingly crowded. Some see these partnerships as new spaces for citizen participation in the UK. Some partnerships are constituting themselves as companies limited by guarantee with charitable status, and in that sense they might be seen as third sector organizations themselves. Others see them as a new, but less visible, form of state control, with accountability to citizens and service users increasingly blurred. For existing third sector organizations the move from government to governance poses a new challenge, as they balance new roles closer to the centre of policy making and implementation with the need to retain their autonomy, distinctive contribution and freedom to criticize.

Growing without Growing

The current revitalization of mutuality offers considerable opportunity for innovation in the social economy, and the government's legal proposals can only help. But experience of demutualization in the older mutuals gives plenty of warning of the danger that such enterprises will lose their democratic base and thus their distinctive contribution to local economies over time. Many housing associations (who tend to be registered as mutuals) have been driven to merge in order to compete effectively in the financial market. There have also been many criticisms within the wider third sector that service-providing organizations, especially those funded by government contracts, are losing their associational character. At the same time, there are fears that increasingly aggressive 'commercial' approaches to fund raising are resulting in a loss of public trust.

Leadbeater and Christie (1999) argue that mutuality is most likely to be sustainable where mutuals are well run, serve appropriate markets and are on the 'right scale'. But what is the 'right scale' and how can it be sustained? We still do not know enough about the life cycles of organizations or about ways in which they can grow without losing their distinctive associational characteristics. Federal models in the traditional voluntary sector among user-led organizations offer some precedents, but these have been underconceptualized and underresearched (Taylor and Lansley, 2000). More needs to be learnt from these models as well as from those leading-edge businesses that are organizing along decentralized lines and from mutuals in other countries if third sector organizations, including social enterprises, are to reap the benefits of economies of scale and yet stay close to the ground.

Resourcing

The income of the third sector in the UK shows a general upward trend, with a shift away from income donated through grants and gifts and towards income earned through contracts, other trading and return on investments – the shift towards social enterprise noted in the Cabinet Office report cited at the beginning of this chapter. However the sector's income is concentrated in the largest organizations, with almost 90 per cent of the income accounted for by 10 per cent of organizations.

Within this there are both positive and potentially negative trends. Among the positive trends are the recognition by the government of the need to invest in the third sector infrastructure. Its recent cross-cutting review of the role of the voluntary and community sector in service delivery has emphasized the importance of investment in the voluntary and community sector infrastructure to ensure that these organizations have the support they need to contribute not only to the delivery but also to the planning of services (HM Treasury, 2002). Government has already put money directly into neighbourhoods through the Community Chest and the Community Empowerment Fund to ensure that communities are adequately represented in the new local strategic partnerships.

A second positive is that the government is responding to pressure to promote social investment (Mayo *et al.*, 1998; Mulgan and Landry, 1995) by introducing a number of initiatives to encourage investment in social enterprise, by extending to social enterprise the kind of support that has long been available to small businesses and by developing a venture capital fund tailored to their needs.

Both these developments, along with the opportunities offered by the proposed changes in charitable law, could help to develop a new investment-oriented approach towards the third sector. But there have been positive developments in grant aid, too, with the advent in the mid-1990s of the National Lottery and its Charities Board, which has since developed a range of grants programmes. However, this new funding stream has not been without its problems. In the early days there were concerns that the Lottery would have a negative effect on charitable giving. More recently, the decrease in Lottery sales has given rise to concern, along with evidence of increasing 'vetting' of Lottery grants by the government, with implications for the independence of its decision making.

On the debit side, while there has been a considerable increase in funding for organizations in the third sector to provide services, there are, as this chapter has already suggested, questions about the sustainability of this contribution as funding begins to level out. There is particular concern about the capacity of smaller organizations to sustain quality services on contract with public sector purchasers who are looking to save money. If the third sector is to take a greater responsibility for the delivery of welfare, and especially if it is to develop new and more effective services, then it needs to be adequately resourced.

Investment will be particularly important if new and emerging social enterprises are to gain access to the welfare market. Although third sector organizations such as care cooperatives and development trusts are winning government contracts, there is considerable scope for expansion, since cooperatives and similar organizations are still minor players in this market compared with other European countries.

Another concern is the phasing out of the Single Regeneration Budget which has been a significant source of income for third sector organizations across the country, particularly in disadvantaged communities. It is being replaced by a 'single pot' given to regional development agencies (RDAs) to support economic and social regeneration. There are fears that this will be spent on large-scale economic development, with little attention paid to social regeneration or the third sector's contribution to the economy. Other sources of grant aid, like the Lottery, are shorter-term and unlikely to fill the gap.

Finally, while the financial environment for social enterprise is now changing and the potential for social investment is being enhanced, there is still a long way to go. The structure of the banking industry in the UK, with considerable power concentrated in five major banks, is not conducive to social or local investment in what are seen as risky enterprises and there is still of lot of persuasion and education to be done. Many UK organizations have lobbied the government to consider introducing a Community Reinvestment Act similar to that in the USA, which would increase the transparency of investment decisions in disadvantaged neighbourhoods, but government and financial institutions in this country have not been sympathetic to this reform. There has also been some discussion of ways to use welfare benefits to support the unemployed in developing their own enterprises, but this is very difficult political territory and little progress has been made beyond isolated experiments.

In conclusion, therefore, the profile of the third sector has steadily increased since the New Labour government took office in 1997. This was not the first postwar government to take an increased interest in the sector, but what is significant is that, under this government, there is more potential understanding of the breadth of the sector, of the importance of a social economy and of new institutional forms to allow the sector to flourish. This new interest poses considerable challenges as well as opportunities, but it offers an environment in which the sector can flourish. This depends on two things: first, the capacity and will within the sector both to seize the new opportunities that exist and yet to preserve its distinctive contribution; second, the capacity and will across government and other partners to support what the sector, in all its diversity, does well and not to try and reshape it into a pale imitation of either business or the public sector.

NOTES

1. The historical part of this chapter draws on material developed in collaboration with Jeremy Kendall but not previously published. While my use of this material is my responsibility alone, I would like to acknowledge my indebtedness to Jeremy's previous work.
2. The Community Sector Coalition defines the distinction as that 'between the professional voluntary sector, employing paid staff and often providing services under contract to local and central government, and community-based groups, which are often very small, unfunded and with no professional staff' (Taylor and Lansley, 2000). However, the terms are often used more loosely
3. Best value was introduced by the new government to replace the compulsory competitive tendering regime of the previous administration. While competition was still an element of the new policy, competition on the basis of price was no longer the primary definition of 'value'.

4. This language can be used to encompass the whole of the third sector. But it has been particularly associated in the UK with mutuals, community-based organizations and organizations which combine social with economic objectives.

REFERENCES

6, Perri and Diana Leat (1997), 'Inventing the British voluntary sector by committee',
   Non-Profit Studies, 1 (2), 33–45.
Bagguley, Paul (1994), 'Prisoners of the Beveridge dream? The political mobilization
   of the poor against contemporary welfare regimes', in Roger Burrows and Brian
   Loader (eds), *Towards a Post-Fordist Welfare State*, London and New York:
   Routledge.
Beveridge, William (1948), *Voluntary Action*, London: George Allen and Unwin.
Black, Antony (1984), *Guilds and Civil Society in European Political Thought from the
   Twelfth Century to the Present*, London: Methuen.
Blair, Tony (1998), *The Third Way*, London: Fabian Society.
Brenton, Maria (1985), *The Voluntary Sector in British Social Services*, Harlow:
   Longman.
Brown, Richard (1991), *Church and State in Modern Britain*, London and New York:
   Routledge.
Cabinet Office (2002), *Private Action, Public Benefit: a Review of Charities and the
   Wider Not-for-Profit Sector*, London: Cabinet Office.
Cahill, Michael and Tony Jowitt (1980), 'The new philanthropy: the emergence of the
   Bradford City Guild of Help', *Journal of Social Policy*, 9 (3), 359–82.
Chesterman, Michael (1979), *Charities, Trusts and Social Welfare*, London:
   Weidenfeld and Nicolson.
Commission on the Future of the Voluntary Sector (1996), *Meeting the Challenge of
   Change: Voluntary Action into the 21st Century*, London: NCVO.
Davis Smith, Justin (1995), 'The voluntary tradition: philanthropy and self-help in
   Britain 1500–1945', in Justin Davis Smith, Colin Rochester and Rodney Hedley
   (eds), *An Introduction to the Voluntary Sector*, London and New York: Routledge.
Deakin, Nicholas (1995), 'The perils of partnership: the voluntary sector and the state,
   1945–1992', in Justin Davis Smith, Colin Rochester and Rodney Hedley (eds), *An
   Introduction to the Voluntary Sector*, London and New York: Routledge.
Dearlove, John and Peter Saunders (1991), *An Introduction to British Politics*,
   Cambridge: Polity Press.
Esping Andersen, Gosta (1990), *The Three Worlds of Welfare Capitalism*, Cambridge:
   Polity Press.
Finlayson, Geoffrey (1994), *Citizen, State and Social Welfare in Britain 1830–1990*,
   Oxford: Clarendon Press.
Giddens, Anthony (1998), *The Third Way: the renewal of social democracy*,
   Cambridge: Polity Press.
Gladstone, Francis (1979), *Voluntary Action in a Changing World*, London: Bedford
   Square Press.
Hadley, Roger and Stephen Hatch (1981), *Social Welfare and the Failure of the State:
   Centralized Social Services and Participatory Alternatives*, London: George Allen
   and Unwin.
Harrison, Brian (1987), 'Historical perspectives', in National Council for Voluntary
   Organisations, *Voluntary Organisations and Democracy*, London: NCVO.

HM Treasury (1999), *Enterprise and Social Exclusion*, Report of National Strategy for Neighbourhood Renewal Policy Action Team 3, London: HM Treasury.

HM Treasury (2002), *The Role of the Voluntary and Community Sector in Service Delivery: a Cross-cutting Review*, London: HM Treasury.

Home Office (1998), *Getting It Right Together*, London: Home Office.

Kendall, Jeremy and Martin Knapp (1996), *The Voluntary Sector in the UK*, Manchester and New York: Manchester University Press.

Knight, Barry (1993), *Voluntary Action*, London: The Home Office.

Leadbeater, Charles and Ian Christie (1999), *To Our Mutual Advantage*, London: Demos.

Lewis, Jane (1995), *The Voluntary Sector, the State and Social Work in Britain*, Aldershot, UK and Brookfield, US: Edward Elgar.

Lindow, Vivien (1994), *Self-Help Alternatives to Mental Health Services*, London: MIND.

Mayo, Ed, Thomas Fisher, Pat Conaty, John Doling and Andy Mullineux (1998), *Small is Bankable: community reinvestment in the UK*, York: Joseph Rowntree Foundation.

Mulgan, Geoff and Charles Landry (1995), *The Other Invisible Hand*, London: Demos

Owen, David (1964), *English Philanthropy 1660–1960*, London: Oxford University Press.

Passey, Andrew, Leslie Hems and Pauline Jas (2000), *The UK Voluntary Sector Almanac 2000*, London: NCVO.

Pearce, John (1993), *At the Heart of the Community Economy: community enterprise in a changing world*, London: Calouste Gulbenkian Foundation.

Perkin, Harold (1989), *The Rise of Professional Society*, London: Routledge.

Prochaska, Frank (1988), *The Voluntary Impulse*, London: Faber and Faber.

Rein, Martin (1989) 'The social structure of institutions: neither public nor private', in Ben Gidron, Ralph Kramer and Lester Salamon (eds), *Government and the Third Sector: emerging relationships in welfare states*, San Francisco: Jossey-Bass.

Salamon, Lester and Helmut Anheier (1998), 'Social origins of civil society: explaining the nonprofit sector cross-nationally', *Voluntas*, 9 (3), 213–48.

Social Exclusion Unit (2000), *A National Strategy for Neighbourhood Renewal: a consultation document*, London: The Stationery Office.

Taylor, Marilyn and John Lansley (2000), 'Relating the central and the local: options for organizational structure', *Nonprofit Management and Leadership*, 10 (4), 421–33.

Taylor, Marilyn, Joan Langan and Paul Hoggett (1995), *Encouraging Diversity: Voluntary and Private Organisations in Community Care*, Aldershot: Arena.

Thane, Pat (1982), *The Foundations of the Welfare State*, Harlow: Longman.

Wolfenden, John (1978), *The Future of Voluntary Organisations*, Report of the Wolfenden Committee, London: Croom Helm.

Yeo, Stephen (2001), 'Co-operative and mutual enterprises in Britain: a usable past for a modern future' (*s.yeo@pop3.poptel.org.uk*) and summarized in Stephen Yeo (2001), 'Making membership meaningful: the case of older co-operative and mutual enterprises (CMEs) in Britain', in Nicholas Deakin (ed.), *Membership and Mutuality*, Report no. 3, London: Centre for Civil Society.

7. The Netherlands: from private initiatives to non-profit hybrids and back?

Paul Dekker

INTRODUCTION

Private non-profit organizations have a strong position in Dutch society, not only economically but also culturally. They are seen as embodiments of national identity, that is, as representing what are imagined as typical Dutch traditions of private responsibility for common interests, of religious pluralism and of a non-authoritarian state that is pragmatically looking for partnerships in society. However, the area of private non-profit organizations is hardly ever described in commonly understood international terms as a 'third sector' or 'non-profit sector'. The Dutch use their own non-economic terms to talk about organizations in the area between state agencies and business firms: 'private initiatives' and 'societal midfield'.

The oldest term is private initiative (*particulier initiatief*), used to describe the origins of many organizations: groups of citizens in voluntary associations and pursuing issues that supersede individual interests. Until the 1990s the term was also used in the abbreviated form, 'het PI', indicating the field of non-profit service providers that were the offspring of the private initiatives (but had turned into vested interests). Nowadays the abbreviation is seldom used and the term 'private initiative' itself has become somewhat ambiguous since it can now mean private commercial initiatives as well.

The term 'societal midfield' (*maatschappelijk middenveld*) was introduced in the 1970s and focuses on the functions of organizations as intermediaries, mainly between the individual citizen and the state, but also between groups in society. On the one hand, the organizations in the societal midfield represent the interests of their specific group at government level and try to influence public policy making. On the other hand, many of the organizations are of service to the government, for instance by implementing and monitoring policies. The term primarily depicts interest, advocacy and political organizations, but the societal midfield discourse normally includes other voluntary associations and all non-profit service-delivering organizations as well. This even includes public service providers in their role as intermediary organizations, that is, the role they may play in expressing values and voicing the interests of their clients in order to integrate these groups into society, link them to politics and so on. The focus of the societal midfield is similar to that of the 'mediating structures' of Berger and Neuhaus ([1966]1977), but without the more informal elements of families and neighbourhoods that these authors include, and with the suggestion of an institutional cluster of interconnected organizations. From the beginning, the term was associated with the existence of 'pillars' (see below) encompassing organizations with the same denomination or ideology, from kindergarten to political party.

'Civil society' (in English) was welcomed in the 1990s as a modern and international alternative to 'societal midfield'.[1] Nowadays the two appear to be used more or less as equivalents, but on further consideration they often stress different aspects of the same organizations, respectively their vertical (citizen–state) and horizontal (citizen–citizen) intermediary role.

'Private initiatives', 'societal midfield' or 'civil society' are common terms in the Netherlands where they have more social and political than economic connotations. The term 'non-profit' is used to characterize both private and public not-for-profit organizations, and the term 'non-profit sector' is used for all these organizations together. Economists and the general public may have problems in understanding why one might want to distinguish a private non-profit sector from the government or public sector. In daily life it is often hard to find the differences between a public and private facility; regulations mostly apply to both, and political debates are about single policy fields such as education, health care, welfare or social housing, not about private non-profit organizations in general.

'Third sector' and 'social economy', current terms in neighbouring countries, are hardly ever used in the Netherlands. The Dutch terms *'sociale economie'* and *'mutualiteit'* are almost exclusively used in Flanders. This does not mean that cooperatives and mutual societies are of no importance in the Netherlands.[2] The point is that the benefits and disadvantages of these forms are discussed in relation to 'normal' business forms and not in a framework of private not-for-profit organizations or in an alternative social economy discourse.

This chapter will stick to the non-profit vocabulary. The concept of a private non-profit sector finds no response in Dutch debates (Dekker, 2002a), but if one has to choose an international term, this economic term comes closest to what the majority of the offspring of Dutch 'private initiatives' have in common. In the final section we will briefly return to the social economy.

The chapter starts with a historical sketch of partnership in the Netherlands before and after the Second World War. After a brief description of the present situation of the Dutch third sector, trends of blurring boundaries and hybridization between public and private non-profit and for-profit organizations are elaborated. After speculation about the disappearance of the sector and a discussion of strategic options for non-profits between becoming real enterprises and a return to civil society, the chapter ends with concluding remarks about reasons to keep non-profits as a separate organizational form in the modern welfare state, and about the perspective of professional autonomy.

PILLARIZATION AND PACIFICATION

The Dutch welfare state is characterized by high levels of private non-profit delivery of collectively financed services. In the area of education, about 70 per cent of primary and secondary pupils receive their education at private schools which get money from the government according to the same financial schemes as the public schools. To explain this situation, we have to go back at least to the second half of the nineteenth century, to pillarization. Of course, as in other countries, the roots of non-profits can be traced back to earlier times, to guilds and congregations, but that is less important for the understanding of the present situation.

Pillarization (*Verzuiling*) is the vertical segregation of various population groups along religious or political lines. It is the result of 'bottom-up' and 'top-down' building of associations, and linking existing organizations into blocks, from the second half of the nineteenth century on. There were at least two, and there may have been up to five, pillars. Catholic organizations definitely formed the most encompassing and homogeneous pillar. Also the existence of a Protestant or Calvinist pillar has rarely been contested, but this pillar remained more diverse, probably because it was never controlled by a single hierarchical church. Separate networks of organizations developed, from a loose liberal Protestant one to several tighter orthodox clusters. Whether the liberals and the socialists formed a pillar of their own is still a matter of discussion. Some claim that these groups had formed too few organizations in too small areas to deserve the label of a pillar.[3] Pillarization had its strongest hold on society between 1920 and 1960.

The existence of the pillars as such stimulated the development of what was later to be called the non-profit sector. Pillars got their own hospitals, burial funds, newspapers, economic interest organizations, radio and, later on, television broadcasting associations, women's organizations, choirs and soccer clubs. Calvinists and Catholics also got their own schools; the socialists and liberals were content with the public schools.

A landmark in the development of government–denominational relations was the state financing of denominational schools (cf. Bax, 1988; Burger and

Veldheer, 2001). Private schools had been formed long before pillarization, by churches, but also by economic interests and enlightened wealthy citizens. From the eighteenth century on, the state got more and more involved and municipalities started public schools. In the first half of the nineteenth century, the government claimed that the public schools had a general Christian character. The Catholics especially disputed this claim. The government gradually increased support for the public schools, but did not provide financial means for private schools. This provoked opposition from Catholics and Calvinists, who did not want to pay taxes for public schools and also pay for their own private schools. They strove for equal treatment of public and private schools. Their struggle was initially rewarded with a few small successes. Full recognition of their schools was reached in the historical compromise between liberal and confessional parties in 1917: the 'pacification' or 'accommodation'. Liberals received universal suffrage and confessionals received full recognition and equal financial rights for private schools in the constitution of 1920.

The importance of the pacification can hardly be overstressed. By spillover processes, the idea of shared responsibility of the state and pillarized private initiatives for the common good became the dominant model for new policies of the expanding welfare state after the Second World War.

The Catholic principle of subsidiarity and the Calvinist principle of circles of sovereignty differed philosophically on the relationship between state and civil society (with the Protestants more in sympathy with Locke's primacy of society and the Catholics closer to Montesquieu's acknowledgment of political authority) but in practical politics they were in agreement on a small role for government and strong public responsibilities for private actors. The Calvinist principle of circles of sovereignty is basically a plea for independence and self-determination of social units in society. The principal areas or circles of society, such as the family, business, education, the arts and churches, should not be subjected to the authority of the state, but govern themselves. This entails the role of the state being as small as possible and the role of the circles as large as possible. The subsidiarity principle of the Catholics is embedded more in an organic idea of society. A higher organ of society may not do what a lower organ or the individual can do, but it is the higher level that should decide to decentralize or to leave responsibilities to the lower level; it is less the natural right of the lower level.[4]

Liberals and social democrats in the Netherlands have both adapted themselves to this view and supported strong public–private relationships as alternatives to strong government and to no collective action at all. The legacy of pillarization is that private action for public purposes, often publicly paid, has become accepted as a normal state of affairs.

PUBLIC–PRIVATE PARTNERSHIP IN THE WELFARE STATE

The development of the welfare state after the Second World War led to the expansion of publicly financed but privately provided welfare state services. The scheme of full recognition and public payment of private, mainly denominational, organizations was also adopted for a number of other services, such as health care, welfare work, housing and media. But only in the case of education was equal financial treatment of public and private services given a place in the constitution. Pillarization provided the organizational framework for the development of the welfare state, and the 'politics of accommodation' (Lijphart, 1968) supplied essential guidelines for its administration, such as the acceptance of extensive freedom of action for the pillarized organizations and the principle of proportional representation for the distribution of facilities between the pillars and of benefits between the respective segments of the population. However, the successful liaison with a growing welfare state was not without consequences for the function and character of the pillarized institutions. As service industries they modernized, increased in scale and professionalized. Their ideology and denomination became less and less relevant and the networks of pillarization eroded.[5] The crisis in government finances of the late 1970s and early 1980s led to large-scale mergers and the disappearance of many pillarized organizations.

The 'reform of the welfare state' after the mid-1970s was a mixed blessing for the non-profit sector. Reforms were directed towards cutbacks in public expenditure, slimming down of the civil service, territorial and functional decentralization, privatization and deregulation. Many non-profit organizations felt the need (or were forced) to reorganize, scale down or commercialize as a result of the decreasing levels of government funding. In addition, deregulation meant the end of the non-profit monopoly in certain areas and gave newcomers the opportunity to enter the domain previously dominated by non-profits. On the one hand, non-profits have experienced a reduction of direct government interference and a growth of independence. On the other hand, they have lost tasks and resources, and have been forced to accept commercial newcomers in their fields. Privatization also stimulated non-profit activity (cf. Kramer *et al.*, 1993). The term 'privatization' is often associated with the private commercial sector, but there were also state agencies moved over to the private non-profit sector, for instance in health and housing. Some notable examples of government agencies that moved to the non-profit area are municipal housing organizations, government health care institutions and some state museums.

At the beginning of a new century, the conclusion may be drawn that the overall result of privatization for the non-profit sector has not so much been a loss of 'market share' as a strong incorporation of the ways of the market into the behaviour of its organizations. In a few years a terminology of entrepreneurship, marketing and market niches has become quite popular among the offspring of old pillarized private initiatives. An important stimulus in this culture shift has been the growth of new service providers at the margins of the public sector as a result of functional decentralization. The new managers of these organizations want autonomy and they criticize bureaucracy, but they also want financial guarantees and other securities from the state – not so different from the leaders of denominational organizations earlier. One could say that privatization has continued the pillarization tradition of the private provision of public services.[6]

As already indicated, subsidiarity has become a guiding principle in politics and policy making. Traditional preferences for either the market (liberals), the state (social democrats) or the non-profit sector (Christian democrats) are not very pronounced any more. Most parties have become rather pragmatic on these issues and governments (always coalitions) differ only slightly. The overall posture of the government towards non-profits is also difficult to qualify, because the (legal) status of non-profit organizations is not much of an issue. Usually the stance towards types of non-profits depends more on their field of activity and the government's posture towards that particular field of activity than on their legal status.

With regard to public attitudes, it is important to note that people often do not know whether organizations are really public or 'private public', and indeed it is sometimes hard to know: many 'public libraries' are private foundations, and so are 'regional hospitals'. The organizations are often the result of mergers of private organizations with different religious backgrounds or non-religious philosophies of life, and are now just organizations for everybody and thus public. Where schools are concerned, for many people the difference is between confessional and non-confessional schools, and they do not see a difference between a real public (municipal) school and a 'general' private school. Private non-profit organizations are most of the time not seen as a specific class of institutions. It is interesting to note that Dutch public opinion turns out not to be especially in favour of non-profits if one looks at their rating in population surveys of a longer list of private and public institutions one can 'tend to trust' or 'tend not to trust'. Eurobarometer data about institutional trust show that the relative position of the charitable and voluntary organizations and non-governmental organizations is not exceptionally positive in the Netherlands. In Italy, France and Belgium, where overall trust levels are lower, the relative position of non-profits is better. Thus non-profits are well accepted in the Netherlands but, compared with other countries, they do not enjoy a particularly high level of public trust (Dekker, 2002b).

THE PRESENT SITUATION IN FIGURES

The Dutch non-profit sector is very large by international standards.[7] Measured as a percentage of full-time equivalences (FTEs) of non-agricultural paid employment in 1995, the Netherlands has the largest non-profit sector of all 22 countries studied in the second phase of the Johns Hopkins 'comparative non-profit sector project'.[8] Table 7.1 shows some international comparative data for the 13 OECD countries included in this phase of project. As the first column shows, in the Netherlands, Belgium and Ireland the employment share of the non-profit sector is above 10 per cent, clearly above the other Western European countries (and far above the non-OECD countries of the project, ranging from 0.4 per cent in Mexico to 3.7 per cent in Argentina).

Table 7.1 also gives some information about the structure of the non-profit sector with regard to the three main fields of activity of non-profits for all 22 countries of the project: what is the share of non-profits in these fields in the total non-profit sector of a country, and how important non-profits are compared to public services and for-profits per field of activity.[9]

In the Netherlands, health, social services and education and research account for almost 90 per cent of all non-profit employment, which is the highest share, but not an exceptional one. More marked is the UK's small share (because of the national health system). What is more surprising for the Netherlands is the large share of health: smaller than in the USA and Japan but far above the share of health in the non-profit sector in other European countries. It is surprising because, from the history of the Dutch non-profit sector and the constitutional protection of private schools, one would have expected a leading position for education. Looking in the last three columns at the shares of non-profits in the total employment per field of activity, we see that Dutch non-profits do have the biggest share in the educational field after Ireland.[10] In the field of social services, Ireland and Spain pass the Netherlands, but across the row non-profits in the Netherlands appear to have a dominant position as regards the share of employment.

The figures in Table 7.1 are all about paid employment. The non-profit sector also attracts unpaid or voluntary labour. Although measurements of volunteering are less reliable than measurements of paid work, the Dutch finding of volunteering FTEs being about 6.1 per cent of total non-agricultural paid employment is so much higher than that of other countries[11] that we can be fairly sure that the Netherlands combines the highest levels of both paid and unpaid labour among the 22 countries of the second phase of the Johns Hopkins project. The volunteer input in other countries with (in terms of paid employment) a large non-profit sector is much smaller: 2.6 per cent in Ireland, 2.5 per cent in Belgium and 1.8 per cent in Israel.

Table 7.1 Non-profit sector employment, by country and in main fields of activity, 1995

	Size of the non-profit sector[a]	Three fields in the non-profit sector[b]			Non-profits in the three fields[c]		
		Health	Social services	Education and research	Health	Social services	Education and research
Netherlands	12.9	42	19	27	70	71	65
Ireland	11.5	28	5	54	41	100	72
Belgium	10.5	30	14	39	–	–	–
Israel	9.2	27	11	50	44	29	37
United States	7.8	46	14	21	47	54	22
Australia	7.2	19	20	23	17	61	21
United Kingdom	6.2	4	13	41	4	22	36
Germany	4.9	31	39	12	23	55	10
France	4.9	15	40	21	12	41	12
Spain	4.5	12	32	25	10	84	17
Austria	4.5	12	64	9	15	62	6
Japan	3.5	47	17	22	60	56	25
Finland	3.0	23	18	25	12	13	15

Notes:
[a] Non-profit (full-time equivalents paid) employment as % of total non-agricultural employment.
[b] Non-profit employment as % of total non-profit employment.
[c] Non-profit employment as % of total (public, non-profit and for-profit) employment per field of activity.

Source: Johns Hopkins comparative non-profit sector project.

Public revenues (including private health insurances) make up 59 per cent of the income of the Dutch non-profit sector, fees and charges 38 per cent, leaving only 3 per cent to private giving. Private giving is a minor source of income everywhere in Europe, except in Spain where giving accounts for 19 per cent of the revenues of the (relatively small) non-profit sector (the next highest is 13 per cent in the USA). Compared to the other countries with a large non-profit sector, the Dutch sector is relatively strongly dependent upon fees and charges (38 per cent against 19 per cent in Belgium and 16 per cent in Ireland). The larger dependency on public funding in Belgium and Ireland (both 77 per cent) is interesting for the Dutch debates because it is often supposed that here the offspring of the private initiatives have become extremely addicted to subsidies.

The comparative findings that the Dutch non-profit sector is 'the biggest' but not extremely big, that voluntary work is not pushed aside by paid professionals, that education is not the biggest field of activity of Dutch non-profits and that dependency on public money is substantial but smaller than in other countries with a big non-profit sector, are a useful input for Dutch debates about private initiatives and societal midfield. National history telling with unique concepts easily creates myths about what is typically Dutch and what are general tendencies. Simple comparative quantitative analyses may have many shortcomings, but they are good enough to question these myths.

Table 7.2 offers more information about the structure of the non-profit sector in the Netherlands. Public funds constitute the largest share (59 per cent) of non-profit revenues in the Netherlands; private earnings (payments of clients, membership fees and so on) are the second most important source with 38 per cent; and private giving covers only 3 per cent of the non-profit sector revenue. The division of paid and unpaid labour and of the financial resources differs markedly between fields in the non-profit sector. In the Netherlands, as well as in other countries (Van Til, 2000), a distinction can be made between typical 'welfare state services' fields (the three main fields mentioned in Table 7.1 – health, social services, education and research – and the capital-intensive field of social housing) and 'the rest', which includes more membership and advocacy organizations than are normally associated with the idea of civil society.[12]

The 'welfare state' non-profit services dominate the non-profit sector in the Netherlands. They account for 84 per cent of total expenditures and 90 per cent of total paid employment. Since these groups are so dominant, their sources of income determine to a large extent the revenue structure of the entire non-profit sector. Private giving is insignificant for these services, as the share of 1 per cent indicates. For the other Hopkins groups combined, the share of private giving is 17 per cent.

Table 7.2   Structure of the Dutch non-profit sector, 1995 (%)

	Employment (FTEs)		Expenditures	Revenues[a]		
	Paid	Unpaid		Public	Fees	Giving
Health	42	7	28	96	3	1
Education and research	27	14	20	91	8	1
Social services	19	21	13	66	31	3
Housing and development	2	0	23	7	93	0
Sub-total 'welfare state services'	90	42	84	66	33	1
Culture and recreation	4	37	7	27	65	8
Economic interest organizations	2	1	2	0	100	0
International	1	2	2	45	20	35
Environment	1	4	2	23	60	16
Law, advocacy and politics	1	6	1	4	85	11
Philanthropy and voluntarism	0	0	1	0	94	3
Religion	1	8	1	0	18	82
Sub-total 'other areas'	10	58	16	19	65	16
Total non-profit sector	100	100	100	59	38	3

Note: [a] Percentages of total revenues; public = tax money and social premiums (including private health care insurances); fees = fees, charges, membership dues; giving = private giving.

Source: SCP (Ary Burger)/Johns Hopkins comparative non-profit sector project.

BLURRING BOUNDARIES AND HYBRIDIZATION

So much for the 1995 figures. In the publicly funded and publicly regulated welfare services such as education, health care and social services, non-profits and public agencies have been converging for a long time. Regulations that accompanied public funding made the private organizations more like their public sector counterparts, but there are also other forces at work. Hupe and Meijs (2000), in their study on what differentiates non-profit from government agencies in the fields of primary education and social housing, found little substantial difference, but they also identified converging forces. They refer to the isomorphism approach of DiMaggio and Powell (1983), which explains why organizations look so similar. This states that homogenization is largely affected by political influence and regulation (coercive isomorphism) and professionalization (normative isomorphism). Next to highly similar targets, legal framework and financial structure, convergence is also stimulated by the tendency to copy each other's practices and products (mimetic isomorphism).

These mechanisms apply not only to government and non-profit organizations, but also to non-profits and for-profits in the same field. For-profit practices are introduced in non-profits because of government policies that actively encourage competition or just because modern professional standards demand business-like management styles and accounting procedures. In several fields, non-profits have to face competition from new commercial initiatives. After a long phase of 'going public' in the development of the Dutch welfare state, we see now the stage of 'going private' (Hupe and Meijs, 2000) and trying to find more earnings on the market.

The recent history of social work provides a fine illustration of relevant policy changes in this respect. Today most social work is provided by local non-profits financed by local government. These non-profits usually offer a broad range of activities (day care, youth work, general social work, sociocultural work, minorities, activity programmes and so on) combined in a single organization. Many of them came into existence some ten years ago, after (not always voluntary) mergers between organizations geared towards specific activities, for instance only day care, or only elderly care. The broad social work organizations have a close relationship with their financier and commissioner: local government. The introduction of competition in this field gives local governments the opportunity to redefine their relations with the broad organizations.

Contracting is the main form by which local governments stimulate competition between providers. A contract can be put out for a single service or for the whole range of activities, and the local organization will have to subscribe to keep the work. A relatively new development is to invite tenders for certain social services and for social security arrangements with regard to the long-term unemployed ('integration courses'). Competition comes from non-profits from other parts of the town/country and from commercial providers. At the moment this practice is not widespread as many municipalities like to retain their local providers, but there is clearly a trend towards more competition and competitive tendering. According to government plans, municipalities have received more money and more freedom to decide about unemployment policies from 2001 on, but a condition is that the municipalities themselves will not implement these policies, which should involve private (for-profit or non-profit) organizations, although not necessarily selected through competitive tendering.

Above and beyond the introduction of for-profit management styles and the spread of commercial work ethics, non-profits also take up commercial activities. This 'hybridization' by combining commercial and non-profit elements is apparent in social housing. With the privatization of local government organizations and the ending of subsidies to non-profits, the role of government is restricted to supervising the social function of the housing organizations. Non-profits still have the original target of providing sufficient affordable homes. In order to perform their social function, they now engage in profitable activities.

Broadcasting may serve as another example of a hybrid arrangement. Public television in the Netherlands is basically provided by non-profit associations. Most of these non-profits have a pillarized background that is of decreasing importance. They are allotted public money and broadcasting time according to their respective number of members, but they are also allowed to raise some money from commercial activities. Until recently the non-profits had a monopoly of sorts on the publication of weekly broadcasting programmes and their radio and television guides were an important incentive for membership. A Dutch judge has limited this monopoly, but it seems questionable whether the 'private–public' versus commercial Dutch broadcasting system will long survive European competition rules.[13]

Two more examples of hybridization must suffice here. Elementary schools are the first example. Since 1920, the Dutch constitution has prescribed a dual system of public and private non-profit education. In the classrooms, most differences between the two kinds of schools have already faded away through secularization and converging professional standards, but the 1990s saw a degree of amalgamation in governance. Many municipalities are trying to increase the administrative autonomy of public schools. Since 1996, they have been able to choose independent bodies with a board of parents or full privatization in a foundation. Since 1998, even 'partnership schools' that offer public and private education are allowed. There is still some debate about this legal innovation and there are still a lot of bureaucratic obstacles, but the growth of semi-public autonomous schools seems to be a clear trend. Recently a bill has been presented to parliament to formalize the possibility of having public and private education offered by one school, that is, to have real mergers of the two constitutional types.

The last example is elderly care. It was started by private initiatives and until the 1980s home nursing services were organized in 'cross associations', often several in each municipality in accordance with the local strength of the Catholic, Protestant and neutral 'pillar'. The small 'cross associations' have been merged with other facilities into big regional organizations (130 in the entire country) that no longer have any membership accountability but behave as enterprises, basically paid by social security money. Their managers want to get paid and want to operate like real managers in business; commercial employment services for nurses and additional commercial services for the clients are introduced as subsidiary companies, and so on. At the moment there are a lot of complaints about the work of the home care organizations and attempts are being made to restrict them to the 'core business' of care, but in the long run it seems unlikely that entrance of full commercial enterprises onto the home care market can (or should) be avoided.

PROSPECTS

Through de-pillarization and privatization, major parts of the Dutch non-profit sector have become less visible as separate spheres in society. As is the case in other countries (cf. Evers *et al.*, 2002, Laville and Nyssens, 2001; Van Til, 2000), boundaries around the sector have blurred and the hybridization of public and private and non-commercial and commercial service delivery may even make the non-profit idea obsolete at the level of single organizations. Various developments have resulted in the unfolding of a broad field of ambiguous service providers primarily differentiated with regard to sector. Examples are mergers of public and private schools into collaborative constructions, the combination of commercial and social tasks in housing corporations and insurance companies, the inclusion of new commercial activities in hospitals, social welfare foundations that are searching for new markets and set up temporary job agencies, and the overall internal modernization of old private initiatives into business-like organizations.

Figure 7.1 describes the non-profit sector at the end of the twentieth century in a phase in which there is a long-term trend developing from old private initiatives towards ambiguous non-profit/profit service delivery sectors. In these sectors, the kind of services delivered, professional standards and features of clientele will probably become more important than the legal status and economic background of the organizations that are involved. The perspectives of policy making will be marked by a number of new trends that call for research to review its agenda. Quality control, financial accountability, user

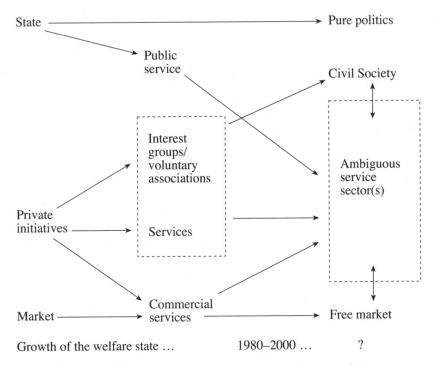

State ———————————————————————→ Pure politics

Public
service

Civil Society

Interest
groups/
voluntary
associations

Ambiguous
service
sector(s)

Private
initiatives ——→ Services

Commercial
Market ——→ services ————————————→ Free market

Growth of the welfare state ...   1980–2000 ...   ?

Figure 7.1   Developments and prospects of the Dutch non-profit sector

rights and the transparency of service clusters demand new regulation, but policies will often not differentiate between types of organizations. More and more people will get vouchers or money, depending on their needs, not on specific services; professional standards will apply to employees wherever they work; patients will have rights wherever they are treated; insurances will adopt rules for the refund of services wherever these are delivered; and the government will be involved with overall volumes of services (budgetary politics) and individual consumption (basic services, vouchers) rather than with the success or failure of individual organizations.

Weakening boundaries around the non-profit sector and hybridization of non-profits are also discussed in relation to other countries (cf. Anheier and Kendall, 2001). The sector is considered to be 'in danger' and strategies are being discussed to revive it. In Dutch discussions about the prospects of the non-profit service providers (mainly in the 'welfare state services' part of Table 7.2) there seem basically to be two strategic options: the 'civil society' option of trying to find a way back to the roots of such organizations and getting citizens involved again, or the 'social enterprise' option of admitting that these organizations have become part of the service economy.

The civil society option is the favoured option for many supporters of the non-profit sector, and it is true that many of the ideals underlying civil society (citizen involvement, public discourse, self-reliance, voluntary action) have a strong tradition in this sector and are still recognizable in the goals and activities of many local clubs and associations, as well as in larger membership and advocacy organizations in other areas of the Dutch non-profit sector (Table 7.2). However, it is hard to imagine how this option would apply to the big professional service providers of the welfare state. More important, too close an association between civil society and the ideals of the non-profit sector implies that these ideals are less relevant for the rest of society. Civil society becomes a national park for non-profits: here and nowhere else the old dreams of voluntary action, citizenship and solidarity should come true.

The enthusiasm for the idea of the civil society among proponents of the non-profit sector rarely leads to serious discussions about the way in which non-profits can contribute to civil society. Civil society is not a centre for change, but is celebrated as a happy discovery: we are civil society (and you are bureaucrats). The American organizational theorist Charles Perrow (2001, p.34) goes further than that: he suggests 'in roughly declining level of importance' the following criteria to judge whether a non-profit organization contributes to civil society: a '*public, collective good* is produced, using *volunteer labour* in substantial amount, with room for *social interaction* that is *not on organizational terms*, and *below market wages* are paid'.

In this view, a 'public, collective good', which is designed for all relevant groups outside the organization, is better than a collective good that is just for the members or a specific sub-group of society. The substantial volunteer labour criterion implies that goals and operations of the organizations would have to be changed if about half the volunteers stopped their contribution (and thus the threat of exit can change goals and operations). Free social interaction means that members of the organization socialize as persons and not as employees restricted by the organization's interests. Payment of below market wages to employees must be possible because of compensation gratifications such as the enjoyment of contributing to a common good or the higher quality of social interactions. According to the fulfilment of these criteria, Perrow talks about 'good', 'intermediate' and 'bad' non-profits. His criteria are disputable, but a clearly normative approach like this is in my view a good starting point for debates and research on implications for non-profits of aiming instead of claiming to be part of civil society.

As regards the *social enterprise option*, the idea of the 'social enterprise' has been discussed in Europe in recent years in different traditions and institutional settings (cf. Defourny, 2001; Laville and Nyssens, 2001). In the Netherlands the social enterprise (*maatschappelijke onderneming*) is less about alternative economics and new economic developments than it is a reform concept for established non-profit service providers. Social enterprises are like normal enterprises except that they do not distribute profits among their managers, owners, shareholders (plc, Ltd) or members (cooperative) but use their surpluses to fund the organizational goals.[14] The legal form is an association or (operating) foundation. Authors disagree as to how idealistic or 'social' the goals of a social enterprise must be (see contributions in Dekker, 2002a), but they agree that the social enterprises should not be protected by the state with rights and benefits because of their non-profit status, and that they must operate in free markets that might well include for-profit enterprises.[15] As non-profits with specific goals they can have tax benefits and subsidies to do things that the state considers to be in the public interest. But this has to be done in a more or less contractual way, avoiding dense public–private relationships. In addition, to make the social enterprises behave as real enterprises, it is in general considered better to support the consumers rather than the providers of services. These consumers might or might not choose non-profits because of their identity, because of a lack of trust in for-profits or for reasons of quality (because the non-profit attracts volunteers or private giving). In some areas the for-profits might win and in other areas they might be pushed out, or even be unable to compete from the outset through lack of purchasing power.

Seen from the Christian–democratic tradition of protection of (denominational) private non-profits, this modern mix of ideas about entrepreneurship, competition and consumer rights sounds quite revolutionary, but, compared to the civil society option, it definitely offers a more realistic perspective for the survival of non-profit providers.

The concept of the social enterprise does not exclude civil society aspirations. Giving clients, volunteers or external stakeholders a greater say, developing the civic skills of clients, community building, support for voluntary associations in the neighbourhood, and so on – these can be part of mission statements or targets to spend surpluses. However, there is no clear reason why these aspirations would only apply to private non-profits, given that, as indicated, many of these organizations are nowadays hard to distinguish from their public and other private counterparts. While non-profits have made changes, public organizations and for-profits have also made adjustments, incorporating original features of the non-profits. Non-profit schools have been bureaucratized, but public schools have adopted much of the non-profit legacy of voluntary action and self-governance. If non-profit schools still do better in parent participation, this should not be cultivated as a non-profit advantage, but be a reason to look for improvements in public schools. Social service providers work in more business-like ways these days, but grocery chains feel compelled to be more oriented towards the local community and to offer employment opportunities to deprived groups. The integration of non-profits into large-scale semi-state and semi-commercial networks of provisions has laid a foundation for the spread of civil society and non-profit aims.

Although the scope of civil society aspirations should not be limited to non-profits, there are still arguments for the protection of the non-profit form as such. We briefly consider here three current reasons. First, compared to public service providers, private providers are still better able to deal with cultural diversity in the population. Services that are highly salient in this respect, such as educating children, homes for the elderly and other long-term full-time care and assistance with moral and psychological questions, are traditional fields for private initiatives. Old religious and ideological cleavages have often lost their significance, but the old arguments may apply to new groups in a multi-cultural society. An example in Dutch society is the development of a 'new pillar' of Islamic schools.[16] The benefits of these new non-profits are controversial because of possible negative effects on learning the Dutch language and on the integration of immigrants, but in general non-profits can positively buffer the tension between the equality of citizens and their peculiarities as pupils, patients and people with problems.

A second argument for non-profits is that they are still better able to attract voluntary resources. They can appeal to religious obligations, group loyalties and sense of community; they might be more easily trusted because of their smaller scale or the status and more immediate accountability of their leaders; or they can meet a more diffuse demand for identity and exclusiveness among potential volunteers and philanthropists.

'Surpluses of purchasing power' provide a third argument. Citizens sometimes want to spend more money on collective services than they are supposed to, or than they are allowed to do. For reasons of equality it is difficult to allow people to spend extra money on their children's public school or on the public nursing home of their parents. This leads to the absurd situation where people can spend whatever they can afford on private goods but not on merit goods, or where they have to choose between poor public services or pure private commercial services. Non-profits can organize group solidarity between the large-scale solidarity of the welfare state and the individual escape to the market. Again, non-profits can buffer the tension between the equality of the citizens and their specificity in terms of wealth and willingness to spend extra money for the benefit of a smaller group of citizens. Politically this is a very controversial argument in the Netherlands: how much in the way of parental contributions is acceptable for primary schools where the basic expenses are paid by (or should principally be covered by) public money? How much inequality is acceptable between primary schools as basic facilities for all citizens? As Table 7.3 shows, the European publics do not easily accept unequal outcomes of

Table 7.3 Opinions about inequality in some EU countries (in % of the population aged 19–79)

Is it just or unjust (or right or wrong) that people with higher incomes can . . .		UK	DE	SE	NL	ES	F
buy better health care than people with lower incomes?	just	42	11	11	10	9	2
	unjust	38	74	75	84	84	87
buy better education for their children?	just	44	11	11	7	8	6
	unjust	38	72	73	85	84	84

Note: Together with the 'neither/nor' and the 'don't know' answers, these figures add up to 100 per cent.

Source: International Social Survey Programme (1999, weighted results).

income inequality in the sphere of basic social services, and the Dutch seem to be quite equality-minded compared to the inhabitants of the United Kingdom, but also to the Germans and the Swedes.

The question of equality and minimal standards of collective provisions will probably be an important topic in the years to come. Shall we stick to the ('social–democratic') model of generally accessible high-quality general public services, ('liberally') accept that public services are minimal services and that the better-off look around for better facilities on the market, or can we find a ('communitarian') way to use group solidarities for the benefit of all?

CONCLUSION

To clarify the present state and relationships of organizations in the Dutch non-profit sector, the chapter started with a brief history of pillarization from the second half of the nineteenth century and the 'pacification' in 1917, to the preferred public–private partnerships of the post-1945 welfare state. The heritage of all these 'p's was a huge non-profit sector, illustrated with figures from the Johns Hopkins comparative non-profit sector project, and a strong acceptance of private initiatives in the public sphere. However, current developments and insecure prospects are cause for serious concern for many non-profits. It has long been difficult to tell whether providers are public or private non-profits, but in recent years the situation has become increasingly complicated and opaque. Former state agencies develop into non-profits, for-profits penetrate the homelands of non-profits, non-profits commence commercial activities and hybrid organizations develop all over the place. As institutional cluster(s) in the Dutch economy, the non-profit sector is in the process of dissolution. It is unclear as yet how much impact present debates about civil society and social entrepreneurship can have on this development. The ideal of citizen-driven civil society organizations is probably too remote from the economic and bureaucratic reality of the non-profit service industries. The same is probably true of imported ideas about the social economy.[17] The pragmatic Dutch version of the social enterprise is the easiest idea to adapt in this environment. It can be helpful to find forms to protect the non-profit status of organizations, but it does not put new positive targets on the agenda of non-profits and it does not help the non-profit sector to develop a common 'post-pillarized' identity.

In discussions in the Netherlands about the results of the Johns Hopkins project and in contributions to a book about the future of the non-profit sector that appeared as a follow-up to this project, the non-profit vocabulary was clearly rejected as being too economistic and too negative (Dekker, 2002a). Apart from 'civil society' and 'social enterprise', two concepts came to the fore when authors with very diverse ideological stances and political positions discussed the future of our bureaucratized and commercialized non-profit sector: 'private initiative' and 'professional autonomy'. The call for new private initiatives goes in the same direction as the pleas to remodel the sector according to civil society ideals of voluntary action for the common good and dominance of volunteers in the organizations (cf. Perrow, 2001). The pleas for more professional autonomy and more room and respect for the street-level professionals in the service-delivering organizations are directed against state bureaucrats as well as market-oriented managers. They apply to schools, hospitals, nursery homes and social work organizations, independent of their economic characteristics. It is no longer a question of non-profits versus public and commercial organizations, but concerns the strengthening of a professional ethos in caring organizations against bureaucratic and economic threats. Although there are still good reasons for wanting to protect private non-profits as a special kind of organization in the public sphere, the antithesis of professionalism versus market and state might well be the more important issue for the future of Dutch civil society and the welfare state.

NOTES

1. The term was popular in particular among secular and progressive people who considered the (pillarized, mainly denominational) 'societal midfield' as the power base and play ground of the governing Christian–democratic party. After the defeat of this party in the 1994 elections (but long before its resurrection in the 2002 elections) and the rediscovery of intermediary organizations by the new social–liberal coalitions (1994–2002), there was a revival of the 'midfield' vocabulary.
2. Quite the opposite: (former) mutuals are strong in the insurance industry (but increasingly integrated in and indistinguishable from for-profits), there are still many – and among them some big – cooperatives in agriculture and the food industry, and the 400 local Rabobank cooperatives (offspring of the initiatives of the German mayor Friedrich Wilhelm Raiffeisen around 1850) and their common 'daughter' Rabobank Nederland form the biggest consumer bank in the country.
3. One can argue that socialist and liberal pillars were not really pillars because the first lacked the upper classes while the latter failed to attract the lower classes. Liberal organizations in particular were often primarily non-religious. They became pillarized through selective membership, not because of a positive ideological identity. One may say that, because of the encompassing denominational segregation in many areas, socialist and liberal organizations had to link and to function as pillars, too. See Bax (1988) for these discussions and for theories about the causes of pillarization.
4. The difference in ideology is still recognizable in the legal form of confessional schools: most Catholic schools are foundations (mirroring the clerical hierarchy and with a representative of the bishop on the board); most Protestant schools are associations, started more from below by parents.
5. The political end-games of depillarization were the mergers of the Catholic and socialist labour unions in the mid-1970s, and of the Catholic and the two larger Protestant parties into the Christian Democratic Party in 1980.
6. Cf. Glenn (2000) who contrasts the positive attitude and pragmatism of politics and government in the Netherlands (and Germany) with the fundamental controversies about the relationship between 'faith-based' organizations and government in the USA.

7. Data about the Netherlands have been gathered by my former SCP colleague Ary Burger. In other parts of this chapter I also draw on our common work (cf. Burger *et al.*, 2000).
8. Entities are defined as non-profits if they are organizations (they have an institutional presence and structure), private (they are institutionally separate from the state), not profit distributing (they do not return profits to their managers or to a set of 'owners'), self-governing (they are fundamentally in control of their own affairs) and voluntary (membership in these organizations is not legally required and they attract some level of voluntary contribution of time or money; see Salamon *et al.*, 1999, pp.3f). Of course, in practice these criteria are sometimes difficult to apply and many disputable decisions must be made in order to arrive at a similar selection of organizations. The last two criteria in particular are difficult: what is 'fundamentally', what is 'some level'? In the Netherlands large numbers of vested non-profits that deliver welfare state services appear to be borderline cases in these respects.
9. See Salamon *et al.* (1999) for a classification of organizations according to the International Classification of Nonprofit Organizations (ICNPO).
10. To add a non-employment indicator: 75 per cent of Dutch pupils in primary and secondary schools go to private non-profit schools, but in Ireland this share is 83 per cent (Japan, 69 per cent; Belgium, 61 per cent; the other countries, between 5 and 29 per cent).
11. France is second with 4.7 per cent, followed by 4.4 per cent for the UK and 4.0 per cent for the USA. Sweden, which was not in the second phase of the Hopkins project, scored 7.4 per cent in 1990. The number of volunteers according to populations surveys is at about the same level in Sweden and the Netherlands, but higher in the USA.
12. This is of course a very rough split of the sector. Besides the fact that most organizations are neither bureaucratic state-dependent service providers nor autonomous citizens' initiatives but mixtures of these prototypes, it is easy to mention examples that do not fit in the simple sectoral divide: there are self-help groups in the health field, heavily subsidized concert halls with fully professional orchestras in the field of culture and recreation and NGOs in the international field that devote much of their energy to implementing the government's development policies. But these are minor exceptions in quantitative terms and the rough split is useful for a better understanding of the diversity of the Dutch non-profit sector.
13. In general, arrangements that are clearly neither plainly public nor obviously private are vulnerable to European attention. The occurrence of friction between European rules and national arrangements is likely in fields that show the characteristic public funding and private delivery of the Dutch non-profit sector.
14. In the Netherlands the 'maatschappelijke onderneming' was primarily developed in the 1990s by the non-profit consultant Steven de Waal and by researchers and politicians of the Christian–democratic party (among them Jan Peter Balkenende, who became prime minister after the 2002 elections).
15. The stress on free entrepreneurship probably has several reasons: the problems of present bureaucratic regulation, the necessity to comply with EU free competition policies, but also a broader cultural shift towards 'Everyone a business-person, some in nonprofits' (Van Til, 2000, pp.111f).
16. The first Islamic primary school was founded in 1988; in 2002, there were already 35 schools with 9000 pupils. The demand is greater, but supply is restricted by lack of teachers and competing requests for an allowance to found a school.
17. Of course this might change because of intellectually stimulating European discussions or financially attractive EU initiatives, but the historical sociopolitical framing of the field and the present perspectives of non-profit social enterprises and civil society do not leave much room for another overall concept. Thus far 'social economy' remains a label for a small number of (EU-financed or evaluated) projects that are directed towards social integration and creating alternative employment. That is not a relevant perspective for the large majority of Dutch non-profits. They offer subsidized jobs and unpaid work for the 'social activation' of long-term unemployed, but so do their public counterparts. The normal voluntary work they accommodate is independent of labour market problems. Although the situation on the labour market has been changing since 2002, the main problem of the Dutch non-profit sector is not how to create new jobs for the unemployed but how to become more attractive as an employer (Dekker, 2004). There are still huge shortages of teachers, nurses and others.

REFERENCES

Anheier, H. and J. Kendall (eds) (2001), *Third sector policy at the crossroads*, London: Routledge.

Bax, E.H. (1988), *Modernisation and cleavage in Dutch society*, Groningen, NL: Universiteitsdrukkerij.

Berger, P. and R. Neuhaus ([1966]1977), *To empower people*, 20th anniversary edn, ed. Michael Novak, Washington: AEI Press.

Burger, A. and V. Veldheer (2001), 'The growth of the non-profit sector in the Netherlands', *Non-profit and Voluntary Sector Quarterly*, 30 (2), 221–46.

Burger, A. and P. Dekker, with T. van der Ploeg and W. van Veen (2000), 'The nonprofit sector in the Netherlands', Working Paper no. 70, SCP, The Hague (available from *www.scp.nl*).

Defourny, J. (2001), 'Introduction', in C. Borzaga and J. Defourny (eds), *The emergence of social enterprise*, London and New York: Routledge, pp.1–28.

Dekker, P. (ed.) (2002a), *Particulier initiatief en publiek belang* (Private initiative and public interest), The Hague: SCP (available from *www.scp.nl*).

Dekker, P. (2002b), 'On the prospects of volunteering in civil society', *Voluntary Action*, 4 (3), 31–48.

Dekker, P. (2004), 'The role of the third sector in the Netherlands', in A. Zimmer and C. Stecker (eds), *Strategy mix: Social and labour-market integration* (in press).

DiMaggio, P.J. and W.W. Powell (1983), 'The iron cage revisited', *American Sociological Review*, 48, April, 147–60.

Evers, A., U. Rauch and U. Stitz (2002), *Von öffentlichen Einrichtungen zu sozialen Unternehmen* (From public service to social enterprise), Berlin: Sigma.

Glenn, Ch. L. (2000), *The ambiguous embrace*, Princeton: Princeton University Press.

Hupe, P.L. and L.C.P.M. Meijs, with M.H. Vorthoren (2000), 'Hybrid governance', Working Paper no. 65, SCP, The Hague (available from *www.scp.nl*).

Kramer, R.M., H. Lorentzen, W.B. Melief and S. Pasquinelli (1993), *Privatization in four European countries*, New York: M.E. Sharpe.

Laville, J. and M. Nyssens (2001), 'The social enterprise', in C. Borzaga and J. Defourny (eds), *The emergence of social enterprise*, London and New York: Routledge, pp.312–32.

Lijphart, A.J. (1968), *The politics of accommodation*, Berkeley: University of California Press.

Perrow, C. (2001), 'The rise of non-profits and the decline of civil society', in H.K. Anheier (ed.), *Organisational theory and the non-profit form*, London: Centre for Civil Society/LSE, pp.33–44.

Salamon, L.M., H.K. Anheier, R. List, S. Toepler, S.W. Sokolowski and Associates (1999), *Global civil society*, Baltimore: The Johns Hopkins Center for Civil Society Studies, Johns Hopkins University.

Van Til, J. (2000), *Growing civil society*, Bloomington: Indiana University Press.

PART III

The Third Sector, the State and the European
Union

8. The state and the third sector in modern welfare states: independence, instrumentality, partnership

Jane Lewis

The idea that social welfare systems encompass more than state provision had to be rediscovered in the last quarter of the twentieth century, but is now well established in the literature. However, the approach to 'welfare mixes' (Evers and Svetlik, 1993) differs considerably between different networks of academics and commentators. In the English speaking literature, the most common conceptualization has been the 'mixed *economy* of welfare', which emphasizes, first, the range of providers of welfare (the state, the market, employers, the family and the third sector) and, second, the increasingly plural sources of finance for social provision (for example, Johnson, 1998). However, in Evers's original formulation of a 'welfare mix', issues of politics and governance were also prominent. The mixed economy approach tends to identify which element dominates a particular kind of social provision, the underlying assumption being that they are *alternatives*, albeit that there is increasing recognition in the United Kingdom of the extent to which it is profoundly difficult to sort out the precise nature of the public and private mix (that is, state and market) of finance and provision in respect of health, education or pensions (for example, Burchardt *et al.*, 1999).

However, when political issues are added, it becomes yet more difficult to keep the different elements in the welfare mix in their separate boxes as alternative providers and financers. In respect of the third sector, the whole issue of its place *vis-à-vis* the state, for example, becomes more complicated. As Deakin (2001, p.110) has asked: is the democratic state a necessary condition for the existence of free associations, or can they survive without a framework of law and citizen rights, and does democracy, in its turn, require associations? The associations comprising the third sector are of course more than just service providers. As part of civil society, their embeddedness in and interdependence with the state and the market are more striking than their separation from these other parts of the public sphere. Nevertheless, the argument remains that associations warrant the attention of academics and policy analysts only in so far as they are able to establish an *independent* presence, whether in terms of financial support or of governance.

The most influential comparative approach to social welfare systems has developed the concept of a 'welfare regime' (Esping Andersen, 1990), which focuses on the social relations of welfare and in particular on the relationship between social entitlements and labour markets. While Evers and Svetlik focused on the relationships between the state, the market and the third sector, Esping Andersen focused on those between the state, the market and the family. The last of these was elaborated by feminist analysts (Lewis, 1992; Orloff, 1993) and has only recently assumed a more important place in the mainstream literature (Esping Andersen, 1999; Myles and Quadagno, 2002). In the welfare regime literature, the third sector is conspicuous by its absence. In part this is due to the fact that the comparative analysis of welfare states has focused much more on cash provision, where the relationship between paid work and state benefits is most direct, rather than on services such as health or education, but in large part it is because the third sector is held to be of less analytical importance. This is because such a large proportion of its funding comes from the state (65 per cent of earned income and 40 per cent of grant income in the UK (NCVO and CCS, 2001, p.18)), which makes it possible to justify collapsing the third sector into the state. Again, the assumption is that, if third sector provision is not a clearly demarcated alternative to the state and the market, it does not warrant separate attention.

Certainly, it is the relationship between the third sector and the state that is most ambiguous and arouses most concern and debate, but it is difficult to dismiss the role of the third sector in either the period of welfare state growth (Skocpol, 1992) or that of 'retrenchment' (Pierson, 1994, 2001) and 'restructuring' (Ferrera and Rhodes, 2000; Scharpf and Schmidt, 2000). Indeed, during the period of welfare state growth consideration of gender roles in families is intimately linked to an understanding of the significant part played by voluntary associations. Broadly speaking, in the absence of suitable opportunities for employment, middle class women in particular extended their caring role to 'domesticate the public' (Baker, 1984; Lewis, 1991; Skocpol, 1992; Koven and Michel, 1993), something that became much less significant with the expansion of state welfare. The importance of the link between the work of voluntary associations and the family was rediscovered in the late twentieth century by those theorists who have invested both with the capacity of building social capital.

Voluntary organizations at the beginning of the twentieth century tended to be more financially independent of government. Nevertheless, historically, free associations have been *integral* to the conceptualization of citizenship and of social solidarity and collective action (Harris, 1990; Lewis, 1995). In this analysis, the interdependence of the third sector and the state becomes crucial to understanding the very nature of European welfare regimes. In the United States, where associations played a major part in early social policy development, early initiatives (in the form of pensions for veterans and maternal and child welfare policies) were not generalized to the whole population. In many European countries the hugely important contribution of the 'mutuals'[1] was made part of the new core programme of modern European social provision, social insurance. (This was the case even in the UK prior to the First World War, although by the mid-twentieth century the role of the mutuals was confined largely to financing house purchase.)

In the more recent period of welfare state restructuring, third sector organizations have once more come to the fore in many countries as potential alternative employers and providers of welfare to the state. Kendall and Knapp (2000) have suggested that, in respect of care services for older people, for example, the expansion of third sector provision has played an important part in enabling governments to restructure welfare provision (or to 'recalibrate' it, to use Pierson's (2001) term). While the picture of the third sector in the last decade emphasizes its resurgence, it still tends to portray the sector as subservient to, and indeed to all intents and purposes as the instrument of, the state; the picture is primarily one of non-profit organizations delivering services at the behest of, and often under contract to, the state.

But voluntary associations have played an important role as campaigners as well as service providers in respect of welfare, and they have long been recognized as part of the fabric of the liberal democratic state. The main issue becomes that of how independent they are of the state. Leaving social provision to the third sector in the manner advocated by many American commentators (for example, Wolfe, 1989; Olavsky, 1992) does not necessarily make them independent providers if the work is done under tightly specified contracts and government is the paymaster. Becoming an alternative provider of welfare may signal a relationship with the state that is above all instrumental, with little acknowledgment being given to the role of voluntary organizations beyond that of service provider.

There is some evidence to suggest that the nature of welfare restructuring in Europe at the beginning of the twenty-first century is opening up a space for a new, explicitly articulated awareness of the political and democratic as well as strategic importance of associations to the polity, for all that the danger of instrumentalism on the part of the state and of subservience to it is ever-present. In policy documents at the level of the nation state and the European Union, there is evidence of both an explicit discussion of the meaning of a partnership between the state and the third sector that is respectful of the independence of the latter, and an effort to give this form and substance. While the instrumental use of voluntary organizations by governments remains a 'clear and present danger', this is increasingly recognized in the political debates and there is also increasing evidence of the means to challenge it in the particular context of European welfare state restructuring.

EXPLANATIONS AND EMPIRICAL OBSERVATIONS

Explanations of the existence and nature of the third sector have been dominated by economists, who have tried to explain the persistence of the sector with the notion of market and/or government failure to meet demand, for example, from minority groups (Weisbrod, 1988). Hansmann (1987) has suggested additionally that, where information asymmetries exist, contract failure occurs. Market mechanisms may fail to provide consumers with the adequate means to police producers and, where consumers cannot evaluate services and need protection by providers, non-profit organizations will appear more trustworthy. This kind of explanation tends to put the state, the market and the third sector in separate boxes, such that the relationship between the state and the third sector in particular becomes at best complementary and often alternative and conflictual. There is little room for the kind of conceptualization of associations as part and parcel of the fabric of the state that empirical historical research has shown was certainly the case in nineteenth century Britain (Harris, 1990; Lewis, 1995) and also in Norway (Kuhnle and Selle, 1992).

Salamon (1987) has also stressed the interdependence and partnership between the state and third sector arising from voluntary failure, rather than conflict. He argued that under certain circumstances cooperative (financial and political) relationships could be forged between the non-profit sector and the state in addressing social problems. This might occur where resistance to direct state action was strong and yet there was demand for particular kinds of social and economic protection, or where it was advantageous to the state to enlist the cooperation of the non-profit sector. While Salamon thus acknowledged the possibility of cooperation, he did not recognize the extent to which in some European countries associations were *integral* to the conceptualization of the state (rather than, say, the corollary of a limited state (see Thane, 1990)).

Most recently, Salamon and Anheier (1998) and Anheier (2001) have suggested that the size and funding structure of the third sector is explained by the nature of the 'welfare regime' (drawing on Esping Andersen's (1990) typology). Thus in the so-called 'liberal model', low government social welfare spending is associated with a relatively large non-profit sector (in the USA and UK); in the social democratic model (Sweden), high government welfare spending is associated with a relatively small non-profit sector (measured in terms of employment). Thus, in these two models, state and non-profit sector provision are seen as 'alternatives'. In the corporatist model, high welfare spending is paralleled by a large non-profit sector (in France and Germany) because government and the third sector are perceived as cooperators rather than as alternative providers. In this model, associations are portrayed as a key element of pre-modern social relations that have been incorporated into the corporatist welfare state (see also Crouch, 1999). Thus this 'social origins' model of explanation allows for state and third sector provision to be seen either as alternative or complementary. In large measure this is because it pays more attention to political as well as the economic variables. However, the measures of associations in the sector have been limited to size and the source of funding, which is a problem given the complicated nature of the sector.

Indeed the observations regarding the 'moorings' of the third sector (Anheier, 2001) require substantial elaboration, especially in terms of which parts of the voluntary sector have prospered and why. In the UK, the welfare mix at the beginning of the twentieth century comprised a very large non-profit sector (larger than the state if medical charities are included). During the first three quarters of the twentieth century the size and relative importance of the non-profit sector shrank, with the decline being particularly pronounced during the period of the 'classic welfare state' (the 1950s and 1960s), when the UK's social provision (but not levels of taxation) more closely resembled that of the Scandinavian countries than that of the USA (Titmuss, 1974). In the UK the 'old Left' in the postwar decades regarded 'charity' as inferior and inherently less desirable than state provision, while the 'new Right' of the 1980s preferred the market to the state or the non-profit sector (Giddens, 1999). The dramatic change in the nature of the UK welfare regime during the postwar period finds no parallel in the rest of Europe, but what is interesting is that in neither its pre- nor post-Thatcher incarnations was priority given to the third sector in the welfare mix.

Associations were broadly regarded as complementary or supplementary to the state until the 1980s (Kramer, 1981); after that they were indeed more likely to be treated above all as alternative providers of welfare services under contract, in other words, as the junior player in what was termed (for primarily ideological reasons[2]) 'the independent sector' (comprising the market and the third sector). Voluntary associations found it very difficult to sustain their campaigning work as grants were turned into contracts for service. The nature of the relationship has changed again since the election of a Labour government in 1997, in favour of an explicit 'partnership' at the level of overarching policy goals and increasingly at the local level, despite continuity in terms of many of the mechanisms – particularly contract – linking the state and the third sector.

In the case of Sweden, interpretation of the nature of the third sector's embeddedness depends largely on the way in which the size of the non-profit sector is measured. Even though the non-profit sector as a whole is relatively small, as Anheier (2001) has noted, the non-service-providing elements of the third sector are very large in Sweden, as is membership as opposed to employment (see also Rothstein, 2002). It is therefore possible to argue that generous state provision and finance of welfare has been paralleled by the largest growth in the kind of spontaneous association that is for the most part independent of government (concerned chiefly, in the Swedish case, with leisure and cultural pursuits), and that is most strongly associated with the formation of social capital. In other words, as even a brief exploration of these two cases shows, it would be premature to characterize the relationship between the state and third sector organizations as instrumental, as a partnership or as independent on the basis of only a limited number of cross-sectional variables.

REDISCOVERING THE IMPORTANCE OF THE THIRD SECTOR

The Third Sector in Academic and Public Debate

Spontaneous association has long been argued to be of crucial importance to the modern democratic state, and in the wake of the Second World War the importance of the part played by civil society in western democracies was highlighted in contrast to totalitarian regimes (for example, Lindsay, 1945; Beveridge, 1948). More recently Putnam (1993) has focused on the specific aspects of social interactions that matter for well performing governments and ultimately for democracy. In his study of 20 Italian regions, Putnam demonstrated the effects of social capital on the performance of regional government, defining social capital as the norms of generalized reciprocity and trust, and as networks of civic engagement. In this argument, associations and voluntary organizations are part of such networks and help to inculcate such norms. Following de Tocqueville, associations are seen as functioning as 'schools of democracy' and thus as creators of social capital.

The concept of social capital was picked up and developed in the USA in the late 1980s, first as a way of challenging the rational individual action paradigm (Coleman, 1988). The attention to social capital represented a wider appreciation of the extent to which no one is an 'unencumbered self' (Sandel, 1996), and stressed interdependence and hence the obligations people have towards one another. It is significant that the concept was elaborated in a country where associations have historically been seen as occupying a separate space from the state, and in which increasing concern was being expressed about the growth of 'selfish individualism' (classically by Bellah *et al.*, 1985), which was believed to be threatening the very foundations – that is, family and community – on which liberal market democracies depended (see also Fukuyama, 1999).

Social capital was conceptualized as a set of informal values and norms that permit cooperation and foster trust. Trust and cooperation were held to be learned in the private sphere of the family and in the free associations of civil society, and, in Putnam's (1993) formulation, then to be generalized into the public sphere of politics and the market. In a recent discussion paper on social capital produced by the UK government's Performance and Innovation Unit (Cabinet Office Performance and Innovation Unit, 2002), the possible benefits of building social capital for the economy are given as much space as those for the political sphere. However, the building of social capital was argued to be something that had to happen outside the state. Indeed, the main measure of social capital has been membership of voluntary associations. In other words, virtuous causality runs in only one direction, from voluntary, spontaneous association to the wider polity. But this is problematic in so far as people who trust more may be more readily drawn to membership of associations, whereas people who trust less may not join in the first place (Stolle and Rochon, 1998). In addition, the assumption that the social capital fostered by voluntary associations has a 'bridging' and 'linking' function has been questioned. Associations can be as much a means of 'bonding' (the extreme example given is usually the Mafia) as 'bridging'.

The concept of social capital as the 'glue' that seems to be increasingly missing in society was also taken up in the UK in the wake of the emphasis given to the importance of market individualism by successive Conservative governments. However, Hall (1999) has argued that there is no evidence of any erosion of social capital in the UK to match that in the USA (summarized by Putnam (2000) in terms of 'bowling alone'). Hall attributes this to a range of factors, including the part-time (rather than full-time as in the USA) participation of women in the labour market, education reform together with the transformation of the class structure (given that participation in associations is correlated with higher social class and educational achievement) and the acceptance of voluntary action alongside government provision. Yet even if there is no sign of any huge decline in participation in associations, there is some evidence of the decline of social trust. Between 1990 and 1995, those reporting that they trusted other people declined from 44 to 30 per cent in the UK (NCVO and CCS, 2001). Furthermore, in 1996, fewer people in the UK reported trusting charities than teachers, the police or the BBC, which in turn casts doubt on the value of associations *per se* in building trust. Nevertheless, the 2001 UK Home Office Citizenship Survey reported that overall 76 per cent of people said that they could trust some or many people in their neighbourhoods (only 2 per cent said that they trusted no one) (Prime *et al.*, 2002).

This evidence can be interpreted in such a way as to support those who argue for the importance of the separation of associations from the state and see the means of building social capital as a process of 'spontaneous renorming' (Fukuyama, 1999). After all, some of the largest charities in the UK became vehicles for government activity at an early stage (Ware, 1989), while others became service deliverers under contract during the 1980s and 1990s and therefore shared in the public's growing distrust of governments. Public opinion surveys asking about trust in third sector organizations may well have tapped negative attitudes about the declining quantity and quality of welfare provision, with which many voluntary organizations became associated, rather than views about the more independent and often smaller associations.

However, in the final event, this means that more is being said about trust in government than about trust in associations and, as the Swedish case shows (Rothstein, 1998, 2002), it is possible to create 'just institutions', which in turn create a belief in the possibility of intervention to achieve greater equality, and which are paralleled by strong, independent voluntary organizations (see also OECD, 2001). Generalized levels of trust appear to be the highest in Scandinavia and have been maintained there, whereas in the USA they have declined strongly (Putnam, 2000). Levi (1998) has argued that governments can realize their capacity to generate trust only if citizens consider the state itself to be trustworthy. From a gender perspective, the family policies in the Scandinavian countries that are explicitly directed towards enabling women to enter the public sphere of work and politics are important in explaining the trust that women develop in state institutions and policies (Stolle and Lewis, 2002). This political and institutional trust enables women also to trust other citizens more extensively. In the welfare politics of the continental corporatist countries, the strong linkage between third sector organizations and the state in respect of the delivery of the major social services of modern states, particularly health, social care and education, and the commitment to consensus building ensures a baseline of agreement in which third sector organizations are included.

All this suggests that for social capital to flourish it needs to be embedded in and linked to formal political institutions (Levi, 1998; Skocpol, 1996; Tarrow, 1996). Thus social capital is held not to exist independently in the realm of civil society, which in turn means that the capacity of citizens to develop cooperative ties may also be determined by state policies. If this is true, the state can play a role in fostering social capital, and we arrive at a notion of the relationship between state and associations that has more to do with interdependence than with independence and alternatives. Certainly Putnam's (2000) most recent contribution suggests that it needs the combined effort of employers, the mass media, voluntary associations, individual citizens and government to restore levels of social capital in the USA. If social capital is important both for individual well-being (for example, social networks are important for finding employment) and for societal stability, cohesion and prosperity, and is, in addition, unequally distributed, the case for the government playing a part in building social capital seems strong.

The Third Sector in Welfare State Restructuring

During the 1990s, all European welfare states substantially restructured. The pressures to do so have been manifold and there is substantial debate about their respective importance and effects. However, what became clear by the turn of the century is the apparent determination on the part of all EU member states to defend the European social model in the face of common pressures from more 'global' competition, and from the demands of ageing populations in particular. Indeed it is possible to characterize much of the restructuring as more a matter of 'recalibration' (Pierson, 2001) than of 'dismantling' (Pierson, 1994). Restructuring has involved a new emphasis on particular principles: responsibilities as opposed to rights and equality of opportunities rather than outcomes, both of which have resulted in a focus on getting people into work and to some extent a demand for more self-provisioning, for example in respect of pensions. This has commonly been referred to as a shift towards an 'active' welfare state and relies on a new conceptualization of the work/welfare relationship.

There has also been more emphasis on what might be termed 'marketization', meaning *both* a more mixed economy of welfare (although in the case of pension provision, for example, private provision varies hugely, from 2 per cent as the result of recent Swedish reforms to 40 per cent in the UK) and, more significantly, the introduction of market principles into the public sector. In the UK the result has been much more blurring of the public/private boundaries in terms of finance and provision (Burchardt *et al.*, 1999). In the field of service provision, where third sector organizations are particularly active, associations are expected to meet the demands of the 'contract culture', the main mechanism in the lexicon of the 'new public management' by which market principles have been introduced into public services. But most recently (as the next section of the chapter shows) more emphasis has been put at nation state and EC level on formulating a new partnership between the state, the market and voluntary organizations, to supersede both the old hierarchical principles of the classic welfare state and the pure contract culture that endeavoured to make the market and the third sector alternatives to the state. Furthermore, the concept of partnership includes the recognition of both the economic and the political importance of the third sector.

Theorists of globalization predicted that more open economies necessarily mean more competition and put pressure on the social costs of labour. Thus the predictions envisage a 'race to the bottom' in respect of social provision. Recent studies have failed to show clear-cut decline, even in the UK during the 1980s (Hills, 1990, 1995; Glennerster and Hills, 1998). Indeed, the evidence suggests that, while expansion has come to an end in most, but not all fields of welfare, there is little sign of a 'race to the bottom' (Stephens *et al.*, 1999; Castles, 2001). Looking beyond Europe and the USA, Alber and Standing (2000) have again tended to confirm this view, albeit they have detected a trend to lower social spending relative to a given level of wealth.

However, the importance of the globalization discourse, as opposed to any of the more empirically measurable drivers associated with the phenomenon, is important. As in the case of monetary and fiscal policy, the neoliberal prescriptions of the Washington Consensus have constituted a new framework of ideas about the proper conduct of social policy, dictating private rather than public provision, allocation by markets rather than on the basis of need, selective rather than universal provision, charging rather than tax-based finance, and decentralization rather than central planning. These have influenced the pattern of welfare state change, for instance by justifying the call to strengthen responsibility by matching entitlements to benefits with the requirement to train or to work. The main point is that the globalization discourse directs the attention of governments to labour markets and competitiveness and, as Atkinson (1999) has noted, the power of this discourse to change attitudes and norms, for example, in respect of the political *will* to redistribute (regardless of the extent to which it results in measurable cuts in social programmes or the employment and pay of unskilled workers) should not be underestimated. Even in the absence of a 'race to the bottom', governments may adopt a more cautious approach and the new-found emphasis on the obligation of individuals to engage in the labour market is part of this. Certainly, the European Commission has stressed the importance of adult labour market participation in order to increase competitiveness (CEC, 1993, 1995, 2000a, 2000b). Both the EC (CEC, 2000a) and the OECD (2000) have emphasized the importance of policies to 'make work pay' and, in the words of the EC, of strengthening 'the role of social policy as a productive factor' (CEC, 2000b, p.2).

The arguments that wrap up concern about internal demographic challenges in the form of low birth rates and ageing populations into a notion of intergenerational conflict (Thomson, 1991; Kotlikoff, 1992) also serve to promote this approach. The conclusion from this work on 'generational accounting' is that current levels of social provision, particularly in respect of pensions, are unsustainable, thus justifying privatization and making the individual responsible for providing a larger proportion of his or her pension. Alternatively, the Belgian Presidency document on redrawing the 'architecture' of welfare states promotes the employment of women in order to broaden the tax base, particularly in the continental European, Christian Democratic corporatist welfare states (Esping Andersen *et al.*, 2001). Overall in the European context, the competitiveness agenda has promoted policies aiming at labour market 'activation' and at services that can be justified under the umbrella of 'social investment', especially in education, but also in health. As Goodin (2001) and Gilbert (2002) have observed, there has been some convergence among western welfare states towards stressing the importance of so-called 'active' rather than 'passive' welfare[3] and an 'enabling' role for the state.

This approach to social provision has major implications for third sector organizations, which may as a result be expected to play a greater role in provision, but also to demonstrate their 'added value', and to play more of a role as providers of employment, or in providing a way into the labour market via 'active volunteering'. The European Commission's Social Economy Unit (which operated until the reorganization of the Commission in 2000) was active in promoting an enterprise approach to the third sector, with voluntary organizations seen as a key player in regenerating communities, delivering social services and training the socially excluded. This approach brought together the desire to promote a new relationship between work and welfare with a determination to tackle social exclusion.

It is the linking of these ambitions that has meant that welfare state restructuring in Europe over the past decade has been undertaken in order to promote social cohesion and to defend the European social model. The policy intent has been to bolster social solidarity. This is in large part what Torfing (1999) means when he describes the Danish version of 'workfare' as an 'offensive' reform strategy, or what Timonen (2001) is also getting at when she describes the Finnish and Swedish changes as 'defensive'. Even in the UK the policy intent is no longer to promote the 'independent sector' (that is, market and third sector) as a means of 'rolling back the state'. There is rather a reassessment of what the third sector has to offer in and for itself, while the desirability of a 'welfare state' has not been in question since the Labour government was elected in 1997 (although, given the context of the low wage, low skill productivist model established in the UK during the 1980s and early 1990s, welfare-to-work, labour market activation and social investment strategies inevitably look different in practice from those of the continental European countries).

The reasons for this 'change in order to defend' approach to social provision in EU member states has much to do with Pierson's (1994) arguments about the nature of the politics of retrenchment. His arguments focused on 'institutional stickiness' and the fact that policies had produced politics, that is, they had created constituencies, for example, of old age pensioners, who were ready to defend the policies that were important to them. In consequence, any politician wishing to 'retrench' had to seek to 'avoid blame'. But 'blaming' politicians for retrenchment was not activated solely by the self-interest of particular constitutencies. Because welfare has always involved talking about the conditions under which cash and services may be provided for strangers, there has also always been a moral dimension to the debate. This is often believed to have been strongest in the English-speaking countries, because of the persistence of the preoccupation with desert, but it has also been a powerful force pulling in a rather different direction in the Scandinavian countries. Thus Rothstein (1998) has argued that the creation of 'just institutions' in those countries has fostered a high regard for equality and trust in government, which is in turn a crucial prerequisite for high levels of taxation. In any event, Schmidt's (2000, p.231) comment that 'no major and initially unpopular welfare state reform could succeed in the medium term if it did not also succeed in changing the underlying definition of moral appropriateness' must be taken seriously, touching as it does on what is understood by politicians and people as the very purpose of welfare.

In most continental European countries during the 1990s, welfare reform has been undertaken with the express purpose of saving rather than fundamentally changing the welfare system, and of preserving and promoting social solidarity. Apart from the UK prior to 1997, there has been no explicit aim to promote the market and third sector organizations as alternative providers to the state. The third sector has historically been integral to conceptualization of the polity and to social provision in Europe. Welfare state restructuring has involved renegotiating and formalizing the notion of partnership in the belief that the third sector can be part of the determination to promote the obligation to work and to create an active welfare state, as a means to greater competitiveness and to tackling social exclusion. This is not without dangers. In particular voluntary organizations may find it hard to escape state instrumentalism, in respect of the terms for service provision and the desire of governments for employment creation. It remains to be seen whether the new discourse and practice of partnership at the national and EU level has the potential to avoid the marginalization of the third sector and how far it can also serve to promote a new commitment to a vigorous civil society.

NEW PARTNERSHIPS

In his 2000 Goodman lecture on 'Civic Society', Gordon Brown, the UK finance minister, drew a picture of civic society as encompassing individual freedom alongside the 'rejection of self-interested individualism and of state power for the idea of association and common endeavour' (p.6). Partnership between the third sector and the state was thus portrayed as part of the renewed commitment to social engagement and an ethical state. The basis for such a partnership was described in terms of a morally based and internally sustained 'covenant', encompassing shared values, common purposes and mutual obligations, rather than the market principles of a 'contract'. In the following year, Ralf Dahrendorf's Goodman lecture on 'Challenges to the Voluntary Sector' was sceptical of such a possibility. The third sector should not, he argued, be harnessed to state action, nor should it fill the gaps left by the state, or become an alternative service provider and hence a quasi-governmental organization. He asked: 'Is not the seemingly mutual embrace of government and the voluntary sector a threat especially to the weaker partner of the love affair? Is there not an issue of independence, which is the oxygen of charity but stifled by the flirt with political power?' (Dahrendorf, 2001, p.8). Dahrendorf's concern about the room for independent – in the sense of unfettered – action on the part of third sector associations is shared by many (Lewis, 1999), but the turn-of-the-century 'partnership' commitments at the national and European levels have paid conspicuously more attention to this issue. The idea of partnership is far from new (Lewis, 1996),[4] but it has undergone significant changes in emphasis in recent years.

In the UK, a 1997 Labour Party document promised to 'establish a Compact with the Voluntary Sector', and undertook to replace a 'contract culture' with a 'partnership culture' and to guarantee the independence of the sector. Partnership with the voluntary sector was seen as 'central to Labour's policy of achieving social cohesion in a one-nation society' (Labour Party, 1997, p.1). The 1998 Compacts (for England, Wales and Scotland) between government and the sector gave an unequivocal undertaking to 'recognize and support the independence of the sector, including its right with the law to campaign, to comment on Government policy and to challenge that policy, irrespective of any funding relationship that might exist' (Home Office, 1998).

The undertaking to recognize that voluntary organizations have a role beyond that of contractors for services stands in marked contrast to government policy of the late 1980s and early 1990s. In addition to recognizing the independence of the voluntary sector, the national Compacts promised to pay attention to the need of the third sector for strategic funding, for adequate consultation and for better working relationships. Third sector organizations undertook to maintain high standards in funding and accountability, to inform and consult members, users and supporters, and to promote good practice (*http://www.thecompact.org.uk/*).

In the UK, hundreds of local partnership arrangements now exist for the provision of social services in relation to the New Deal for the unemployed, Education Action Zones, Health Action Zones, New Start, New Deal for Communities, New Commitment to Regeneration and Sure Start (programmes for under-fives). One third of England was covered by such compacts in 2001 and all local authorities in England will have local compacts by 2004. Evidence as to the effects on voluntary organizations has tended to be positive (Balloch and Taylor, 2001; Glendinning *et al.*,

2002), while evidence on the effects of partnership as an approach to solving social problems is more mixed (for example, Geddes and Bennington, 2001). The French Compact (Charte d'engagements réciproques entre l'Etat et les associations) was signed in 2001 and in the same year the EC issued a discussion paper on 'relations with NGOs', which emphasized their importance as 'components of civil society' (CEC, 2000a) and spoke of the need to establish 'civil dialogue' alongside the more familiar 'social dialogue' between unions, employers and government. This document recognized the role of third sector organizations in relation to the building of participatory democracies, representing the views of specific groups of citizens, contributing to policy making, project management and, with enlargement of the EU in prospect, European integration.

There remains a fundamental tension between the demands of the new public management and the contract culture for highly specified accountability, and the emphasis of the new partnerships on building trust. In their study of local compacts in England, Craig *et al.* (2002) have observed that the power relations between the partners remain unequal, which has led them to suggest four possible scenarios for the future of such compacts: (a) that voluntary organizations may indeed become, at the local level, equal partners, (b) that they may become 'incorporated' and effectively lose their independence, (c) that there may be a shift in power away from local government and towards the voluntary and community sector organizations, or (d) that the compacts may prove irrelevant in the complex task of negotiation between the partners in diverse local environments. The outcomes are hard to predict and many of the worrying features of the new partnerships are very similar to the problems that were identified in the 'contract culture' of the late 1980s and 1990s. But the new compacts give explicit recognition to the different nature and purpose of non-profit organizations and their importance to civil society, which is a large part of the reason why they have proved more popular with the sector.

Once agreed, compacts have the potential to provide principles against which consultation processes and funding arrangements can be checked, and act as a framework for review of the partnership between the statutory and voluntary sectors (Craig, 2001). Indeed, it is important to recognize the notion of partnership between the third sector and government as part of the 'new governance' identified by political scientists (for example, Rhodes, 1997; Geddes and Bennington, 2001). At the national level, the Compacts in the UK may offer little more than a redress in the balance between instrumentality and independence, but the effects may be more profound at the local level, not least because of the relative weakness of local government in the UK. There is more chance of genuine partnership working at the local level, which would result in a significant shift towards 'community governance'.

As Deakin (2001) has noted, the commitment to state/third sector partnerships is a far cry from the business philanthropy of the USA. The politics of welfare in EU member states draws on the legacy of a civic culture, on professionals who are locally based, and on an ethic of the public good (Paterson, 2000).

CONCLUSION

European states have not withdrawn from the field of social welfare, but rather they have adopted new patterns of regulation and service delivery. Third sector organizations are crucial to these – possibly 'Third Way' – strategies (Blair and Schröder, 1999). It remains to be seen whether this revamped partnership will result in the 'isomorphism' of the 1980s 'contract culture' (whereby voluntary organizations came increasingly to resemble the government bureaucracies they were replacing in respect of service delivery), or how far it will create something different, as much or more in respect of governance than as an effective way of tackling social problems. The third sector may be viewed above all in terms of potentially employment-creating organizations, especially in countries with above-average unemployment rates, which would fit with the European Commission's focus on social policy as a 'productive factor', or it may be viewed as a means of achieving further cost containment in service delivery via the mechanism of contract. Either would emphasize the economic role of the third sector as an alternative provider to the state and would fatally undermine the place of the sector in a genuinely pluralist welfare mix and as part of the underpinning of democratic societies. However, the new commitment to partnership, promoted by government and embraced by third sector organizations, explicitly recognizes the political and moral dimensions of non-profit organizations and promises to respect them. If it succeeds, it may be able to contribute to the building of a new civic culture.

NOTES

1. The mutuals were not included in the pioneering Johns Hopkins mapping project, which is a major impediment to understanding the differences between the nature of the relationship between the state and third sector associations in the European context.
2. Stephens *et al.* (1999) have argued that welfare state change was ideologically driven in the 1980s in only the UK and New Zealand.
3. For a critique of the active/passive dichotomy, see Sinfield (2001).
4. Its popularity has shown a dramatic increase in recent years, however. The term 'partnership' was used 38 times in the UK House of Commons in 1989, but 6000 times in 1998 (NCVO and CCS, 2001, p.19).

REFERENCES

Alber, J. and G. Standing (2000), 'Social dumping, catch-up, or convergence? Europe in a comparative global context', *Journal of European Social Policy*, 10 (2), 99–119.

Anheier, H. (2001), 'Dimensions of the third sector: comparative perspectives on structure and change', working paper, London School of Economics: Centre for Civil Society, London.

Atkinson, A.B. (1999), 'Is rising inequality inevitable? A critique of the transatlantic consensus', UN University World Institute for Development Economics Research Paper.

Baker, P. (1984), 'The domestication of politics: women in American political society, 1780–1920', *American Historical Review*, LXXXIX (June), 620–47.

Balloch, S. and M. Taylor (eds) (2001), *Partnership Working*, Bristol: Policy Press.

Bellah, R., R. Madsen, W. Sullivan, A. Swidler and S.M. Tipton (1985), *Habits of the Heart: Middle America Observed*, Berkeley: University of California Press.

Beveridge, W. (1948), *Voluntary Action. A Report on Methods of Social Advance*, London: Allen and Unwin.

Blair, T. and G. Schröder (1999), *Europe: The Third Way – die Neue Mitte*, London: Labour Party and SPD.

Brown, G. (2000), 'Civic society in modern Britain', Arnold Goodman Charity Lecture, 20 July.

Burchardt, T., J. Hills and C. Propper (1999), *Private Welfare and Public Policy*, York: Joseph Rowntree Foundation.

Cabinet Office Performance and Innovation Unit (2002), 'Social Capital: A Discussion Paper', April (http://www.cabinet-office.gov.uk/innovation/2001/futures/attachments/socialcapital.pdf).

Castles, F. (2001), 'The dog that didn't bark: economic development and the post-war welfare state', in S. Leibfried (ed.), *Welfare State Futures*, Cambridge: Cambridge University Press.

Coleman, J.S. (1988), 'Social capital in the creation of human capital', *American Journal of Sociology*, 94 (Suppl.), 95–120.

Commission of the European Communities (CEC) (1993), *Growth, Competitiveness and Employment – The Challenges and Ways Forward into the 21st Century*, Luxembourg: CEC.

Commission of the European Communities (CEC) (1995), *Equal Opportunities for Women and Men – Follow-up to the White Paper on Growth, Competitiveness and Employment*, Brussels: DGV.

Commission of the European Communities (CEC) (2000a), *Report on Social Protection in Europe 1999*, Com (2000) 163 final, Brussels: CEC.

Commission of the European Communities (CEC) (2000b), *Communication from the Commission to the Council, the European Parliament, the Economic and Social Committee and the Committee of the Regions: Social Policy Agenda*, Brussels: CEC.

Craig, G. (2001), *Evaluating the Significance of Local Compacts*, York: Joseph Rowntree Foundation.

Craig, G., M. Taylor, M. Wilkinson and K. Bloor, with S. Monro and A. Syed (2002), *Contract or Trust? The Role of Compacts in Local Governance*, Bristol: Policy Press.

Crouch, C. (1999), *Social Change in Western Europe*, Oxford: Oxford University Press.

Dahrendorf, R. (2001), 'Challenges to the voluntary sector', Arnold Goodman Charity Lecture, July.

Deakin, N. (2001), *In Search of Civil Society*, Basingstoke: Palgrave.

EC (2000), 'The Commission and non-governmental organisations: building a stronger partnership', Discussion Paper, EC, Brussels.

Esping Andersen, G. (1990), *The Three Worlds of Welfare Capitalism*, Cambridge: Polity Press.

Esping Andersen, G. (1999), *Social Foundations of Post-Industrial Economies*, Oxford: Oxford University Press.

Esping Andersen, G., D. Gallie, A. Hemerijck and J. Myles (2001), *A New Welfare Architecture for Europe? Report to the Belgian Presidency of the EU*, Brussels: CEC.

Evers, A. and I. Svetlik (eds) (1993), *Balancing Pluralism. New Welfare Mixes in Care for the Elderly*, Avebury: Aldershot.

Ferrera, M. and M. Rhodes (eds) (2000), *Recasting European Welfare States*, London: Frank Cass.

Fukuyama, F. (1999), *The Great Disruption: Human Nature and the Reconstitution of Social Order*, London: Profile Books.

Geddes, M. and J. Bennington (eds) (2001), *Local Partnerships and Social Exclusion in the EU*, London: Routledge.

Giddens, A. (1999), 'The role of the voluntary sector in the third way', Arnold Goodman Charity Lecture, 15 June.

Gilbert, N. (2002), *The Silent Surrender of Public Responsibility*, Oxford: Oxford University Press.

Glendinning, C., M. Powell and K. Rummery (eds) (2002), *Partnerships, New Labour and the Governance of Welfare*, Bristol: Policy Press.

Glennerster, H. and J. Hills (eds) (1998), *The State of Welfare*, Oxford: Oxford University Press.

Goodin, R.E. (2001), 'Work and welfare: towards a post-productivist welfare regime', *British Journal of Political Science*, 31, 13–39.

Hall, P.A. (1993), 'Policy paradigms, social learning and the state: the case of economic policy-making in Britain', *Comparative Politics*, 25 (3), 275–96.

Hall, P.A. (1999), 'Social capital in Britain', *British Journal of Political Science*, 29 (3), 417–61.

Hansmann, H. (1987), 'Economic theories of non profit organisations', in W.W. Powell (ed.), *The Non-Profit Sector. A Research Handbook*, New Haven: Yale University Press.

Harris, J. (1990), 'Society and the state in twentieth century Britain', in F.M.L. Thompson (ed.), *The Cambridge Social History of Britain 1750–1950*, vol. 3, Cambridge: Cambridge University Press.

Hills, J. (ed.) (1990), *The State of Welfare*, Oxford: Oxford University Press.

Hills, J. (1995), *Income and Wealth*, vols 1 and 2, York: Joseph Rowntree Foundation.

Home Office (1998), *Getting it Right Together: Compact on Relations between Government and the Voluntary and Community Sector in England*, Cmnd 4100, London: The Stationery Office.

Johnson, N. (1998), *Mixed Economies of Welfare: A Comparative Perspective*, London: Prentice-Hall Europe.

Kendall, J. and M. Knapp (2000), 'The third sector and welfare state modernisation: inputs, activities and comparative performance', working paper 14, London School of Economics, Centre for Civil Society.

Kotlikoff, L. (1992), *Generational Accounting. Knowing Who Pays, and When, for What We Spend*, New York: Free Press.

Koven, S. and S. Michel (eds) (1993), *Mothers of a New World. Maternalist Politics and the Origins of Welfare States*, London and New York: Routledge.

Kramer, R. (1981), *Voluntary Agencies in the Welfare State*, Berkeley: UCLA Press.

Kuhnle, S. and P. Selle (1992), 'Government and voluntary organisations – a relational perspective', in S. Kuhnle and P. Selle (eds), *Government and Voluntary Organisations*, Aldershot: Avebury.

Labour Party (1997), *Building the Future Together: Labour's Policies for Partnership between Government and the Voluntary Sector*, London: Labour Party.

Levi, M. (1998), 'A state of trust', in V. Braithwaite and M. Levi (eds), *Trust and Governance*, New York: Russell Sage Foundation.

Lewis, J. (1992), 'Gender and the development of welfare regimes', *Journal of European Social Policy*, 3, 159–73.

Lewis, J. (1995), *The Voluntary Sector, the State and Social Work in Britain*, Aldershot, UK and Brookfield, US: Edward Elgar.

Lewis, J. (1996), 'The boundary between voluntary and statutory social service in the late nineteenth and early twentieth centuries', *The Historical Journal*, 39 (1), 155–77.

Lewis, J. (1999), 'Reviewing the relationship between the voluntary sector and the state in Britain in the 1990s', *Voluntas*, 10 (3), 255–70.

Lindsay, A.D. (1945), 'Conclusion', in A.F.C. Bourdillon (ed.), *Voluntary Social Services. Their Place in the Modern State*, London: Methuen.

Myles, J. and J. Quadagno (2002), 'Political theories of the welfare state', *Social Service Review*, (March), 34–57.

NCVO and CCS (2001), *Research Quarterly*, no. 11, December.

OECD (2000), *Economic Studies*, no 31, 2000/2, Paris: OECD.

OECD (2001), *The Well-being of Nations: The Role of Social and Human Capital*, Paris: OECD.

Olavsky, M. (1992), *The Tragedy of American Compassion*, Washington, DC: Regnery Pubs.

Orloff, A. (1993), 'Gender and the social rights of citizenship. State policies and gender relations in comparative research', *American Sociological Review*, 58 (3), 303–28.

Paterson, L. (2000), 'Civil society and democratic renewal', in S. Baron, J. Field and T. Schuller (eds), *Social Capital: Critical Perspectives*, Oxford: Oxford University Press.

Pierson, P. (1994), *Dismantling the Welfare State? Reagan, Thatcher and the Politics of Retrenchment*, Cambridge: Cambridge University Press.

Pierson, P. (ed.) (2001), *The New Politics of the Welfare State*, Oxford: Oxford University Press.

Prime, D., M. Zimmeck and A. Zurawan (2002), *Active Communities: Initial Findings from the 2001 Home Office Citizenship Survey*, London: Home Office.

Putnam, R.D. (1993), *Making Democracy Work: Civic Traditions in Modern Italy*, Princeton: Princeton University Press.

Putnam, R.D. (2000), *Bowling Alone: The Collapse and Revival of American Community*, New York: Simon and Schuster.

Rhodes, R. (1997), *Understanding Governance*, Buckingham: Open University Press.

Rothstein, B. (1998), *Just Institutions Matter. The Moral and Political Logic of the Universal Welfare State*, Cambridge: Cambridge University Press.

Rothstein, B. (2002), 'Sweden: Social capital and the social democratic state', in R.D. Putnam (ed.), *Democracies in Flux: The Evolution of Social Capital in Contemporary Society*, Oxford: Oxford University Press.

Salamon, L. (1987), 'Partners in public service: The scope and theory of government–nonprofit relations', in W.W. Powell (ed.), *The Non-Profit Sector. A Research Handbook*, New Haven: Yale University Press.

Salamon, L. and H. Anheier (1998), 'The social origins of civil society: Explaining the nonprofit sector cross-nationally', *Voluntas*, 9, 213–48.

Sandel, M. (1996), *Democracy's Discontents: America in Search of a Public Philosophy*, Cambridge, Mass: Harvard University Press.

Scharpf, F.W. and V.A. Schmidt (eds) (2000), *Welfare and Work in the Open Economy*, vols I and II, Oxford: Oxford University Press.

Schmidt, V.A. (2000), 'Values and discourses in the politics of adjustment', in F.W. Scharpf and V.A. Schmidt (eds), *Welfare and Work in the Open Economy*, vol. I, *From Vulnerability to Competitiveness*, Oxford: Oxford University Press.

Sinfield, A. (2001), 'Managing social security for what?', in D. Pieters (ed.), *Confidence and Changes: Managing Social Protection in the New Millennium*, Amsterdam: Kluwer Academic.

Skocpol, T. (1992), *Protecting Soldiers and Mothers. The Political Origins of Social Policy in the United States*, Cambridge, Mass: Harvard University Press.

Skocpol, T. (1996), 'Unravelling from above', *American Prospect*, 25, 20–25.

Stephens, J.D., E. Huber and L. Ray (1999), 'The welfare state in hard times', in H. Kitschelt, P. Lange, G. Marks and J.D. Stephens (eds), *Continuity and Change in Contemporary Capitalism*, Cambridge: Cambridge University Press.

Stolle, D. and J. Lewis (2002), 'Social capital – an emerging concept', in B. Hobson, J. Lewis and B. Siim (eds), *Contested Concepts in Gender and Social Politics*, Cheltenham, UK and Northampton, MA, USA: Edward Elgar.

Stolle, D. and R. Rochon (1998), 'Are all associations alike? Member diversity, associational type and the creation of social capital', *American Behavioral Scientist*, 42 (1), 47–65.

Tarrow, S. (1996), 'Making social science work across space and time: A critical reflection on Robert Putnam's *Making Democracy Work*', *American Political Science Review*, 90, 389–97.

Thane, P. (1990), 'Government and society in England and Wales, 1750–1914', in F.M.L. Thompson (ed.), *The Cambridge Social History of Britain, 1750–1950*, vol. 3, Cambridge: Cambridge University Press.

Thomson, D. (1991), *Selfish Generations? How Welfare States Grow Old*, Wellington: Bridget Williams Books.

Timonen, V. (2001), 'In defence of the welfare state: Social policy restructuring in Finland and Sweden in the 1990s', unpublished D.Phil thesis, University of Oxford.

Titmuss, R. M. (1974), *Social Policy*, London: Allen and Unwin.

Torfing, J. (1999), 'Workfare with welfare: Recent reforms of the Danish welfare state', *Journal of European Social Policy*, 9 (1), 5–28.

Ware, A. (1989), *Between Profit and State. Intermediate Organisations in Britain and the US*, Cambridge: Polity Press.

Weisbrod, B.A. (1988), *The Nonprofit Economy*, Cambridge, Mass: Harvard University Press.

Wolfe, A. (1989), *Whose Keeper? Social Science and Moral Obligation*, Berkeley: University of California Press.

9. The European Union and its programmes related to the third system

Peter Lloyd

INTRODUCTION

One of the sparks that ignited interest in the policy community for the idea of the third system came in 1998 from a little known internal European Commission publication from what was then known as DG5. In this paper, entitled *The Third System and Employment – A Reflection* (perhaps the first time the label acquired some official as opposed to academic currency) the following statement appeared:

> The social economy *and* the activities oriented to meet the needs unsatisfied by the market can lead to the development of a new sense of entrepreneurship particularly valuable for economic and social development at local level. This sense of entrepreneurship is closer to the aspirations and values of people that do not seek profit making but rather the development of socially useful activities or jobs. These forms of entrepreneurship have a useful role in promoting social cohesion and economic local [*sic*] performance. (CEC 1998d, p.4, original emphasis)

It introduced the notion that there are alternative forms of enterprise with different aspirations and values that can contribute to economic and social development and that these are associated with something called the 'third system'. It was on the basis of these 'reflections' and some Italian-led discussions in the European Parliament that a whole series of debates began to take place inside and outside the European Commission about how to define the third system and about how useful it might be as a policy instrument. What follows is itself a 'reflection', based on the author's experience as a participant in some of the debates and EU programmes. The chapter sets out to look at the emergence of the concept of the third system in one specific context: through the evolving policy portfolio of the European Union. In doing this it is drawn to explore both the nature of the concept itself and the *realpolitik* of drawing the third system into the policy mainstream. The basic argument here is that the third system has been having its brief moment in the limelight of the European policy debate but that, thus far, there can be little confidence that this will see its general adoption in the mainstream of macro rather than micro policy.

The chapter proposes that the story of the third system in the EU so far is (a) a struggle for an agreed definition, (b) a tale of competing interests with different viewpoints seeking to mould the progression of policy development to align with their own agendas, and (c) a resolution that sees it chiefly as just one instrument among many in the toolkit of actions to generate local jobs. In the end the chapter argues that, while it is possible to see recognizable foot-prints of the third system in the current regulations for the 2000–2006 struc-tural funds programmes and in some specific pilot actions, there is no real basis as yet for it to be seen in more than the most narrowly defined of policy roles.

COMPETITIVENESS WITH COHESION: THE POLICY PLATFORM

To provide a context for the discussion that follows it is necessary briefly to characterize the European Union (EU) approach to economic development. This takes as its starting point the need to pursue competitiveness *with* cohe-sion as parallel, rather than sequential, objectives. It is a model designed to ensure global competitiveness and, in parallel, to offer a route to social inclu-sion (CEC, 1994a, 1994b). Success is measured both by indicators of economic progress and by the record of employment creation. In accordance with this, general anti-poverty and social exclusion policies in the EU have also become pivoted on employment promotion and labour market reintegra-tion.[1] Indeed, in 1997, the commission's *Agenda 2000* declared that the primary means of promoting economic and social integration would be through the structural funds strategies of generating employment and the insertion of the excluded into the labour market. For the third system, the EU idea that social and economic goals can be pursued simultaneously and that social aims can be pursued by business means offers a potentially fertile terrain for experiment and policy making.

The platform for third system approaches is also conditioned by the scale of intractable unemployment in the EU15 over the past decade and by the pres-sure that will arise from the accession of a further ten states with low GDP per capita and high unemployment by 2004. Any new approach that claims to offer both new sources of job creation and labour market insertion for excluded groups certainly needs to be actively considered. Specifically, during the period when the policies for the current (2000–2006) Structural Funds Programme were being put in place, the problem facing this job-driven model on which so much depends was the existence of 16 million unemployed people and an inability, even in high growth years, to match job entrants with employment. Given that competitive success under conditions of economic globalization demands greater productivity and for jobs in many sectors to rise more slowly than output, the challenge was clearly considerable. The arrival of the new accession states was always going to raise the stakes on the job creation/insertion model still further by adding directly to EU unemployment and by bringing in new regions to challenge the current allocation of structural funds assistance to existing regions. Small wonder the employment issue dominated the councils and summits of the late 1990s and was incorporated so firmly by the Amsterdam Treaty (CEC, 1998a).

In accordance with this, European Union responses to unemployment and social exclusion during the last policy cycle were designed to work on three main levels:

- the macro economy, with the single market and European Monetary Union (EMU) providing a platform to generate enhanced global competitiveness and the jobs that should follow as new start-ups and expanded businesses take up Europe's growing market share;
- the structural level, through the incorporation of supply-side measures for employability, adaptability, entrepreneurship and equal opportunity (the Employment Guidelines, CEC, 1998b) into National Action Plans to raise flexibility and overall workforce quality; and
- the territorial level, with a focus on regional development through the Structural Funds enhanced by new approaches aimed at capitalizing upon entirely new sources of jobs through the Local Development and Employment Initiative (CEC, 1995, 1996, 1998c) and the Territorial Employment Pacts (CEC, 2000a).

More recently, as EMU has moved to its apogee with the creation of the Eurozone Twelve there has been a growing concern also to guard against those spatial and social inequalities that the more open marketplace is expected to exacerbate. In this respect, the search has been very much one for any new policy devices capable of performing the miracle of creating new sources of jobs with minimal public expenditure that will absorb the unemployed and, without running into problems of either displacement or unfair competition, help private enterprise to focus on its drive for global competitiveness. While the orthodox solution is seen to depend heavily on the expansion of small and medium enterprises across the board, a further recent manifestation of this search for the 'holy grail' has been an expanded interest in the third sector. In particular, the potential of that range of activities variously labelled 'not for profits', social economy organizations or third sector organizations (TSOs) has been attracting special attention. All this is set within a general movement at EU level and within many member states to generate new forms of partnership to open the doors to new, more economic, pluralism, particularly at the local level.

THE THIRD SYSTEM: LABELS AND DEFINITIONS

The Third System as a Generic Label

One of the most fascinating but, at the same time, disabling features of attempts to draw the third system and the social economy into the policy mainstream has been the struggle to agree on a definition and a succinct and acceptable label for the overall portfolio of activities under its umbrella. The individual components that make up the third system or social economy approach – social and community enterprise, cooperatives, community development financial instruments (CDFIs), integration enterprises (entreprises d'insertion), intermediate labour market organizations (ILMs), credit unions and so on – are well understood and appear as part of the national policy portfolios of many member states. But there is as yet no acceptance of any one generic and inclusive label to encompass all these activities and others like them and bring them under one banner. Much of the following in this chapter describes the rise and perhaps the fall (for the moment at least) of one contending generic label – the third system – as an inclusive emblem (if not a formally defined categorization) for activities that fall neither into the private for-profit nor into the state sector, but that represent the elements of some third component of the contemporary economy. The merit of the third system as a label is a capability to be both flexible and inclusive in a way that does not demand the acceptance of some bounded definition that would be too restrictive. The disadvantage of the third system as a banner is, of course, that it might well be seen as *too* inclusive and *too* flexible.

Interlocking Definitions: Third System, Social Enterprise, Social Economy

As previous contributors to this volume have shown, the third system (CEC, 1998d) can be seen as sitting between the private for-profit (distribution) and the public or state sector of the economy. Being formally part of neither, it has its own internal integrity through a clear focus on combining economic aims with social objectives. The third system can, however, derive much of its power in delivering its mission not only from within itself but also from a process of close engagement with the other two sectors. It is this openness, where organizations that have a primarily social purpose can extract benefit from engagement with the private as well as the public sector, that gives the third system as an idea its distinctiveness and power (as opposed, say, to the social economy). Through complex arrangements of partnership, stakeholding and joint venturing as well as by trading business methods and alternative value systems both ways between firms and social organizations there is an openness to the possibilities of hybridization.[2] Sadly, however, like all hybrids, the third system has a degree of equivocal parentage that makes it hard to find strong voices ready to speak up for it and that makes it an easy focus of criticism from those with more strongly held opinions to the left and right of it and who demand to know what *exactly* it is.[3]

As we indicated earlier, it is much easier to defend the idea of the third system from an exploration of the key elements that constitute it. The 'base molecules' of the third system are its *social enterprises* (and there is a growing chorus of voices willing to speak up for them). They can be visualized as combining with other kinds of 'molecules' (private firms, public agencies, local partnerships, charitable bodies and so on) to create a wide variety of hybrid forms and new sorts of phenomena that add a sense of wider social values to the search for jobs and opportunities to address market failure. It is this that provides the essence of the third system approach.

Social enterprises are defined in their widest sense by Laville and Nyssens (2001) as 'enterprises initiated by groups of citizens who seek to provide an expanded range of services and more openness to the community – they place a high value on independence and economic risk taking'. Evers (2001) helps to identify the sort of wider contribution they can make through his idea of *civic capital*. This is a resource contributing to 'trust and democratization' that social enterprises can both create in their communities and reveal as properties within themselves. Through this, it can be argued, the third system, with its constantly evolving social enterprise forms, has the potential to empower and integrate people, and use trust to reduce transaction costs, and to create the conditions to mobilize goodwill and free volunteer labour. Essentially the special property of the social enterprise is its ability to mobilize social capital 'through reciprocal relationships that integrate a dimension of service to the community' (Laville and Nyssens, 2001). If at the same time some social enterprises can supply quality local services in the face of market failure and create new sources of jobs, then perhaps the level of current interest is not entirely misplaced.

Once again, it is the openness and fluidity that pervades the notion of the third system through what Laville and Nyssens (2001) call the 'new dynamic of social enterprise' that justifies seeing it as distinct. The third *system* then can be considered as a process in motion or a movement. At its core it maps a different sort of emergent economy, the *social economy*, whose players, notions of value and ultimate objectives are different from the orthodox. At its margins it interfaces with the private and state sectors. By contrast, the third *sector* is a structural/political entity where the issues are about boundaries, what constitutes the legitimate membership and questions of positioning in relation to existing power structures. The key players at the core of the third sector undoubtedly lay claim to most of the special values that characterize the third system, but, taking on board the idea of the third *system* in addition to the third *sector* brings more. It allows a concentration on dynamics, openness, hybridization and constant change as opposed to closure and the determination of the boundaries of the system by reference to questions like 'who is in and who is out?', 'is being not-for-profit enough?' or 'does there need to be a genuine ethos of solidarity?' These are undoubtedly vital and interesting questions and the way the third system has evolved in practice owes much to the way the answers have been revealed to produce different shapes in opportunity structures from country to country. What this chapter goes on to explore is how, in the face of the actual emergence of the third system as a 'process in motion', the European Union has tried to understand and utilize it in policy frameworks.

The Third System as a Contested Terrain

Being clear about definitions (even if, as has been discussed above, it were possible to be prescriptive) gives no real hint of the contested terrain on which the third system actually sits. This is, however, vital to any understanding of how European policy with respect to it has emerged. At the most basic level discussions about the third system have a propensity easily to bring into play deeper debates about those social and political movements (mutualism and cooperative action versus shareholder equity and private profit) that lie deep in its ideological roots. The fact that views on these issues evoke sharp differences from left to right across the political spectrum, and that historical experience offers different lessons from state to state, provides a crucial backdrop to the way the third system has been regarded in European debates. Is it, for example, the focus for a radical critique of neoliberal political economy or is it just another manifestation of 'institutional searching' that offers no challenge to the existing order? In Italy, Spain and France, for example, there is a tendency for the third system to be more readily identified with solidarity-oriented and left-leaning approaches, while in the UK, by contrast, there is tendency for it (though the label is unrecognized) to be pulled increasingly toward the US 'not-for-profits' model.

Discussions about the third system also run into those more prosaic but no less sensitive issues lightly touched on above about how it relates to (or is distinguishable from) the established third sector. One way of looking at the third sector within the EU context is, for example, to see it as bounded *political* space occupied by that set of organizations and institutions which lay claim to legitimate membership and that see themselves as the essential core. From this viewpoint the third sector sees itself as *the* sector with an established position in representing the views of its members to the European institutions. (For a discussion of the contested issue of the so-called 'platform' of third sector organizations in relation to the EU, see Geyer, 2001.) By contrast, the third *system* is not a membership body but a more open, dynamic and non-exclusive system that values its porosity and promotes flexibility in alliances both within and outside the third sector. This sort of 'promiscuity' in dealing with the private sector can, however, be seen in some quarters as challenging or at least weakening the hard-won struggle of the established third sector to establish a position in the corridors of power. The easy juxtaposition of 'third sector and third system' that pervades the policy literature may, therefore, be less comfortably reflected in the world of European *realpolitik*.

From a positive viewpoint, however, the intrinsic value of the third system as an idea comes from precisely the possibility that it can straddle both the realm of economy/employment and the wider sphere of governance, civil society and social justice: that it can carry both *instrumental significance* as a creator of jobs and producer of services and *ideological weight* as a non-exploitative and socially conscious means of fostering cohesion and good governance. This source of strength can also be a serious source of weakness since the third system can often be forced to defend itself on two fronts. Even if it can be shown to work at the instrumental level and can indeed create new sources of jobs for the excluded, there may still be suspicions from established interests about how far it has more radical aspirations to advocate an alternative model of a more general kind. There are strong echoes of this in the debate taking place between a US 'not-for-profits' model that offers no challenge to neoliberal orthodoxy and a European model that has a more strongly defined solidarity-oriented political position (Salamon and Anheier, 1996). From the more open perspective of the third system, however, it becomes less problematic (at least instrumentally if not ideologically) to incorporate the US 'not-for-profits' model. A wide third system perspective would see this as a classic hybrid ('market-led, value-driven') distinguishable primarily by its being embedded within and not in any way seeking to challenge the American neoliberal model. More ideologically founded positions would, however, make a clear distinction between the US not-for-profits and European social economy models.

There is scope here, at the very least, for lively debate. This is particularly intense where the private for-profit sector suspects that state subsidies may be used in some countries to promote forms of social enterprise through what they see as unfair competition. Even the social partners/trades unions can find some aspects of the third system proposition about which they have strong reservations. Trade unions become particularly concerned when they perceive a threat that relatively secure public sector employment for their members will be allocated to 'integration enterprises' from the third system where there are concerns that job quality and working conditions may be undermined.

Defining and positioning the third system is then not simply a technical or taxonomic question. It has a clear *political* dimension on many levels. While the third sector offers the possibility of being 'bracketed' as just another sector, alongside but functionally distinct from the public and private sectors, the third system is, by definition, a much more slippery concept. It is, potentially, the manifestation of another kind of economy, the social economy, that has a different value system, organizations and firms with different motivations, where the relationship with workers and customers is based upon principles of trust and where there is an open attempt to draw private firms onto its terrain and to share its values.

The Problem of Complexity

Notwithstanding politics and ideology, for those who seek to make a strong and clearly defined case for the third system in European policy, even as no more than an instrument for local development and employment, the problem is one of complexity. It is simply hard to get handles on the third system and to specify what it is, who inhabits it, and what is its value added contribution. Looking through the lens of the organizations that inhabit it, the observer is presented with a picture of Byzantine variety. Definition by legal form does little to simplify things. Third system organizations may be charities, foundations, trusts, mutuals, not-for-profit companies and (though this is an object of dispute in some quarters – Defourny and Monzon Campos, 1992; CIRIEC, 1999) member and producer cooperatives. To add further complexity, the particular form these organizations can legally adopt is highly variable from country to country (see Granger, 1999). On top of this, the third system is also colonized both by established members of the third sector and increasingly by newcomers seeking to gain a foothold. At the micro level even local unincorporated associations and grant-aided projects can also be legitimate members (though once again opinions differ).

All this has made even more functionalist attempts to define the third system by the legal form of its members an intense arena for academic debate. Clarity of definition continues to be an aspiration difficult to fulfil and leaves the promoters of the case for the third system as an instrument of policy within the EU struggling to make headway. Nevertheless, as we go on to show, the elements of the third system (whether recognized as such or not) are continuing to appear as observable footprints in European policies as they emerge.

THE COLONIZATION OF FERTILE POLICY GROUND

'Bottom-up' and Local Approaches

The organizations of the third system seem to find themselves straying onto a surprisingly large area of fertile ground within the present policy paradigm. They appear, for example, to have a special ability to satisfy growing local demands for 'bottom-up' approaches and to foster integrated local partnership approaches to social and occupational integration (Lloyd and Ramsden, 2000; Evers, 2003). The third system can be seen as a vehicle for multi-stakeholder collaboration engaging the state and the private sector with social partners and community organizations in a concerted attempt to solve locally problems that either the state alone or market forces have failed adequately to address. It can aspire to deliver more integrated approaches to socioeconomic and urban/rural development by bringing together coalitions of partners and can be a representative form for local social capital by promoting volunteering and self-help and offering a vehicle for the building of relations of trust between people (Lloyd *et al.*, 1996). The organizations of the third system look to have the sorts of attributes that the current policy paradigm is looking for to deliver a genuinely 'bottom-up' approach.

Platforms for Insertion Jobs

A second fertile policy ground for the growth of the third system and its organizations has come from an ability to respond to the rise of intractable unemployment across the EU. Given the inability of the formal economy to provide jobs in sufficiently large numbers to absorb particular groups, and the pressures on state finances, the search has been on for some time for a third way. This has opened the door to the introduction of third system organizations dedicated to the creation of 'insertion jobs': forms of employment dedicated to overcoming the barriers that keep people out of the labour market. While many of these are at the local level they also operate nationally, regionally and in some cases by industrial or occupational sector. At the large scale they have become associated with national 'second labour market' programmes where unemployed and socially excluded groups have been drawn into time-bound programmes of training, occupational integration and work placement. Many of the older established players in the third sector have taken a key role here by virtue of their capacity to deliver these sorts of schemes in a way that fits with governments expectations. To do this, many of them have had to become more flexible and businesslike in their ambitions and have adopted the attributes of social enterprises in a third system.

A Device to 'Prospect for New Jobs'

A third feature of the third system portfolio that can be seen to have acquired some competitive weight in providing policy solutions has come from attempts to address three long-standing problems: (a) a rising demand for social, personal and community services, (b) a need to find ways to meet these demands while constraining levels of direct state expenditure and rates of taxation, and (c) the persistence of spatially localized pockets of deprivation where these service gaps are extreme regardless of the economic cycle (Borzaga, 1999).

In this context the European Commission's *Local Development and Employment Initiative* (LDEI) was particularly important as an original fountainhead of new ideas about the use of local enterprises to create sustainable employment (CEC, 1995, 1996). Specifically, what LDEI introduced was the idea that local action could be taken to search out new job slots to fill unmet service needs in the caring, environment and leisure and cultural sectors. One of its key features was to encourage local authorities and others to open a new policy front: the exploration of the *demand side* in the local context. The policy lever was to establish what additional governance mechanisms were needed to convert 'latent' demands for services into 'real' local job opportunities and to install instruments to render them 'solvent'.

From the perspective of those who support them, the organizations of the third system have a special ability to sit in the gap between a public service under pressure and a private for-profit sector that supplies services only where their activities can offer a reasonable return on investment. Birkholzer (1996) sees this gap as being created by the emergence of what he calls a 'shadow economy'. In this, the socially marginalized are economically and fiscally disconnected from the mainstream. Along with a drive by local people themselves to find their own solutions, governments, traditional third sector bodies and TSOs can come in to occupy the space. The suggestion is that these 'shadow spaces' can be filled by the creation of a new form of community-based social enterprise economy.

Empirically, then, there is evidence that the third system (or at least the phenomenon that it purports to describe) is a rapidly expanding feature of the European economic and social landscape. Its expansion has come in response to fast-changing conditions. It looks, from one viewpoint, as if the current standing of the third system is less the product of a fully worked out philosophy about how economy and society can confront new conditions than an empirically observable set of practical responses to real events (to unemployment, social exclusion and deficits in welfare and collective services provision) particularly, but by no means exclusively, at the local level.

We now turn to explore the practice of the European institutions in dealing with the third system. In many ways this is an example of what the EU is best at, running an experimental process that breaks the boundaries and allowing alternative groups to obtain access to policy-making agendas. The political realities, however, are never switched off and it is what follows the experiment that gives some hint of how that contested terrain that we described earlier responds to real differences in power. We begin by tracing the 'footprints' of the third system concept within the regulations and guidance for the structural and territorial policies of the EU.

THE THIRD SYSTEM AND EU STRUCTURAL AND TERRITORIAL POLICIES

The Employment Guidelines and the Social Economy

In December 1997 the Council of the EU adopted a series of employment guidelines following discussions at the Amsterdam Summit and the Luxembourg Jobs Summit (CEC, 1998b). This formed part of the new title on Employment within the Amsterdam Treaty. Among the numerous measures to bolster employability, flexibility, adaptability and entrepreneurship, the guidelines recognized the potential for job creation in the social economy under the entrepreneurship pillar (Guideline 12), suggesting that member states will

> investigate measures to exploit fully the possibilities offered by job creation at local level in the social economy and in new activities linked to needs not satisfied by the market, and examine, with the aim of reducing, any obstacles in the way of such measures. (CEC, 1998d, p.11)

Guideline 12 became, in effect, the 'passport' for the third system in European regulations, the regulation that can be waved at the sceptics within national administrations to ensure its passage. As many of those consulted by the Commission (specifically about *Acting Locally for Employment*, CEC, 2000c) were quick to point out at the time, however, it offers only the narrowest of interpretations of the wide terrain of the third system that we have just mapped. Guideline 12 connects job creation with the local level and with market failure. It is carefully constrained to the uncontroversial. As we have already seen, it also has powerful antecedents. The Commission's Local Development and Employment Initiative (LDEI) had already made a strong case for the ability of new forms of local organization to 'prospect for' and 'actualize' new jobs sources, filling gaps chiefly in the areas of personal and social services, new technologies and the environment. It is both economistic and instrumental and strays into few of the contested areas.

Gaining a Foothold in the Structural Funds Programmes, 2000–2006

Despite the difficulty people were having in defining what it actually meant, the term 'third system' had already begun to acquire a limited currency in the regulations and opinions of EU bodies during the framing of the 2000–2006 programmes (Chanan, 1998; EAPN, 1998). For example, it was referred to in the Regulation on the European Social Fund (Article 3.1d) where the 'third system' label was specifically applied. Once again, 'third system' is used sometimes alongside and sometimes in exchange for 'social economy'. The complexities that we explored earlier explain sufficiently why there is a tendency to mix the labels. Nevertheless, by sticking firmly to the well-established position that insertion into the job market is the best way to address unemployment and social exclusion and that they have a special competence for local actions, the organizations of the third system were able find a gateway into EU policy.

Acting Locally for Employment and the Third System and Employment Pilot Action (TSEP)

The European Commission's *Acting Locally for Employment* programme was specifically designed to provide a local dimension to the European Employment Strategy (CEC, 2000c). What it represented was a determined move to tap what was seen to be the 'considerable potential' for action at the local level to unlock new sources of job creation. The way to achieve this was to bring together local actors and to encourage them to pool their energies and resources while the regional and national authorities adapted their policies to support them. These actors were understood to be local authorities, enterprises, local offices of the public employment services, the social partners and, again significant for the discussion here, 'the Third System/the social economy'. Yet again the European Commission resorts to the use of the term 'Third System' in its documentation while being, once again, careful to hedge it with a combined reference to the social economy.

The narrowness of this perception of the third system is challenged by many of those Commission consultees already referred to (CEC, 2000b; see also Lloyd, 1999). For them, the opportunity is lost to see third system organizations as being able to support *all four* pillars of the Employment Strategy both locally and in more general terms. They can contribute to employability and adaptability. They are a source for new forms of entrepreneurship. In the realm of equal opportunities – not just between women and men but also across the board – they would claim that by their very nature and purpose they have a particularly important role. Once more, the third system finds itself confined to the narrow channel of providing new jobs in local areas by tackling market failures. This limited vision has served to distort, deflect and even suppress the ability of the third system to claim a more appropriate place in the emerging framework of European policy.

Under the banner of *Acting Locally*, however, a very specific opportunity presented itself for the third system to display the breadth of its potential contribution. This was the *Third System and Employment Pilot Action* under Article 6 of the European Social Fund. Once again, the brief was narrowly constrained to employment (but this time with a specific focus on social and neighbourhood services, the environment and the arts). Under the pilot some 81 projects were supported and, this time, something of the true variety of the wider third system was allowed to emerge.[4] Indeed, one project carried out by CIRIEC at the University of Liège was specifically charged with 'producing an inventory of the Third System in the EU as a whole'. CRIDA in Paris was given the money to examine the 'socio-economic functioning of the third system'. Similarly Fondazione Cesar in Bologna was financed 'to organize a series of seminars analysing the role of the Third Sector in the market economies of four different Member States of the European Union'. In parallel, a *capitalization group* of academics was appointed to assist in thinking through some of the broader issues while the projects were under way and encouraged to produce a series of synoptic reports (available from the Europa website). It was inevitable that, under this stimulus, debates about the role of the third system tended to spread way beyond the limiting brief imposed by its positioning under the banner of *Acting Locally for Employment*. This presented a difficulty because it served to expose the tension between the narrow interpretation of the role of the third system in European policy that we have been tracing throughout this chapter and the complexities that inevitably emerge once the windows are thrown open to wider definitions.

Part of this difficulty arises from the need in a funded programme to set clearly definable outputs to account for the expenditure. As we have shown, it has been the spectre of unemployment that gave the third system its *laissez-passer* into debates about European policy. It is then the ability to generate employment that forms the primary measuring rod for benchmarking and transmitting information about performance. This is not, of course, inappropriate.

However, the programme is tightly constrained in this way to see the third system chiefly through its contribution to local job creation and to some degree, the final judgment of the policy merit rests heavily on the *number of quality jobs* generated by the projects; there is a tendency to regard it as having in some way 'failed'.

What is lost, of course, is the ability of the third system to deliver that most intangible of outcomes, *social capital and relations of trust between people and communities*. What the third system needs also to be valued for is its ability to tackle Birkholzer's 'shadow economy' in a way that can deliver jobs, quality services and a degree of local solidarity to the fabric of society as a whole. A wider frame of reference that attempted to capture the overall social and civic capital contribution as well as employment contribution of the projects would have served to present the *Third System and Employment Pilot Action* in a much more favourable light.[5] Europe-wide policy for the adoption of third system approaches is, then, highly constrained both in terms of the way the third system and its organizations are defined and in the ways in which this follows through into indications of relative success or failure.

The Committee of the Regions (COR) seems, however, to have grasped this essential point in its latest Opinion (CEC, 2001) with statements like the following: 'social economy enterprises are an essential part of the plural European economic and social model'; and 'social economy organizations help local authorities to transform passive social security and employment benefits into active investment for sustainable development'. Here the social economy (and one assumes the third system) is not simply seen as a locus of action for improving employment as in Guideline 12 but as a set of particular organizational entities capable of acting as direct instruments for the delivery of both economic and social objectives.

CONCLUSIONS

The third system has, then, been granted an opportunity to have its brief moment in the limelight of the European policy debate. There is, however, no particular reason to believe that this will see it formally established as a major component of employment and social inclusion policy. Part of the difficulty with the third system for the policy makers clearly lies in the difficulty of defining it in a consistent way that can have similar meaning across the EU15. Part lies in giving it operational form and proving that it can deliver real outcomes. Perhaps the greatest difficulty lies in attempting to insert such a macro concept into existing structures of power and influence, many of which see it as at best an irrelevance and at worst a threat. Perhaps even considering the third system as a candidate for the mainstream might be regarded as naïve. As Evers (1995) points out, the third system forms 'part of the public sphere of modern democratic societies within civil society as a whole' and exercises its influence as a focus for independent forums of discussion and debate. Once coopted to the mainstream its intrinsic value may be reduced. In essence, as an Italian TSEP workshop participant vociferously pointed out, the third system is the terrain for the 'wild horses' of civil society. To 'corral' its players by seeing them as no more than 'job prospectors' and an alternative to the public service is to deny their power as a democratic force as well as an instrument for service delivery. Nevertheless, aspects of the third system can legitimately claim to make a social welfare contribution by the quality of their service provision and can expect a degree of public support at least for this part of their role.

Despite what has just been said, some elements important to the third system are already in place in European policy. The first is the *social economy*. This is already recognized within the Structural Funds Regulations and in the Employment Guidelines. The second is more indirect. This is the weight being given to 'acting locally' for employment and its strong emphasis on *local part-nership*. Together they offer a policy platform which, regardless of whether the term 'third system' is used or not, will enable those who wish to promote actions with a combination of economic and social aims to press their case. In this respect, the existence of the third system and its players has already exerted an effect on mainstream policy development through the impact of local initiatives on the mind-set of public authorities.

The critical task, then, is not so much to adopt the third system as a formal plank of European policy but to engage in a well-thought-out process of (at the very least) benign regulation to allow it to evolve. The best way forward for policy would be to provide a degree of strategic intervention to support its autonomous evolution, through structural funds or otherwise. The objective is to preserve and recover lessons from the best aspects of third system-type activities and to change or remove the worst. The danger is, however, that reaction to the third system as a 'grand idea' draws such a weight of opposi-tion that a sense of balance in the argument is lost. This could be at the expense of more basic intervention strategies aimed at raising the overall scale, sustain-ability and quality of some of the organizations that already exist.

The adoption of the third system as a 'grand' objective of European policy is, then, unlikely to succeed. More seriously, the danger of losing this battle is the collateral damage that will see the merits of this valuable complementary approach to economic and social policy blighted and its development set back. Disabling questions of definition and narrowly defined purpose have, for example, cast a long shadow over the reporting of the results of the *Third System and Employment Pilot Action*. This serves to obscure its real value as a showcase for the creativity and dynamism of people and projects where economic and social solidarity objectives are pursued in parallel.

De facto, however, what might be labelled 'third system activities' have been growing in number in many European member states in recent decades. Some have emerged spontaneously from national and local politi-cal movements under the incentive structures available within each country. Others have emerged as a direct by-product of the activities of the European Commission in sponsoring local actions to combat unemployment and social exclusion. The merit of the current European debate about the third system is that it provides the opportunity to move forward from the concept of piloting ideas and initiating start-ups to examining the requirements for sustainability among those projects that have been seeded already. The debate thus becomes inevitably widened from one solely about project 'best practice' to an examination of the contribution of the third system as a whole. The key policy questions then become what might be needed to sustain the momentum of its growth and simultaneously to preserve its quality. It is this much-needed widening of the debate which is proving most difficult to handle within the constraints of discussions about the application of the structural funds.

NOTES

1. Following the rejection of the Fourth Poverty Programme in 1994.
2. This can be seen as one distinctive element of what Peck and Tickell (1995) have described as a process of 'institutional searching'.
3. In this way it suffers a similar fate to Anthony Giddens' (1998) idea of the 'Third Way'.
4. Some indication of the sheer range of the projects and their multifaceted contribution can be gained from the final programme evaluation document produced by Ecotec (2002) and available on the Europa website.
5. Another pilot action running in parallel with TSEP was 'Local Social Capital'. Once again, there is a bounded definition: 'Local Social capital means an intermediary organization – operating at regional or local level – capable of providing back-up for people who pool their resources with a view to carrying out micro-level projects which promote employment and social cohesion.' No doubt the same constituency of third system organizations were bidders but the two pilots were not seen as both being about the third system.

REFERENCES

Birkholzer, K. (1996), 'Social economy, community economy and third sector: Fashionable slogans or building blocks for the future?', in Bauhaus Dessau Foundation (ed.), *Peoples Economy*, Dessau: Bauhaus Dessau Foundation, pp.41–4.

Borzaga, C. (1999), *The Role of the Third System – Neighbourhood Services*, report of the Capitalisation Group – Third System and Employment Pilot Action, Brussels: European Commission DG Employment and Social Affairs Website.

CEC (1994a), *Growth, Competitiveness, Employment: The Challenges and Ways Forward into the 21st Century*, Luxembourg: Office for Official Publications of the European Communities.

CEC (1994b), *European Social Policy: A Way Forward for the Union*, Luxembourg: Office for Official Publications of the European Communities.

CEC (1995), *Local Development and Employment Initiatives: An Investigation in the European Union*, Internal Document, Luxembourg: Office for Official Publications of the European Communities.

CEC (1996), *First Report on Local Development and Employment Initiatives*, SEC (96) 2061, Luxembourg: Office for Official Publications of the European Communities.

CEC (1998a), *Joint Employment Report*, SEC (98) 1688, Luxembourg: Office for Official Publications of the European Communities.

CEC (1998b), *The 1998 Employment Guidelines: Council Resolution of 15 December 1997*, Luxembourg: Office for Official Publications of the European Communities.

CEC (1998c), *The Era of Taylor-made Jobs: Second Report on Local Development*, SEC (98) 25, Luxembourg: Office for Official Publications of the European Communities.

CEC (1998d), *The Third System and Employment – A Reflection*, DGV (A4), Brussels: Commission of the European Communities.

CEC (2000a), *Guide to Territorial Employment Pacts, 2000–2006*, SEC (99) 1933, Luxembourg: Office for Official Publications of the European Communities.

CEC (2000b), *Opinion of the Economic and Social Committee on the Social Economy and the Single Market*, CES, 242/2000, Luxembourg: Office for Official Publications of the European Communities.

CEC (2000c), *Acting Locally for Employment: Commission Consultation*, COM 2000/196.

CEC (2001), *Opinion Committee of the Regions*, CdR, 384/2001.

Chanan, G. (1998), *The New Structural Funds. What Development Model for Europe?*, London: Community Development Foundation.

CIRIEC (1999), *The Enterprises and Organizations of the Third System: A Strategic Challenge for Employment*, final report to the European Commission on the Third System and Employment Pilot Action, Brussels: CIRIEC.

Defourny, J. and J.L. Monzon Campos (eds) (1992), *Economie Sociale: Entre Economie Capitaliste et Economie Publique*, Brussels: CIRIEC.

EAPN (1998), 'Reinforcing the Impact of the Structural Funds on Social Inclusion and Equal Opportunities', mimeo, September, EAPN, Brussels.

Ecotec (2002) (*http://europa.eu.int/comm/employment_social/news/2002/feb/fiches_ projets_en.pdf*).

Evers, A. (1995), 'Part of the welfare mix: The third sector as an intermediate area', *Voluntas*, 6 (2).

Evers, A. (2001), 'The significance of social capital in the multiple goal resource structure of social enterprises', in C. Borzaga and J. Defourny (eds), *The Emergence of Social Enterprise*, London: Routledge, pp.296–311.

Evers, A. (2003), 'Local labour market policies and social integration in Europe: Potential and pitfalls of integrated partnership approaches', in J. Zeitlin and D. Trubek (eds), *Governing Work and Welfare in a New Economy: European and American Experiments*, Oxford: Oxford University Press.

Geyer, R. (2001), 'Can EU social NGOs promote EU social policy?', *Journal of Social Policy*, 30 (3).

Giddens, A. (1998), *The Third Way: The Renewal of Social Democracy*, Cambridge: Polity Press.

Granger, B. (1999), *The Role of the Third System – Legal and Financial Structures*, report of the Capitalisation Group – Third System and Employment Pilot Action, Brussels: European Commission DG Employment and Social Affairs Website.

Laville, J.-L. and M. Nyssens (2001), 'The social enterprise: Towards a theoretical socio-economic approach', in C. Borzaga and J. Defourny (eds), *The Emergence of Social Enterprise*, London: Routledge, pp.312–32.

Lloyd, P.E. (1999), *The Role of the Third System – Intermediary Support Structures*, report of the Capitalisation Group – Third System and Employment Pilot Action. Brussels: European Commission DG Employment and Social Affairs Website.

Lloyd, P.E. and P. Ramsden (2000), *Local Enterprising Localities: Area Based Employment Initiatives in the United Kingdom*, Luxembourg: Office for Official Publications of the European Communities.

Lloyd, P.E. *et al.* (1996), *Social and Economic Inclusion Through Regional Development*, report for European Commission DG XVI, Luxembourg: Office for Official Publications of the European Communities.

Peck, J.A. and A. Tickell (1995), 'Social regulation after Fordism: regulation theory, neo-liberalism and the global–local nexus', *Economy and Society*, 24 (3), 357–86.

Salamon, L.M. and H.K. Anheier (1996), *The Emerging Non-Profit Sector: An Overview*, Manchester: Manchester University Press.

10. The European Union and the third sector

Jacques Delors

The purpose of this chapter is to confront the main hypotheses put forward in the book's first chapter with my personal intellectual and institutional background. In the 1970s, after a close study of certain social developments in France, I put forward a number of theoretical and regulatory proposals for a legal and financial framework that could promote the development of the third sector in Europe. At a later stage, the sector often benefited from my work, as President of the European Commission between 1985 and 1995, to strengthen economic and social cohesion between regions. Nevertheless, developments at the European level have sometimes been unexpected. Without attempting to draw any lessons, I believe it would be useful to review some of the major milestones of the last two decades.

THE THIRD SECTOR: A 'PRE-CRISIS' APPROACH

I believe the term 'third sector' first appeared in France in grey papers in 1978. I had carried out a study for the European Commission, called '*La création d'emplois dans le secteur tertiaire: le troisième secteur en France*' ('Job creation in the tertiary sector: the third sector in France'), in which I analysed a large number of experiments of a cooperative and voluntary nature. One year later, in an article, 'Pour la création d'un troisième secteur' ('For the creation of a third sector'), co-written with Jocelyne Gaudin, we built on the report to call for the establishment of a legal and financial framework that could promote the development of such initiatives.

But the invention of the 'third sector' concept should be seen in its historical context. In France, the issue and the debate derived from the events of May 1968, and in particular from the slogan 'travailler autrement' ('work differently'), the revival of the concept of worker self-management and the Lip affair. Lip was a watchmaker that went bankrupt; its employees tried to save it by setting up a self-managed cooperative. Independently of these well-known references, the 1970s had seen the emergence of a number of initiatives by young men and women who wanted to start up new activities and were look-ing for other legal frameworks than those available at the time (such as coop-eratives, associations and of course the private-sector profit-making companies). 'Autonomy' was their watchword. Their demand was not a 'right to laziness', but to work in organizations that would provide them with a degree of independence, not only in organizing but also in creating their activ-ities. They were essentially driven by the will to create a small undertaking, even if that was very difficult. They would often say: 'I'm doing what I want to do. There is a demand for it and I am organizing my own work' or 'I am organizing my work within a group with some friends.' To them, this concept of autonomy was really important. Today, however, it no longer seems to be a keyword of the social economy.

I had studied these experiences as a teacher at the Paris-Dauphine univer-sity and as the director of the research centre, 'Travail et société' ('Work and Society'), that I had set up. The idea gradually dawned on me that, in the future, we should create, alongside the market economy and the public sector, a third sector that would allow these initiatives to develop and flourish in a context of adequate and fair legal and fiscal provisions.

At the time, other researchers were interested in the issue but were tackling other aspects of it. They were mainly working on the concept of social econ-omy. Within the social economy, the keyword is not 'autonomy' but 'solidar-ity'. This school of thought has produced many experiments but no founding text since 1968. Later, in France, the responsibility for following up the matter was given to a state secretary (a junior minister in the French government). Currently, both an interministerial delegation and a state secretary deal with the social economy. In 1998, the government asked the economist Alain Lipietz to examine whether a new structure or statute could be created for the social economy, and he recommended to create a label. The issue is therefore still on the political agenda and is the subject of continuing research.

However, to complete this social picture of the period, we should add that the May 1968 events also rekindled the debate on working conditions. In France, the skilled workers of the Renault car manufacturer's plant in Le Mans staged a famous work stoppage which lasted for some time and was the land-mark strike of that period. And one of their demands had to do with the very issue of working conditions. A few years later, a national agency dedicated to the improvement of working conditions was created and a state secretary was appointed to manage it. In short, the qualitative aspects of work also played a role in the exchange of ideas at that time. Nevertheless, the young people who started initiatives in the third sector seldom gave much thought to improving the living conditions of their customers and combating unemployment.

This movement was not specific to France, of course. Italy and Sweden in particular had quite a strong cooperative sector that could depend on very active municipalities. Initiatives were not based on abstract theories developed by academics but were rather derived from practical experience (in particular in Sweden, whose economy then had a significant social component). The municipalities and local authorities had the necessary resources to organize personal services (child care, care for elderly people), which subsequently thrived. The promotion of equal opportunities and of female employment was already well under way in Sweden, Norway, Denmark and Finland, without the third sector having played any particular role in the process. For its part, Italy had always had a fairly powerful cooperative sector. So had the Spanish Basque Country, albeit with just one cooperative, Mondragon.

We also looked at what was going on in the United States, for the student revolt had not been limited to France. Over there, however, the activity creation trend proved short-lived. Of course, the environment is very different in the United States, where the organizations known as 'non-profits' have a very strong legal and financial status. Nevertheless, they present a more phil-anthropic orientation that is specific to the Anglo-Saxon countries, while many continental European countries have a well-established tradition of mutual help, as is pointed out in the first chapter of the book. In the US private sector, the system is considerably more flexible than the European one and lays down practically no restrictions.

CHANGE OF TACK IN THE 1980s

The following years were not very propitious to the development of the sector or to the slightest political move in this area. The study drafted for the Commission and our recommendations issued in 1979 were not followed up, either in Brussels or in France. Nonetheless, they did catch the attention of some officials within DG V, the Directorate-General for Social Affairs and Industrial Relations at the European Commission, and the ideas re-emerged a little later. For my part, my other duties left me no time to take any initiatives, although I continued to monitor the issue.

As the European economies had moved into an adjustment phase, industrial conversion problems had become increasingly important. To address these problems in France, conversion support units had been created to provide flanking measures for the restructuring plans that involved redundancies. They were based on the model of a national agency that had played a remarkable role in stimulating economic development during the 1960s. For instance, in south-west France, it was well known that the Lacq gas field was soon going to dry up and the large extracting company, Elf-Aquitaine, had set up a conver-sion support unit whose purpose was to try to create new activities in the area and thus enable worker resettlement. The problem still remains today. Local development thus went through a first phase consisting of these conversion operations, which involved municipalities, extraction sites, industrial basins or employment areas.

At the European level, when I became President of the European Commission in 1985, I was immediately engrossed in my battle for the single market, and soon after in the flanking policies designed to complement the completion of the internal market. These policies, tied to the Structural Funds,[1] were to expand far more than I had initially expected.

In 1986, therefore, I submitted the paper, 'Making a Success of the Single Act', in which I set out the famous triptych, 'competition, cooperation and solidarity'. My main concern at the time was to build on the Single Act to ensure that the European Community became an area combining these three dimensions. That was a precondition for achieving the Act's other provisions. The main idea suggested in that document was that each region should have its opportunity, and that meant giving the European Community an ambitious policy in terms of resources. I must admit that I did not grant very much attention to local development in that paper. Furthermore, it had been decided to replace project-based financing (hitherto the rule for giving grants from the structural funds) with programme-based financing. These development programmes were to include all the measures and projects likely to increase the gross domestic product of a region, while also creating jobs. In that system, the little seed that was later to lead to the impressive local development movement was rural development.

Rural development is what made it possible to achieve a practical break-through. When it was decided to create assistance programmes for rural development, the aim was clearly not to improve transport infrastructure but essentially to create activities. Fundamentally, rural development was the first area which led the Commission officials to discuss endogenous development and new forms of activity. Certain people even demonstrated some scepticism as to the need for this kind of action. At that time, I received memoranda pointing out that rural development was, after all, only a component of urban development and that the future of the countryside was of marginal importance in an area where conurbations were playing an increasing role. I nevertheless persevered by taking account of the historical, natural and traditional characteristics of rural areas. I must admit that I had never imagined that so much ingenuity and energy would subsequently be devoted to that strand of structural policy. I later noticed the expansion of local development and of specifically local initiatives. In the 1993 White Paper on 'Growth, Competitiveness and Employment' (European Commission, 1993), I recommended that they should be given systematic assistance. However, that was not included in the initial blueprint because, as the Union had lost a million jobs between 1980 and 1985, the priority had become creating jobs within the internal market.

LOCAL DEVELOPMENT AND EMPLOYMENT INITIATIVES

The unexpected event of the 1990s was the merging of local development, supported by the Community structural policies, with a new form of entrepreneurship. As I have pointed out, local development was not clearly and directly encouraged as part of the 1986 reform, but the success of the structural policies – and their limitations – led to some fine-tuning of an approach initially designed in terms of investment, income increase and job creation. The first aim was to demonstrate that the social and economic cohesion policy, whose budget had been doubled, was a positive sum game. In other words, the countries which made a greater contribution to the Community funds also received their share of benefits in the form of investment opportunities in the other countries and exports. Soon, a new qualitative issue emerged: what could be done to take the process further and encourage local initiatives? It gradually became clear, thanks to the visits of the regional leaders to Brussels, that what we were dealing with was not merely a straightforward economic growth function with physical investment and financing on the 'input' side and regional GDP and jobs on the 'output' side. If the Commission was to heed the lessons of this experience, it would notably have to think in terms of local development and employment initiatives (Jouen, 2000).

The fact that regions and local authorities could make their voice heard in Brussels encouraged them to think about their development. Their representatives brought us their conclusions and experiences without our genuinely realizing that we were inducing them to do so, in particular through the Community initiatives.[2] Initially, my position had been to study the programmes put forward by the regions, then finance them within a fairly short period, and finally draw conclusions by trying to understand what had happened. When the Directorate-General for Regional Policy attempted to take stock of these programmes, it realized that the phenomenon was a highly complex one which was governed not merely by the simple growth function I have just mentioned but also by innovative factors that we were not even aware of.

It was only in the 1990s that the industrial model truly came to an end, even though its death had been announced 15 years earlier. We gradually realized that the business start-ups and new activity creation were taking place almost exclusively in the services sector and that the strategy of trying to attract companies from outside to create jobs was no longer working. The secondary sector, industry, accounted for 60 per cent of the economy in the 1950s. The transition to a service-based economy in which this 60 per cent was generated by the tertiary sector was bound to have considerable repercussions. And the process was further amplified by social, demographic and lifestyle changes.

Basically, the question is even clearer today than it was yesterday: what can the market economy do, and what can it not do? For part of the European population cannot afford to buy services at their market price. That is one example among others which explain this change, this continuing mutation, whose outcome cannot yet be predicted. The question is whether we will realize in time just how important the 'third sector' has become, and whether we will be able to create the instruments needed to promote its development. The third sector's development is closely related to local development because it very often involves local community services and it is also a by-product of the industrial conversion process.

I must admit that, between 1985 and 1995, my own position on this issue changed, mainly because I became more acutely aware of the importance of subsidiarity. This prompted me to look into what could be done at levels that were close to the citizens. Two other reasons for my change in outlook were the severity of the unemployment crisis and the fact that there are limits to promoting economic recovery by establishing a favourable environment for economic activity (in terms of infrastructure or even education). These three factors led me to reflect more closely on how to encourage local development. Paradoxically, this was at a time when many experts attached far more importance to globalization than to local development. Yet both ends of the chain must be addressed. That is what we tried to do with the White Paper on 'Growth, Competitiveness and Employment'. We took account of the constraints of globalization, while reminding ourselves that what could be done at local level was also far from negligible. It is that converse process – the need to reconcile the global and local levels – which is not being properly understood in the public debate.

POOR RECOGNITION OF THE THIRD SECTOR AT COMMUNITY LEVEL

When I became President of the European Commission, I was keen to keep in touch with the world of cooperatives, mutual societies and associations. I therefore established a specialist unit within the Commission that could act as their contact, hear their representatives and process the information received. I thought that some day we might succeed in getting the third sector recognized at the European level. However, the goal was somewhat distant and in the end our effort did not yield the results I was hoping for.

The cooperatives, mutual societies, associations and other organizations belonging to the social economy could have followed the example of the regions and visited the relevant Commission departments (the Directorate-General for Enterprise Policy and the Directorate-General for Social Affairs and Industrial Relations) to speak of their experience. In France, the *Mutualité Sociale Agricole* devotes considerable effort to rural development. It endeavours to reintegrate unemployed people in rural areas by promoting, for instance, the development of various types of personal services, for example, home care services. But these organizations failed to make their voices heard and thus to act as representatives of the social innovation movement. We can imagine several reasons for their lack of enthusiasm, but in my view the most probable one is conservatism. Whatever we might think, social economy organizations are attached to their prerogatives and tend to keep a distrustful eye on each other. To use a sporting term, they 'mark' each other closely. The sector innovates in the field, but is anxious to preserve its powers in political terms, both at the national and at the European level. It therefore failed to grasp the opportunities opened up by May 1968 and the tremendous possibilities of the structural policies.

In fact, the regions and municipalities were the ones that approached the cooperatives, mutual societies and associations. They aroused their interest and gave them ideas. This was in marked contrast to what happened during the nineteenth and early twentieth centuries, when the latter sector was particularly innovative and made up for the shortcomings of society by creating new services and strengthening solidarity. Its passion for new activities and new partners seems to have disappeared. My judgment is a little harsh, but probably accurate.

The lack of reaction from certain components of the third sector was perhaps also due to the fact that some organizations, such as the large cooperatives and mutual societies, were established during a bygone industrial era. They were having trouble finding their bearings in the new service-based economy we are now living in.

I felt rather isolated in that effort to create a European third sector. Although my socialist background is essentially of the Nordic variety, I was not given much support. My arguments often fell on deaf ears, in spite of the fact that the Nordic countries have an idea of the state, social dialogue, solidarity and trade movements which is conducive to the emergence of local initiatives. I will mention just one example: during the last years of my period at the Commission, the Swedish employers' organization had created an association that 'lent' its members' managers to business start-ups. In practice, these business executives spent five hours a week counselling people, explaining how to create a business, keep it afloat, run it and so on. That initiative by the Swedish employers is now part of the European Business Network for Social Cohesion established with the support of the Commission in 1994. The experiment was typical of the particular mentality of the Swedish people. That Nordic approach would have been very useful to the Community during the 1980s, and could still be in the future, by inspiring the Commission's general policy in these areas.

Regarding the attitude of the social partners towards this issue, I must confess that I was somewhat disappointed. Admittedly, in those days they were worried by the deterioration in working conditions, recruitment terms, work contracts, and so on. Generally speaking, they tended to follow a macro-economic approach. It is therefore hardly surprising that they should not have been very interested in the working patterns and activities of a sector that was atypical in many respects. Yet it is possible that, at the local level, certain trade union organizations, in particular in Finland, Sweden and Denmark, were more active in this area.

Looking back, I wish I had devoted more attention to the European Social Fund (ESF). I called for reforms, but never succeeded in persuading the ESF to give up the temptation of routine allocation, at least for 20 per cent of its funds, and to be flexible and versatile enough to encourage innovation. That is my main regret. I noticed these rigidities rather late in the day, because one cannot do everything. What we had failed to do was adapt the ESF to the spirit of the Single Act. That reform would have speeded up the convergence between local development and the social economy. It would also have allowed the Directorate-General for Social Affairs and Industrial Relations to become aware of the local development phenomenon at an earlier stage, instead of the initiative coming from the regions.

THE INSTITUTIONAL PITFALLS AND THE NEED FOR NEW INSTRUMENTS

An important aspect of the completion of the internal market was the harmonization of legislation and standards, and in some cases the adoption of new legal statuses to help business growth and the free movement of goods and services. Where cooperatives and associations were concerned, I was hoping that the creation of European company statutes would make these types of organization more popular. The aim was not only to harmonize, but also to promote development. Most importantly, I was hoping that we would generate added value by pooling national experience and that we would be able to combine the best of the German, French or Italian forms of cooperative organization to draw up optimal legal statuses and financial rules.

However, retracing the full course of events from 1985, the fact is that many obstacles arose along the way to giving a European and institutional dimension to the third sector. When I put forward the idea of a European company statute during my first years in Brussels, I added that there should also be a European statute for what is called 'the social economy sector'. The creation of a specialized Commission unit in December 1989 was part of that process. Unlike what happened with the private-sector companies, I think the difficulties came, not so much from national governments wishing to preserve their powers, from subsidiarity or from ideological disagreements, as from the sector itself. 'All the instruments are there. Why do you want to create new ones?' – this objection, which I had already heard in France in the 1970s, came up again in Europe in the 1980s.

In actual fact, I was not really very fond of the term 'social economy', which tended to be associated with generosity and contrasted with the private sector, which was synonymous with profitability. This terminological conflict was stifling substantive debate and innovation: how can you criticize generosity; and, conversely, what more can you expect from profitability? We were unable to move forward. We had to change the paradigm and demonstrate that there was an intermediate grey area which could combine profitability and generosity or, to use the philosophical terms, autonomy and solidarity. This was achieved only much later with the local initiatives and social cooperatives. We were able to create an emblem, which now exists, and around which we must continue to muster energy to determine the right legal and fiscal provisions and so on.

Naturally, we must put all this in perspective. For instance, the voluntary sector is a highly complex universe. The word 'association' can refer to very different systems in the various countries. The term has no doubt been used to conceal what were in fact profit-making enterprises, but it has also made it possible to cover new needs that were ignored by both the market and the public sector. This universe of associations is vast. So the accusation of conservatism applies only to those who say, 'If we touch that, what will become of us?' In France, some years ago, the government announced taxation guidelines for associations and the reactions were defensive rather than welcoming.

The Europeanization of the third sector has progressed over the last five or six years, through practice but also with the help of researchers who are increasingly working as a network and comparing their findings. I welcome the fact, for I do not share the point of view of those pragmatists who believe that all the necessary legal and fiscal provisions and policies are already in place for the development of what we call – rightly or wrongly – the 'third sector'. I think the development of the sector is being hindered by ill-adapted public policies, legislation and tax rules. While tools do exist, they must be further developed and we should not rule out the possibility of creating new ones. But mine is a minority opinion. I think the sector has tremendous potential but cannot fulfil it in its present form. I also have the intuition that without better organization at the local level we cannot achieve equal opportunities in the workplace, and without better organization of the third sector we cannot achieve the solidarity and social interaction tomorrow's society will need. I am convinced that the solution to this problem is to create a genuine third sector, and that this remains to be done. We must establish a totally new sphere, which will feature its share of risk taking and will need certain tax incentives. There will no doubt be some fraud and controls will be necessary, but I am sure it will be worth it. Should we start at the European level? I have my doubts.

NOTES

1. Under the Treaty on European Union (Articles 158 and 159), the structural funds – the European Regional Development Fund (ERDF), the European Social Fund (ESF) and the European Agricultural Guidance and Guarantee Fund (EAGGF) – support the Union's action to strengthen economic and social cohesion, that is to say reduce disparities in the level of development between regions.
2. Financed through the structural funds, the main aim of the Community initiatives is the pooling of experience and transnational cooperation between beneficiaries (regions, cities, NGOs, professional organizations and so on).

REFERENCES

European Commission (1993), *White Paper on Growth, Competitiveness and Employment: the Challenges and Ways Forward into the 21st Century*, OOPEC Supplement 6/93.
Jouen, M. (2000), *Diversité européenne: mode d'emploi,* Paris: Descartes et Cie.

PART IV

What Matters with Respect to the Third Sector?
Theoretical Considerations

11. Alternative paradigms for the mixed economy: will sector matter?

Ralph M. Kramer

INTRODUCTION: CRITIQUE OF THE SECTOR CONCEPT

Between the late 1940s and the 1980s, the number of non-profit organizations in the United States increased from about 50 000 to over 1 400 000; similar patterns of exponential growth occurred in other post-industrial and developing nations worldwide. Originating in the economic and political conditions associated with the postwar 'crisis of the welfare state', the non-profit sector has joined the public sector and the private sector as a pillar of the political economy of modern society.

The first efforts of account for the development and character of the non-profit sector were by economists using neoclassical concepts of state or market 'failure', or trust, as explanatory variables (Hansmann, 1987, 1996; Ortmann, 1996; Steinberg, 1997). These macroeconomic models, however, failed to capture the critical dimensions of the third sector beyond some imputed compensatory functions. Nor did they explain cross-national variations in the size and composition of the third sector (DiMaggio and Anheier, 1990; Lifset, 1989). Economic models have also been faulted for their reductiveness, empirical circularity and ethical obtuseness (Hall, 1998; *Voluntas*, 1997, esp. pp.97–119).

In the twenty-first century, the dominant theoretical perspective on the development and character of the non-profit sector is still a model based on the form of organizational ownership. Typically, it emphasizes the rapid institutionalization of the third sector as the core of civil society, as the state's primary partner in the provision of human services and the promotion of culture and the arts. At the same time, because of the blurring of sectoral boundaries and the extensive interdependence among organizations, the utility of a sectoral model based on ownership form can be questioned for the following reasons.

First, the rapid growth in the number and types of non-profits has been accompanied by their growing dependence on governmental funding that supports their substantial role in implementing public policy. Before the drop-off in funding during the 1980s, non-profit social service agencies in the USA received three times as much revenue from the public sector as they did from their traditional philanthropic sources, which accounted for only 11 per cent of their income (Salamon, 1993).

A second trend has been the growing privatization of many governmental functions, and the rapid commercialization and competition in fields once dominated by non-profit organizations, including health care, education and the social services (Adams and Perlmutter, 1991; Tuckman, 1998). To compensate for declining government funding during the 1980s, many non-profits imposed fees, began charging for services or converted to for-profit status (Ryan, 1999; Salamon, 1993; Skloot, 1988). Others created new structural forms in which hybrid or pseudo-non-profits spun off commercial subsidiaries (McGovern, 1989; Scotchmer and Van Benschoten, 1999).

At the same time, various business and industrial corporations converted to the non-profit form or established non-profit subsidiaries (Claxton *et al.*, 1997; Gray, 1997; Kuttner, 1997; Weisbrod, 1998). For example, in recent decades for-profit companies have expanded their share of hospital and home health care, child welfare and day care, and drug treatment (Clarke and Estes, 1992; Geen and Pollak, 1999). In higher education, roughly two-thirds of the income of private colleges and universities are derived from fees and revenues from commercial activities, which yield close to a billion dollars a year (Weisbrod, 1998).

These new patterns of expansion and commercialization have led to a convergence and blurring of sectoral boundaries. Because most social services are or could be provided by any type of organization – public, private or non-profit – the traditional concept of sector has lost much of its theoretical and analytic power. While 'sector' may well continue to serve a 'symbolic function' in political language (Alford, 1992, p.42), in the mixed social economy 'the sector is an artificial construct, not an institutional reality' (Hall, 1992, p.28).

As Kaufmann (1991, p.91) observed in his description of Europe in the late 1980s: 'There is a growing interdependency of both public and private actors in economic and social policy that renders meaningless the old distinctions of "state and society" or of "public and private" as separate domains.' Hall (1992) offered a similar view of the USA: 'The interpenetration of sectors is an established fact. The epistemological problem is to devise methods that will enable us to grasp its extent and its significance' (pp.105–6).

Efforts to reify the 'guiding construct' of the third sector, to identify its unique substance and coherence, ignore the history of shifting boundaries (conceptual, legal, political, economic and organizational) between societal sectors; such boundaries have always been blurred, permeable and interpenetrated (Brody, 1996a; Musolf and Seidman, 1980; Young, 1999). Other factors contributing to the diminution of differences in the structure, roles and performance of organizations are their increasing dependence on the same funding sources, public policies and regulations, as well as the diffusion across sectoral lines of a common set of principles of the 'new managerialism' (Ferris and Graddy, 1989; Bielefeld and Galaskiewicz, 1998; Locke, 1996).

While there have been few empirical intersectoral studies of the convergence and erosion of boundaries, many sociological explanations have been proposed. Concepts have been borrowed from network, ecological, exchange, open systems, coalition, contingency, resource dependency, and even postmodern theories (Powell, 1990; Gronbjerg, 1993, pp.309–10; Hatch, 1996; Boje *et al.*, 1996). Among the independent variables suggested for comparative intersectoral studies of the role and performance of non-profit organizations in different industries are size, age, structure, fiscal resource systems, decision-making and governance patterns, professionalization and service technology.

However, studies of hospitals, nursing homes, schools, universities and such social services as day care and nursery schools have shown that the organizations in each industry have much more in common with one another than they do with other non-profit organizations in the sector (McGovern, 1989; Mauser, 1998; Krashinsky, 1998). For example, 'ownership-related' differences in hospitals are more closely related to the character of their external environment, geography and the industry itself, which is extremely competitive, professionalized and commercialized (Schlesinger, 1998; Wolf and Schlesinger, 1998).

Furthermore, all organizations, regardless of their type of ownership, are subject to changes in their internal and external environments effected by the same forces of supply and demand, resource dependency and shifting patterns of interorganizational collaboration or competition. These factors help account for the conclusion that most formal differences among organizations tend to be more of degree than of kind (Brody, 1996b; Kramer, 1987).

While their form of ownership has contributed to the legitimacy of non-profits, differences in their performance where they coexist with for-profit organizations may depend more on the extent of competition, size and isomorphism within the institutional and ecological structure of a particularly industry or field of service (Hammack and Young, 1993, pp.398–419).

There is considerable evidence that, as Anheier and Seibel concluded, 'the more one increases differentiation and complexity, the less useful the whole concept of sectors becomes ... the designation of organizations into sectors may ultimately rest on research conventions rather than on strict empirical grounds' (1990, p.381).

That the traditional concept of 'sector' has less meaning today is also supported by the finding that social service systems in Europe, regardless of their organizational mix in different industries, have encountered the same problems of cost and quality control, inequities and inefficiencies such as over- or underutilization, and fragmentation (Evers and Svetlik, 1993). Recent research shows clearly that, the greater the scope and responsibilities of a nation's non-profit sector, the more it is likely to generate the same bureau-pathologies usually ascribed to government (Kramer, 1981; Kramer *et al.*, 1993).

If, then, form of ownership has become a poor predictor of organizational behaviour, alternative concepts are needed for studying the human services industry. Let us turn to four paradigms that are based on the convergence and blurring of sectoral boundaries and that could be used to supplement or complement sectoral studies.

THE POLITICAL ECONOMY OF HUMAN SERVICES

The political economy perspective on human services has its roots in eighth-century European accounts of the relationships between the emerging nation-states and the dynamics of their economies. As the social sciences became more specialized and various disciplines proliferated during the nineteenth century, political economy eventually lost some of its centrality. It was revived in the latter part of the twentieth century as one of the interdisciplinary studies of the growth and development of industrial societies (Benson, 1975; Walmsley and Zald, 1970).

Beginning in the 1970s, new programmes of professional education and training were also established for many components of this vast industry, together with new job titles and career lines, particularly for those who did not have graduate or professional degrees (Anderson *et al.*, 1977; Stein, 1986). Within a few years, 'human services' became the most widely used term for the proliferating specializations within the broad fields of health, education and social welfare.

The scope of professional and research publications in the burgeoning human services industry includes upwards of a dozen specialized fields of service such as education, health care, behavioural (mental) health, personal social services, income maintenance, employment training, rehabilitation, housing, recreation and social development (Wernet, 1994). Most definitions of the human services industry include not only service agencies and their clients, but also local, state and regional organizations that regulate, coordinate, plan, supply resources, advocate and set policies (Dickens, 1996). Each level has multiple stakeholder constituencies: clients, advocacy organizations, professional associations, funders, board and committee members, and regulatory and legislative bodies. The industry also includes various mixed and hybrid organizations that combine non-profit and for-profit characteristics, such as public agencies organized as free-standing non-profit corporations, as well as subsidiaries of for-profit organizations.

Austin, whose *The Political Economy of Human Service Programs* (1988) exemplifies this paradigm, concludes that, in post-industrial societies, the scope, structure and financing of the human services has become one of the three most critical societal concerns, alongside the avoidance of war and the management of the economy (p.15).

Noting the rapid movement of for-profit providers into the human services industry, Austin asserts that 'for-profit firms have the technical capacity to produce any type of human service which is produced by either non-profits or government' (ibid., pp.235–7). While this may be true in theory, a review of empirical studies comparing nursing homes and day care under different auspices concluded that the findings were inconclusive, and that even the cost advantage of for-profit providers faded when measures of quality were used (Gilbert, 1995, pp.135–7). Indeed, comparative studies suggest that relatively few generalizations can be made about the consistent comparative advantages of for-profit or non-profit service providers (Weisbrod, 1998, pp.287–305).

The scope and focus of the political economy paradigm are exceptionally broad, consisting of selected political and economic interactions between organizations and their external or task environment, which is composed of other organizations, interest groups and stakeholders that control important resources. One consequence of the resurgence of interest in political economy has been the widespread diffusion of its various components. As a result, the term 'political economy' is often misused to describe almost any collection of concepts that focuses on selected political or economic aspects of a social process (Roberts-DeGennaro, 1988; Knocke, 1990). As used here, however, 'political economy' is restricted to its meaning as an organizing principle in the work of exemplars such as Austin (1988) and Hasenfeld (1983, 1992).

As applied to organizations, 'political' refers to the various processes through which power and legitimacy are acquired and maintained, goals and tasks determined, and systems of governance and oversight established. 'Economic' refers to the processes by which resources (such as funds, staff and clients) needed for the organization's service technologies are obtained and allocated, and a division of labour established for the production and delivery of services (Hasenfeld, 1983, pp.31–2).

Within a human services organization, institutional rules reflect the outcomes of negotiations and other interactions among various interest groups (for example, boards, staffs, contributors and clients) and their differential access to and control of power. Consequently, it is the changing power and economic relations *within* the organization that determine which policies are adopted, how service technologies are implemented and how decision-making authority is distributed. To maintain its autonomy in an intersectoral environment, the organization engages in various political strategies (competition, cooptation and collaboration) to cope with the forces that affect its resource acquisition and service delivery systems. (These circumstances may explain why many of the interest groups incorporated as non-profit organizations have been described as 'private governments'.) From the perspective of political economy, an organization can be conceived as an arena, or open system, in which the various interest groups or stakeholders that possess needed resources compete in order to optimize their particular values.

Critics of the political economy model, however, point to the difficulty of distinguishing between political and economic factors, the model's overly abstract conception of power and other economic realities, and the problems in operationalizing and validating empirically complex organizational issues (Hasenfeld, 1983, pp.43–9). Others argue that the model underestimates the importance of values and ideologies, which can transcend calculations of power and money in influencing organizational behaviour. Nor does political economy overcome the intrinsic obstacles to empirical research in the human services: imprecise technology in many fields and the lack of consensus about the definitions of outcomes and the criteria for judging effectiveness. Many of these weaknesses are addressed in Austin's list of feasible, high-priority intersectoral research topics, which include detailed mapping studies of human services industries, labour forces, public attitudes, resource flows, professional networks within an industry, and interorganizational service delivery systems (Hasenfeld, 1983, pp.240–44).

After reviewing seven other theoretical approaches to human services organizations and finding each inadequate, Hasenfeld (1983, pp.43–9) concluded that the political economy perspective, as a 'converging framework', a synthesis of some of the other approaches' major themes, came closest to meeting the prerequisites for a theory. The political economy paradigm, in Hasenfeld's view, articulates more specifically than any of the others the external and internal political and economic processes that shape the character of an organization and the interest groups that influence it.

Concepts from political economy thus seem particularly useful in understanding how the external environment and resource acquisition processes affect an organization's service delivery systems, especially in intersectoral industries characterized by interdependence and interpenetration.

THE ECOLOGY OF A MARKET ECONOMY

Hammack and Young (1993) offer a different theoretical framework in which the public, private and non-profit sectors are treated as occupying interdependent niches in a market economy. This holistic perspective is drawn largely from the pioneering work of Hannan and Freeman (1989), who recommended the use of ecological analysis when (a) there are strong inertial pressures to resist change (that is, organizations feel compelled to continue doing what is habitual) and (b) there is an uncertain environment, and change is likely. Under these conditions, the basic assumption is that biotic and organizational populations will behave in similar ways; hence the analysis focuses on large populations of organizations from all sectors rather than on only one.

Ecological studies typically seek to identify the life cycle regularities that shape the birth, development and ageing of populations of organizations over long time spans. Curiously, these studies pay relatively little attention to the role of the state or to ideological, political and economic influences on the life cycle of organizations. An exception is Gronbjerg's (1993) intensive study of 13 Chicago social service and community development organizations, which revealed the slow pace of change. Gronbjerg's findings illustrate a key tenet of ecological theory: once relationships with the environment are established, organizational structures persist, with few modifications in their basic character.

Ecological analysis has been applied in studying the rates of founding and dissolution of such populations of organizations as national labour unions, newspapers, phone companies, wineries and social movements. Some researchers acknowledge, however, that institutional forces, such as the state, may be much more important than ecological forces in understanding the life cycle of human service organizations (Hasenfeld, 1992, pp.38–9).

On the basis of an extensive body of empirical research, four major social processes that affect long-term changes in populations of organizations have been studied: competition for funds, members and other resources, legitimacy, aging and environmental abundance or constraints (Hannan and Freeman, 1989, pp.13–14). Historical and societal forces (political, technological and cultural) are invoked to explain the particular mix of public, private and non-profit organizations within an industry or a nation.

For example, many of the important niches for non-profit sectarian organizations in the provision of educational, health and social services in the USA are the result of the historical separation of Church and state, as well as constitutional restrictions on the role of government. Other niches for non-profits result from the social policy of separating public funding from service provision by contracting with non-governmental organizations to deliver services to persons for whom there is some public responsibility. Traditional niches for non-governmental organizations in the political and market economy also include advocacy, innovation and the promotion of voluntarism (Boris and Steurle, 1998, pp.3–30; Young, 1999).

At the same time, isomorphic forces in the society have eroded some of the claims to distinctive niches based on an organization's form of ownership

(Bielefeld and Galaskiewicz, 1998; Clarke and Estes, 1992). Whether public or private, most universities and hospitals look and act much like each other, and in other ways they resemble commercial enterprises. With some exceptions, the same set of managerial principles and techniques prevail throughout the organizational universe regardless of ownership form (Boje *et al.*, 1996; Locke, 1996). Government contracts, grants and subsidies are awarded to non-profit organizations, for-profit corporations, quangos and hybrid organizations for similar purposes. In the field of child welfare, for-profit organizations in the USA have become the major contractors for state and county governments in the operation of residential treatment, day care and group homes, in addition to being the major providers of drug abuse programmes (Gilbert, 1995; Geen and Pollak, 1999). (Before Congress changed the law in 1996, government agencies could purchase such services only from non-profit organizations.)

Under what conditions, then, is an ecological model useful? In general, ecological models have been most productive in studying a network of organizations in the same industry or field where (a) the environment has been relatively stable, (b) the rates of entry and exit have been low and (c) most of the formal organizations, regardless of their corporate form, have, over a long period of time, adopted similar patterns of bureaucratic structure, and become, in varying degrees, more entrepreneurial, political, professional or secular in their operations.

There is considerable opportunity for the use of ecological concepts because, with few exceptions, little is known about the origins and characteristics of the organizational mix in industries such as the human services (Billis and Glennerster, 1998). And few researchers have studied the relationships between the characteristics of specific social and health services and the relative strengths and weaknesses of different institutional forms at various stages in the processes of funding and service delivery (Hammack and Young, 1993, pp.401–2).

If, however, a population of organizations from various sectors is viewed as a mix or as a network (Powell, 1990), then ecology can be a source of concepts for studying the origin, change, decline and dissolution of organizations in an industry, particularly from a macro or a mega perspective.

NEOINSTITUTIONALISM

Among the earliest rejections of the static public–private dichotomy was that made by Bruce L.R. Smith (1975): 'So great is the interpenetration between the "public" and the "private" sectors, that this basic distinction – on which the political rhetoric and dialogue of modern times has rested – has ceased to be an operational way of understanding reality' (cited in Van Til, 1988, p.95). From the mid-1970s to the 1980s, many prominent social scientists began to refer to the blurring of boundaries between the sectors; they included Kenneth Boulding (1973), Severyn Bruyn (1977), Ira Sharkansky (1979), and Perry and Rainey (1988).

This blurring of sectoral boundaries has usually been regarded as either a cause or an effect of a process of structural isomorphism in which non-profit organizations have become increasingly bureaucratized, professionalized and commercial. Van Til concluded that the prevailing conceptions of the non-profit sector could not explain this process in American society, and he formulated a conception of the 'social economy' as the broad societal context for all forms of voluntary action (1988, p.167).

In a subsequent discussion of these issues, Van Til (1994) adopted a holistic approach in describing the non-profit as a social institution surrounded and influenced by other institutions within an environment whose major elements are donors, intermediaries (for example, foundations, trade associations, university-based research centres and regulators), other non-profit and charitable organizations, and their beneficiaries (clients, members, staff and customers). This conception represents one of the few applications of institutionalism to non-profit organizations, an approach best exemplified by the volume edited by Powell and DiMaggio (1991).

Each discipline in the social sciences has its own view of institutions, but the core denotation of 'institution' concerns the three Rs: rules, roles and relationships. Together, they are conceived as socially constructed abstractions, rather than attributes of individual behaviour or of organizations' informal structures. While not necessarily the products of conscious design, institutions reflect the interconnections between the policy, the economy and society from a distinctive, taken-for-granted perspective (Meyer and Rowan, 1991, p.8).

An extensive body of empirical research by social scientists has been identified with the 'new' institutionalism, much of which builds on older forms of this intellectual tradition (DiMaggio and Anheier, 1990; Scott, 1995; Lowndes, 1996; Selznick, 1996). Case and industry studies using this framework have been made of art museums, colleges and universities, social service organizations, banks, newspapers, commodity markets, corporate philanthropy, hospitals, schools, law firms, textbook publishers and professional organizations, among many others. All proceed from the basic assumption that the form of ownership is less important than the institutional and ecological structure – the extent of competition and isomorphism – of a particular industry (DiMaggio and Anheier, 1990).

The study of social services and community organizations in Chicago by Gronbjerg (1993), cited earlier, is one of the few examples of an open systems and intersectoral approach to the institutional environment. Using concepts from ecological, contingency, resource dependency and institutional theory, Gronbjerg analysed the diverse factors influencing the structure and types of funding relations. Patterns of intersectoral dependence, competition and collaboration were found to be shaped by organizational reputations and resources, government regulations and strategic adaptions to the changing funding environment.

In another urban research project, neoinstitutional concepts were applied by Feeney (1997) to a case study of five non-profit organizations confronting management problems. Feeney used institutional analysis, rather than the traditional rational–bureaucratic model of organization, to identify the distinctive character of non-profit solutions to their management problems. She viewed the non-profits as embedded in larger organizational and community systems, each with various stakeholders, in an environment that included both vertical and horizontal interorganizational networks. She was able to identify cultural factors that shaped organizational behaviour, such as the ethnic and religious groups within the constituencies and the constraints and demands of funders, regulators and members.

Thus institutional analysis can provide a set of tools for decoding complex and dynamic environments, for mapping the often conflicting cultures, values and role requirements of multiple constituencies and stakeholders as well as the interplay between internal and external factors in an organization and in the systems in which it participates, elements usually unobtainable in a standard organizational analysis.

Among the major principles of institutional behaviour derived from empirical studies are the following: (1) institutions persist even though they may be less than optimal if maintained by ideology and the state; (2) there is a striking homogeneity of arrangements in labour markets, states and corporations in their taken-for-granted expectations and self-sustaining processes; (3) regardless of their form of ownership, most organizations tend to respond in a similar manner to similar problems; (4) structures and performance are shaped by vertical and interorganizational networks for funding, goal setting and regulations; (5) the wide variations in regulatory processes among industries reflect differences in political, economic and organizational arrangements; (6) the key sources of institutionalized rules in modern society are the state, the professions and their distinctive myths and ceremonies, public opinion and the network of organizations within an industry.

Like political economy, neoinstitutionalism does not comprise a coherent body of theory; it contains a variety of perspectives, some of which are complementary, that attribute varying significance to formal and informal structures, change and stability, and the role of rationality and norm-governing behaviour in creating and sustaining institutions (Lowndes, 1996).

Nor does institutional analysis supplant other approaches to understanding organizational behaviour; rather, it offers an *integrative* approach to understanding non-profit organizations in their larger contextual and operating environments. Studies using this approach, however, have been criticized for playing down the importance of change and conflict in institutional behaviour, as well as the role of individuals, while overemphasizing the extent of institutionalization, determinism and organizational isomorphism (Reitan, 1998, pp.298–9). Nonetheless, neoinstitutionalism can serve as a source of concepts, theories and empirical studies that allow a systemic or intersectoral view of the human services industry or its components. Alone or in combination with political economy or organizational ecology, this interdisciplinary approach can yield useful insights about organizational behaviour.

MIXED AND OPEN SYSTEMS

Drawing primarily on political sociology, a series of studies published by the European Centre for Social Welfare Policy and Research in Vienna have had considerable influence in Europe, though this research is not widely known in the USA. Evers (1991, 1995) and Evers and Svetlik (1993) offer a paradigm for analysing the mixed economy of the welfare state in which the interactions among four sectors determine human welfare: the state, the market economy, the civil society of voluntary organizations, and the community of households. All four must be taken into account in planning, organizing or evaluating a pluralist welfare mix.

In this schema, non-governmental or non-profit organizations do not constitute a sector; rather, they are regarded as part of an *intermediate area*, 'a dimension of the public space in civil societies' (Evers, 1995, p.159). Within this intermediate area, non-profit organizations relate to the other sectors, and their 'social and political roles may be as important as their delivery of services' (ibid.). This intermediate area also includes many hybrid organizations that combine resources and rationales from government, markets, households, networks and community organizations.

To distinguish this version of the mixed economy of welfare from welfare pluralism as it emerged in England during the preceding 30 years, Evers draws on the revival of the nineteenth-century concept of civil society, which includes non-profits and other types of organizations and associations. Evers tends to minimize the significance of the non-profit/for-profit distinction, citing organizational size, among other variables, as a more salient differential than 'non-profitness', at least in Europe (1991, pp.167–8). He also regards the exclusion of the informal sphere and the neglect of quasi-formal community organizations as serious deficiencies of American debates on the third sector (Evers, 1995, p.170).

The core concept of the welfare mix of Evers and Svetlik (1993, pp.1–50) can serve four policy and research functions: (1) as an analytical, historical and sociopolitical approach to the sources of responsibility for welfare problems, not all of which involve the state, and as a measure of changing welfare mixes; (2) as a descriptive tool for identifying the empirical advantages and disadvantages of various organizational combinations in different countries and their historical roles in each sector; (3) as an approach to evaluating the potentials and limits of different organizational forms (for example, government is best for equity and uniformity but is slow to respond to specific needs; non-profits are sensitive to the needs of cultural–social sub-groups but are usually ineffective in reducing regional inequalities); and (4) as a tool for describing the different political concepts in social policy, such as the changing responsibility between different actors in the social service sector, and in the formal and informal production and delivery of social services.

Presumably another advantage of the welfare mix concept is the avoidance of ideological bias and the stereotype of a public–private dichotomy. And, like political economy, the mixed, open systems approach affords great flexibility in the selection of variables for study. A pluralistic and synergistic approach that includes the cultural context seems particularly useful for comparative studies. For example, studying the effects of government support for non-profits in the USA is a popular topic, but in Germany, and to a lesser extent in Norway, non-profits simply reproduce the conformity of state-based rules and a rigid professionalism (ibid., p.25).

This conceptualization of a mixed economy of welfare has been applied productively in extensive research particularly on services to the elderly (see Evers and Svetlik, 1993). By 'dethroning' third sector organizations and relocating them in an intermediate area, the schema directs attention to the mixed and interdependent auspices of organizational networks in the society and in a community. At least six advantages flow from this perspective. First, 'welfare mix', as a shorthand term for a pluralistic political economy of welfare, can serve as a corrective to the assumption that the state is a single actor with no administrative separation between financing and service delivery. This assumption underlies most international comparative studies of the welfare state, despite the widespread use of different types of non-governmental organizations to implement public policy (Kramer, 1994).

Second, the concept of a welfare mix can be used to highlight the presence of new entries into a service industry or field. With the exception of Weisbrod (1998), most researchers seem to have ignored the continuing privatization of the public sphere and have not studied the performance of the growing number of for-profit organizations in the welfare economy, where the state and non-profit agencies were once the only actors.

Third, the concept of a mix within the human services could be used to direct attention to the range of social policy choices available to governments in implementing their responsibilities for setting standards, regulation and monitoring, and the evaluation of the delivery of public services.

Fourth, such studies could contribute to a better understanding of the constraints and potentials of different organizational forms, as well as how they could be interwoven in a community environment that includes the informal elements of family, neighbours and other volunteers.

Fifth, a comparative international dimension could be addressed by analysing the changing roles and responsibilities among different types of organizations in the same industry in different countries: for example, the advantages and limitations of commercial enterprises, non-profits and informal networks when they substitute for, complement or supplement the state.

Finally, the concept of mix – or pluralism – can encourage research and debate on the advantages and disadvantages, as well as the structural limits and potentials, for different patterns of functional responsibility among government, non-profits, for-profit companies and the informal sector.

CONCLUSION

Little empirical evidence supports the common belief that the form of ownership is one of the most important determinants of organizational performance in industries where for-profit and non-profit organizations coexist. Most of the research findings are at best equivocal, with costs and quality varying with the industry, time, context and scale (Kamerman and Kahn, 1989, pp.34–5). Where significant differences have been found in the performance of for-profit and non-profit organizations, they can be more reliably explained by variables in the external and internal environment rather than by the form of ownership. Such variables include size, age, competition, supply and demand, and service technology. The type of ownership, however, may influence organizational behaviour in so far as it provides an incentive for administration and staff, affects the perceptions of clients and determines the actions of regulatory bodies (Weisbrod, 1998).

The blurring of sectoral boundaries has presented further challenges to the usefulness of sectoral analysis for analysing the performance of non-profit organizations. We have reviewed four of the most promising alternative paradigms, which could complement, if not replace, sector analysis.

To date, few researchers have applied the concepts of political economy to the study of the non-profits. An exception is David Austin, who has developed an exemplary comprehensive political economy model for the human services. Austin's work deserves greater recognition because this framework could be used productively in studying specific industries. Concepts derived from political economy are particularly well suited to the study of the strategies used by organizations to obtain the resources that shape the character of their service delivery systems. In focusing on power as a key dynamic of organizational behaviour, political economy concepts can illuminate the distinctive ways in which external and internal interest groups compete and otherwise influence the resources that enable organizations to strive towards their goals. As a model, concepts of political economy are suitable for studies of a single organization, an industry or components of an industry. Nonetheless, the paradigm's high level of abstraction, formidable scope, and complexity may discourage its use even in intra-industry research.

Perhaps because organization theory has had relatively little to say about the life cycle of organizations, concepts derived from ecology have been applied in intersectoral and macro-level research on a wide variety of organizational populations. Employing a technical, specialized methodology that focuses on birth, change and dissolution, organizational ecology is particularly appropriate for studying those organizations whose external environment is relatively stable and in those industries in which there is a tendency towards equilibrium among organizations in all sectors. It is more productive when restricted to questions regarding the principal factors that contribute either to rates of founding and decline or to adaptive strategies for organizational change.

The application of neoinstitutionalism to the non-profit sector is still at an early stage; the extensive institutional literature consists largely of case studies of various types of government, business and industrial organizations. But institutional concepts could be applied to different types of human service organizations, and these concepts can be combined with other modes of analysis in integrated studies of organizations in their larger contextual and operation environment. In general, however, institutional analysis is more useful for explaining stability of gradual, incremental change rather than the dynamics of organizational transformation.

In many ways, the mixed, open systems model seems to be the most promising of the four analytical frameworks, particularly for smaller-scale studies of fields of service. Evers and his colleagues present numerous examples of the way policy questions can be reformulated within the context of a mixed welfare economy, and then reframed in terms of the range of social policy choices in a specific industry, field of service or problem area. The concept of a mix within an industry may, in directing attention to the presence of for-profit and hybrid organizations, allow for a more detailed picture of the constraints and potentials of different corporate forms, as well as insights into the relationship between corporate form and such organizational variables as size, age, service technology and competition.

For Svetlik (1991, p.11), 'The right question for social policy is . . . not the choice between one sector or another, but how to combine them most effectively in economic and social terms.' At the start of the third millennium, 'the task for experts, administrators, policy makers and interest groups is to find suitable forms of sponsoring, coordinating and regulating different sectors, and providers which will allow and encourage both a democratic public and effective personal control for care services' (p.14).

REFERENCES

Adams, C. and F. Perlmutter (1991), 'Commercial venturing and the transformation of America's social welfare agencies', *Nonprofit and Voluntary Sector Quarterly*, 20 (1), 25–38.

Alford, R. (1992), 'The political language of the nonprofit sector', in R. Merelman (ed.), *Language, Symbolism, and Politics: Essays in Honor of Murray Edelman*, Boulder, Colorado: Westview Press.

Anderson, W., B. Frieden and M. Murphy (eds) (1977), *Managing Human Services*, Washington, DC: International City Managers Association.

Anheier, H. and W. Seibel (eds) (1990), *The Nonprofit Sector: International and Comparative Perspectives*, Berlin and New York: de Gruyter.

Austin, D. (1988), *The Political Economy of Human Service Programs*, Greenwich, Connecticut: JAI Press.

Benson, K. (1975), 'The interorganizational network as a political economy', *Administrative Science Quarterly*, 20, 229–49.

Bielefeld, W. and J. Galaskiewicz (1998), *Nonprofit Organizations in an Age of Uncertainty: a Study of Organizational Change*, Hawthorne, NY: Aldine de Gruyter.

Billis, D. and H. Glennerster (1998), 'Human services and the voluntary sector: a theory of comparative advantage', *Journal of Social Policy*, 27, 77–98.

Boje, D., R. Gephart and T. Thatchenkery (eds) (1996), *Postmodern Management and Organization Theory*, Thousand Oaks, California: Sage Publications.

Boris, E. and C. Steurle (eds) (1999), *Nonprofits and Government: Collaboration and Conflict*, Washington, DC: Urban Institute Press.

Boulding, K. (1973), *The Economy of Love and Fear*, Belmont, California: Wadsworth.

Brody, E. (1996a), 'Agents without principals: the economic convergence of the nonprofit and for-profit organizational forms', *New York Law School Law Review*, 40, 457–536.

Brody, E. (1996b), 'Institutional dissonance in the nonprofit sector', *Villanova Law Review*, 41, 433–504.

Bruyn, S. (1977), *The Social Economy*, New York: Wiley.

Clarke, C. and C. Estes (1992), 'Sociological and economic theories of markets and nonprofits: Evidence from home health organizations', *American Journal of Sociology*, 97, 945–69.

Claxton, G., J. Feder, D. Shactman and S. Altman (1997), 'Public policy issues in nonprofit conversions: An overview', *Health Affairs*, 16 (2), 9–28.

Dickens, P. (1996), 'Human services as service industries', *Service Industries Journal*, 16 (1), 82–91.

DiMaggio, P. and H. Anheier (1990), 'The sociology of nonprofit organizations and sectors', *Annual Review of Sociology*, 16, 137–59.

Evers, A. (1991), 'Shifts in the welfare mix', *Eurosocial*, 57/58, 7–8.

Evers, A. (1995), 'Part of the welfare mix: the third sector as an intermediate area', *Voluntas*, 6, 159–82.

Evers, A. and I. Svetlik (eds) (1993), *Balancing Pluralism: New Welfare Mixes in Care for the Elderly*, London: Avebury.

Feeney, S. (1997), 'Shifting the prism: case explications of institutional analysis in nonprofit organizations', *Nonprofit and Voluntary Sector Quarterly*, 26, 489–508.

Ferris, J. and E. Graddy (1989), 'Fading distinctions among the nonprofit, government, and for profit sectors', in V. Hodgkinson, R. Lyman and associates (eds), *The Future of the Nonprofit Sector*, San Francisco, California: Jossey-Bass, pp.123–39.

Geen, R. and T. Pollak (1999), 'The changing role of the nonprofit sector in providing child welfare services in Maryland: the potential impact of managed care', 'Crossing the Borders', working paper, Spring Research Forum, Independent Sector, 229–48.

Gilbert, N. (1995), *Welfare Justice: Restoring Social Equity*, New Haven, Connecticut: Yale University Press.

Gray, B. (1997), 'Conversion of HMOs and hospitals: what's at stake?', *Health Affairs*, 16 (2), 29–47.

Gronbjerg, K. (1993), *Understanding Nonprofit Funding: Managing Revenues in Social Service and Community Development Organizations*, San Francisco, California: Jossey-Bass.

Hall, P.D. (1992), *Inventing the Nonprofit Sector and Other Essays on Philanthropy, Voluntarism, and Nonprofit Organizations*, Baltimore, Maryland: Johns Hopkins University Press.

Hall, P.D. (1998), 'Review of R. Kuttner, 1997, Everything for Sale', *Arnova News*, 26 (3), 9.

Hammack, D. and D. Young (eds) (1993), *Nonprofit Organizations in a Market Economy*, San Francisco, California: Jossey-Bass.

Hannan, M. and J. Freeman (1989), *Organizational Ecology*, Cambridge, Massachusetts: Harvard University Press.

Hansmann, H. (1987), 'Economic theories of nonprofit organizations', in W. Powell (ed.), *The Nonprofit Sector: A Research Handbook*, New Haven, Connecticut: Yale University Press, pp.27–42.

Hansmann, H. (1996), *The Ownership of Enterprise*, Cambridge, Massachusetts: Harvard University Press.

Hasenfeld, Y. (ed.) (1983), *Human Service Organizations*, Englewood Cliffs, New Jersey: Prentice-Hall.

Hasenfeld, Y. (ed.) (1992), *Human Services as Complex Organizations*, Newbury Park, California: Sage Publications.

Hatch, M.J. (1996), *Organization Theory: Modern, Symbolic, Integrative in Post-Modern Perspectives*, New York: Oxford University Press.

Kamerman, S. and A. Kahn (eds) (1989), *Privatization and the Welfare State*, Princeton, New Jersey: Princeton University Press.

Kaufmann, F.X. (1991), 'The blurring of the distinction "state v. society" in the welfare state', in F.X. Kaufmann (ed.), *The Public-Sector Challenge for Coordination and Learning*, Berlin: de Gruyter, pp.152–64.

Knocke, D. (1990), *Organizing for Collective Action: the Political Economies of Associations*, Hawthorne, NY: Aldine de Gruyter.

Kramer, R., H. Lorentzen, W. Melief and S. Pasquinelli (1993), *Privatization in Four European Countries: Comparative Studies in Government–Third Sector Relationships*, Armonk, New York: M.E. Sharpe.

Kramer, R.M. (1981), *Voluntary Agencies in the Welfare State*, Berkeley, California: University of California Press.

Kramer, R.M. (1987), 'Voluntary agencies and the personal social services', in W. Powell (ed.), *The Nonprofit Sector: A Research Handbook*, New Haven and London: Yale University Press, pp.240–57.

Kramer, R.M. (1994), 'Voluntary agencies and the contract culture: dream or nightmare?', *Social Service Review*, 68 (1), 33–60.

Krashinsky, M. (1998), 'Does auspice matter? The case of day care in Canada', in W. Powell and E. Clemens (eds), *Private Action and the Public Good*, New Haven and London: Yale University Press, pp.114–23.

Kuttner, R. (1997), *Everything for Sale: the Virtues and Limits of Markets*, New York: Knopf.

Lifset, R. (1989), 'Cash cows or sacred cows: the politics of the commercialization movement', in V. Hodgkinson, R. Lyman and associates (eds), *The Future of the Nonprofit Sector*, San Francisco, California: Jossey-Bass, pp.140–67.

Locke, R. (1996), *The Collapse of the American Managerial 'Mystique*, London: Oxford University Press.

Lowndes, V. (1996), 'Varieties of new institutionalism: a critical appraisal', *Public Administration*, 74, Summer, 181–97.

Mauser, E. (1998), 'The importance of organizational form: parent perception versus reality in the day care industry', in W. Powell and E. Clemens (eds), *Private Action and the Public Good,* New Haven and London: Yale University Press, pp.124–36.

McGovern, J. (1989), 'The use of for-profit subsidiary corporations by nonprofits', in V. Hodgkinson, R. Lyman and associates, *The Future of the Nonprofit Sector*, San Francisco, California: Jossey-Bass, pp.168–82.

Meyer, J. and B. Rowan (1991), 'Institutionalized organizations: Formal structure as myth and ceremony', in W. Powell and P. DiMaggio (eds), *The New Institutionalism in Organizational Analysis*, Chicago, Illinois: University of Chicago Press, pp.41–62.

Musolf, L. and H. Seidman (1980), 'The blurred boundaries of public administration', *Public Administration Review*, March/April, 124–30.

Ortmann, A. (1996), 'Modern economic theory and the study of nonprofit organizations: Why the twain shall meet', *Nonprofit and Voluntary Sector Quarterly*, 25, 470–84.

Perry, J. and H. Rainey (1988), 'The public–private distinction in organization theory: a critique and research strategy', *Academy of Management Review*, 13 (2), 182–201.

Powell, W. (1990), 'Neither markets nor hierarchy: network forms of organization', *Research in Organizational Behavior*, 12, 295–336.

Powell, W. and P. DiMaggio (eds) (1991), *The New Institutionalism in Organizational Analysis*, Chicago, Illinois: University of Chicago Press.

Reitan, T. (1998), 'Theories of interorganizational relations in the human services', *Social Service Review*, 72, 285–309.

Roberts-DeGennaro, M. (1988), 'A study of youth services from a political economy perspective', *Journal of Social Service Research*, 11 (4), 61–73.

Ryan, L. (1999), 'The new landscape for nonprofits', *Harvard Business Review*, 77 (1), 127–35.

Salamon, L. (1993), 'The marketization of welfare: changing nonprofit and for-profit roles in the American welfare state', *Social Service Review*, 67 (1), 16–39.

Schlesinger, M. (1998), 'Mismeasuring the consequences of ownership', in W. Powell and E. Clemens (eds), *Private Action and the Public Good*, New Haven, Connecticut: Yale University Press, pp. 85–113.

Scotchmer, K. and E. Van Benschoten (1999), 'Nonprofit pursuit of commercial ventures: Implications for nonprofit public purpose', 'Crossing the Borders', working papers, Spring Research Forum, Independent Sector, 397–418.

Scott, W. (1995), *Institutions and Organizations*, Thousand Oaks, California: Sage Publications.

Selznick, P. (1996), 'Institutionalism "old" and "new"', *Administrative Science Quarterly*, 41, June, 270–78.

Sharkansky, I. (1979), *Whither the State? Politics and Public Enterprise in Three Countries*, New Jersey: Chatham House.

Skloot, E. (1988), *The Nonprofit Entrepreneur*, New York: The Foundation Center.

Smith, B.L.R. (1975), *The New Political Economy: The Public Use of the Private Sector*, New York: Wiley.

Stein, H. (ed.) (1986), *Organizations and the Human Services: Cross-Disciplinary Reflections*, Philadelphia: Temple University Press.

Steinberg, R. (1997), 'Overall evaluation of economic theories', *Voluntas*, 8, 179–204.

Svetlik I. (1991), 'The future of welfare pluralism in the postcommunist countries', in A. Evers and I. Svetlik (eds), *New Welfare Mixes in Care for the Elderly*, Vienna: European Center for Social Welfare Policy and Research, pp.13–24.

Tuckman, H. (1998), 'Competition, commercialization and the evaluation of nonprofit structures', *Policy Analysis and Management*, 17, 165–74.

Van Til, J. (1988), *Mapping the Third Sector: Voluntarism in a Changing Social Economy*, New York: The Foundation Center.

Van Til, J. (1994), 'Nonprofit organization and social institutions', in R.D. Herman and associates (eds), *The Jossey-Bass Handbook of Nonprofit Leadership and Management*, San Francisco, California: Jossey-Bass, pp.44–64.

Voluntas, 8 (1997), Special Issue on Economic Theory, 93–204.

Walmsley, G. and M. Zald (1970), *The Political Economy of Public Organizations*, Lexington, Massachusetts: D.C. Heath.

Weisbrod, B. (ed.) (1998), *To Profit or Not to Profit: The Commercial Transformation of the Nonprofit Sector*, New York: Cambridge University Press.

Wernet, S. (1994), 'A case study of adaptation in a nonprofit human service organization', *Journal of Community Practice*, 1 (3).

Wolf, N. and M. Schlesinger (1998), 'Access, hospital ownership, and competition between for profit and nonprofit institutions', *Nonprofit and Voluntary Sector Quarterly*, 27, 203–36.

Young, D. (1999), 'Complementary, supplementary or adversarial? A theoretical and historical examination of nonprofit–government relations in the US', in E. Boris and C. Steuerle (eds), *Nonprofits and Government: Collaboration and Conflict*, Washington, DC: Urban Institute Press, pp.31–67.

12. Social services by social enterprises: on the possible contributions of hybrid organizations and a civil society

Adalbert Evers and Jean-Louis Laville

INTRODUCTION

Today's developed societies are characterized by a general trend towards 'tertiarization', that is, a growing importance of services in all sectors of life and all areas of economic activity. Forecasts indicate that jobs in service sectors may soon make up about three-quarters of all jobs in the so-called 'developed' countries (Baethge and Wilkens, 2001). This chapter will focus on 'social services', that is, services to which a political community attributes not only an individual value but also a considerable value for groups, localities and society at large. Such a definition of social services clearly exceeds the core area of welfare services such as health and social care and it also includes services in the fields of culture and education. Given the importance attached to their externalities or the collective benefits they generate, the public policies that affect them, ranging from dense regulation to financing and production of social services directly by the state public sector, can have a significant impact.

In most developed countries the role of third sector organizations, especially as far as their role as providers is concerned, is closely linked with the development of social services. It is in the field of social services that they have a special role as pioneers of new ideas, or as organizations that fill gaps, cooperate with the public authorities or even take a para-state role as providers. However, it is not only the respective roles of public authorities and third sector organizations that vary and change when it comes to service provision. In the last decades there has been a massive increase in the role of markets and individual consumers in the provision of social services, as for example in health, education or social care. The result of all this is that, seemingly, in all welfare states insecurity or, to use a more positive term, openness has increased when it comes to the question of how to design these services, who should pay for them and how they should be managed. To what degree will welfare states be able to fund and/or provide guaranteed social services for their citizens? What should be the role of markets and what should be the contribution of civil society and the third sector?

In light of this debate, this chapter aims to show why the notions of *hybrid organizations* and of *social enterprises* may be useful in overcoming two stereotypical viewpoints and answers. The first one is widely held among scholars in welfare studies, defining 'markets, families and government' as 'the three welfare pillars', and thereby simply omitting the role of social associations and a third sector (Esping-Andersen, 2002, p.11). The future of social services can then be situated on a bipolar axis of state and market funding/provision. Perhaps citizens, the civil society and its third sector are seen here merely as a casual 'alternative' form of provision. The second viewpoint is held by many scholars in third sector research and activists who share the perspective of a more 'civic' society (also in matters of welfare services). Anheier *et al.* (2001, p.3) have made it explicit when raising the question as to whether there is something like 'the right level' of a third sector in a given context. However, while sharing their viewpoint that there is insufficient evidence to provide an answer to the question 'how much of a third sector a country needs' (ibid.) we would reject the view that identifies a strengthening of civil society with the size of a sector altogether. Instead, a different analysis concerning the linkages between civil society, the third sector and social services will be given. Its focus is on the intermeshing of principles rather than on sectors, and it opts for 'civilizing' social services throughout the public realm. The arguments will be developed in three steps.

First of all, it will be argued that in the field of social services one observes changes concerning needs and the status of users, interrelated with special features of personal social services, such as their 'proximity' and their relational character. These changes have contributed to 'shifts in the welfare mix' (Evers, 1990). There are indications that the traditional clear-cut separation and the either/or of market-based, state-based and civil society-bound/third sector-based service units have become insufficient (first section).

Secondly, it will be argued that the increasingly mixed character of service systems is affecting the inner structure of social services and the respective providing institution itself. While the last decades have made state–market mixes familiar, all too often a third element has been overlooked: the presence of civil society, with its associations and various forms of community, in what has been termed the 'hybrid' structure of many social service organizations. However, the present forms and outcomes of hybridization processes are ambiguous, especially in the absence of a welfare strategy that responds positively to them (second and third sections).

The third and final thesis is that the approach that is introduced here breaks with the widespread attitude of underlining the differences between a (state-based) public and a (civil society-based) third sector. Principles and resources from the civil society, that are rightly seen as being central to the makeup of third sector organizations, can also play a role in state and municipal social service organizations (fourth section).

CHANGING ROLES OF MARKETS, WELFARE STATES AND CIVIL SOCIETY WITH RESPECT TO SOCIAL SERVICES: THE DRIVING FORCE BEHIND THE EMERGENCE OF HYBRID ORGANIZATIONS

Looking at the patterns of mutual linkages between the welfare state, market elements and civil society, three traditional key characteristics will be presented first. Each of them will be debated in conjunction with a view on personal social services as 'proximity services' (Eme and Laville, 1988, 1994; Laville, 1992; Laville and Nyssens, 2000). Secondly it will be shown that these characteristics have changed in a way that makes space for what are called here hybrid and entrepreneurial forms of services provision. While it is claimed that these observations hold true to different degrees for (liberal, corporatist and social–democratic) welfare regimes in Europe, it is questionable to what degree they matter for the US version of the 'liberal' welfare regime.

Three Hallmarks of European Welfare Systems and their Form of Social Service Provision

The first hallmark can be described as *the primacy of the state and of hierarchical structures* in the process of the development of professional social service systems. When using the word 'primacy', it is indirectly stated that in all welfare states there are roughly two different areas of welfare services. One area has been very much the product of 'bottom-up' processes and this has remained the case to some degree; for example, care services for children and the elderly, cultural institutions and services throughout Europe are still comparatively decentralized. Here there is a considerable role for third sector organizations like associations and/or a special role for the municipalities situated on the fringes of the welfare state. On the other hand there is a sector of services that, irrespective of the influence that private and social initiatives may have had at the beginning, has run through numerous stages of increasing conformity and centralization. In France, for example, health mutuals have led the way to a state public health system (see Chanial and Laville in Chapter 4); sometimes the 'top-down' elements have been strong from the very beginning;

in other cases, as in the British National Health Service (NHS), they have been introduced at a later stage. All in all, until the late 1960s, in most countries the more stable, costly and central welfare services such as social insurance, health care and education were becoming highly professionalized, standardized and centralized. More importantly, for a long time, development in these key areas set standards for welfare reform in other social service sectors, for example in elderly care where one strived for the same universal rights and professional standards as in health and education (for the German historical example, see Evers and Sachße, 2003).

The second hallmark of the classical welfare state can be dealt with more briefly. Until recently this concerned the clear *separation of structuring principles and spheres of influence between the state public and the private market sector*. This was also mirrored in the different steering mechanisms that dominated in each sector. Public administration and private management techniques, the ethos of civil *servants* (sic) working 'in the public interest' and the ethos of skilled industrial work and competition were fairly different. There was not merely a dividing line between public administration and private business – they represented two very different worlds and visions.

A third hallmark concerns *the role and impact of civil society* in the development of institutions of the welfare state and social services. With regard to this it is necessary, first of all, to explain the ways the term 'civil society' is used here. The term encompasses two dimensions (even if they are intertwined) of a society that is to some degrees a 'civic' one. The first constitutional dimension for a civil society is its ability to create a 'public sphere' made up by citizens with the rights to speak out and associate freely. A society is civic to the degree that rivalry between organized interests and associations representing them can be 'civilized' (Dubiel, 2001, p.133). Hence civil society is about the presence of politics in the social life of a (republican and democratic) political community (see, for example, Cohen and Arato, 1995; Habermas [1962] 1990).

A second dimension of a civil society has been brought to the fore by communitarian thinkers (Etzioni, 1995), by the contributions of Putnam (2000), the debates on voluntary action, user involvement and self-help (Borghi and Magatti, 2002), the third sector and welfare pluralism (Evers and Svetlik, 1993; Johnson, 1998). Here the participation of citizens is discussed mostly in terms of their active social participation, their role in service associations, school boards, voluntary work, community life and similar activities.

Civil society, then, means on the one hand a political space, the modern forms of an 'agora' kept alive by critical reasoning, concern for public debates and issues and civically tempered lobbying, for example on issues concerning the decisions of professional politicians on welfare services. On the other hand, civil society is also constituted of associations such as mutuals, cooperatives or voluntary agencies and characterized by the active participation of citizens and users in running public schools or building up care services.

Against this background one could say that the development of welfare states up to the 1970s has both strengthened and weakened civil society and its impact. The impact has been strengthened with regard to the first dimension, the building up of representative systems of collective interest, a public realm and media linked with democracy and the nationwide influence of groups and citizens by organizations of professionals as well as consumer protection groups. However, with the development of the professionalized, hierarchical structures, 'private interest government' (Streeck and Schmitter, 1985) and their corporate systems of service negotiation and provision (for the German example, see Zimmer, 1999), the second dimension of civil society lost impact. The cooperation of lay people and volunteers, the role of local boards and associations, of active membership in mutuals and cooperatives – these forms of active participation became of decreasing importance in an expanding welfare and service state.

With the integration of umbrella organizations and nationwide agencies into the centralized bureaucratic structures of the welfare state, the intertwining of (local) social participation and (central) organizing of political influence weakened. The multiple forms of local social participation lost their political importance in central decision making, and the degree and character of the 'social embeddedness' (Granovetter, 1992) of service structures and their economy changed. Their future became a matter of big politics and professional lobbying rather than of the material contributions of local citizens and groups. On the way to the present civil societies, as Putnam puts it (2000, p.46), citizens became 'reasonably well-informed spectators of public affairs, but many fewer of us actually partake in the game', a statement that was and is still partly true in matters of planning and provision of social services.

A Reversal of Trends: the Changing Faces of Welfare and Social Service Provision in the Last Decades

What has become visible above all is *a reversal of trends as far as the primacy of hierarchical structures in service provision is concerned*. This is demonstrated by attempts to preserve or upgrade the role of federal and municipal levels in general, but it is also a part of the present trend towards decentralization and 'devolution' in social welfare and, more specifically, in social services. One problem with social services, whose basic organizational models were shaped in an industrial age, is largely due to the double impact of mass production ('Taylorism') and bureaucratic centralization: they developed in a way that has been perceived in the last decades as being contrary to their role as personal services, that is, as 'proximity' services. What matters most here with respect to proximity is not the need for 'objective' proximity of many social services (kindergartens or labour offices have to be near enough in order to be useful) but a 'subjective' proximity.

Proximity is 'subjective' when the kind of relationship that arises between the provider and the user determines the quality of the service (Laville and Nyssens, 2000). For example, in some urban regions people will develop a different attitude towards professional child care or demonstrate different degrees of willingness to use elderly care facilities than in other, perhaps rural areas. Further, the subjective factor of local culture and politics, as it is reflected in local concepts of the public good (Calhoun, 1998), matters increasingly in a modern society, to the degree that variations in tastes, preferences and orientations get, in general, more acknowledgment in a 'pluralist' society. After decades of unification around a single nationwide model of health or education services, the readiness to acknowledge such differences is challenging the basic concept of a single generalized 'one for all' model of service provision. That does not exclude national standards, but there is a search for a new balance between what must be general and what ought to be specific. Moreover, another aspect of proximity, the fact that personal social services are 'relational' because the relationship between the provider and the user lies at the heart of the provision (Perret and Roustang, 1993), has gained a new meaning. The idea of 'educating' clients through uniform and standardized services has lost impact and viability in a market society which has created a variety of ways in which there can be both uniformity and room for personalized services.

Hence, even if the concern with central standards is strong, the general tendency is to give more responsibility and autonomy to the single local organizations and service providers. Local service managers, while acting in the framework of general standards, have to find their own strategies in order to respond to local needs. In Germany, for example, hospitals and even schools are seen as organizations that should work with their own budget. With the introduction of social markets and a variety of providers, there is an additional incentive to create a new balance of universal standards and a diversity of service offers that should fit local peculiarities. Obviously, alongside the increasing autonomy of state public and municipal social services, their status difference with respect to third sector-based service providers may shrink.

This leads to the observation that the second characteristic of the classical welfare state, the separation of public administration and private management, of hierarchical redistribution and redistribution by market mechanisms, has considerably weakened as well. What we have been observing for decades is the trend *towards an increasing mixing of structural elements of market and state*. Welfare states increasingly define themselves as purchasers and regulators of services provided by private business. At the same time the new public management has resulted in a restructuring of the public administration according to the routines that have been developed in private enterprises; these changes affect financing and investment, personal management and the takeover of such concepts as quality management, controlling and so on (Pollitt, 2000). While for a long time bureaucratic rules had a strong impact on markets, nowadays market logic, competition and price invade the public and third sector, thereby 'enterprising nonprofits' (Dees, 1998). 'In so doing, they have lost any specific political associations and become generally accepted as legitimate criteria to apply in devising the governance and assessing the performance of third sector organizations' (Deakin, 2001, p.39). In various sub-sectors of social services, such as health and social care, the steering mechanisms of hierarchy, networks and markets overlap and intertwine. In the face of such developments, traditional distinctions between sectors tend to 'obscure' (Abzug, 1999, p.144) such intermeshing and interlinkage. This points to the central thesis of this chapter: to see organizations that are geared by such a plurality of steering mechanisms as hybrids.

The overlapping of several steering mechanisms, as seen especially in the third 'intermediate' sector (for early analyses of this phenomenon, see Billis, 1984; Evers, 1990), has also to do with the position of many social services. In a way, social services are intermediate between individual and collective services. They are not fully collective goods, where exclusion is generally impossible (as for example with an urban environment), but neither can they be seen as sole individual goods. They simultaneously generate private benefits (flowing to the individuals who consume these services) and collective benefits valued by the whole community. Child care services serve individual children but they also affect the living and working conditions of mothers and families, the labour market, and so on. Therefore these services may be considered quasi-collective services – a source of social utility. Generally those who favour different forms of steering mechanisms accentuate different sides of the social services. Those who vote for more market rules and consumer choice, for example cash benefits instead of service provision, focus on the individual benefit, while those who favour public financing and regulation of providers will argue for the need for equality in service provision, avoiding choices in the generation and distribution of child care facilities that they deem unfair within the wider community (Badelt, 1997).

Altogether this means that a case can be made for market *and* state intervention. Furthermore, in changing contexts, past hallmarks of social services that seemed to give a kind of natural preference to provision by public authorities or not-for-profit providers will not work in the same way today. For instance, the well-known asymmetry in information to the disadvantage of the user, and the fact that many social services (for example elderly homes) are 'relational' and 'trust goods', should not automatically result in a disadvantage to or exclusion of commercial providers. Information and trust can nowadays be handled differently; there are new channels for informing consumers better, and commercial organizations providing personal services have often been quite successful in developing marketing strategies and positive corporate identities that help in gaining trust. Again, this prohibits any idea of establishing a 'natural' place or sector when it comes to the provision of social services (Ben-Ner, 2000). Whether solutions for social service systems should follow a more state-led or a more choice- and consumer-led route is more than ever a matter of politics that must take into account a considerable number of aspects and effects.

Finally, there are many signs that the third hallmark of the classical welfare state – an institutionalization of the impact of civil society in terms of rather centralized forms of corporate governance, accompanied by a weakening of the more disperse forms of active social participation of citizens – has also lost its significance. The past decades have produced hundreds of publications that dealt with the *proliferation of user involvement, local initiatives, self help, local public–private partnerships, alliances and the contributions of various third sector actors*, not only as concepts, but as empirical realities. Internationally, civil society has largely recovered in terms of volunteering and membership in associations (Dekker and van den Broek, 1998). This revitalization of the local sphere, as a point from which wider issues, such as economic development and employment, have been raised, has even found an echo in EU policies (Commission of the European Community, 1996). Obviously, the citizen of today is first of all a consumer of standardized products and services delivered by big corporations and service chains, but that does not mean that his role as a co-producer of services and an active participant, be it in schools, care services or with respect to cultural services, has vanished.

Once again it may be useful to look at the links between changing habits, orientations and needs on the one hand and the role played by the historical extension of personal social services on the other. Their proximity flows from, or is reinforced by, the way in which the service itself is organized, in particular with respect to the degree of involvement of the users. They can participate either in the functioning of the service or in its conception (acting as members of the board of administrators, having a say about the mode of organization) or they can contribute by adhering to the (for example pedagogical) values defended by the organization. This is not new at all. In kindergartens run by a private foundation and in those established and run by a group of cultivated, well-off parents, this was already the case a hundred years ago. However, what is new following the massive building up of social services by the welfare states in the three postwar decades is the belief that social services as public sector-related mass services should or could have a similar 'personalized' and plural quality (for an early analysis, see Gartner and Riessmann, 1974). Consequently, the extension of social services under conditions of more general rights, education and social competence creates a basis for putting direct participation, social cooperation and day-to-day voluntary contributions back on the agenda. A society whose civic character had for a long time been defined solely by its forms of centralized conflict regulation and participation in the large public space has been reconceptualized as a civil society by the addition of a second feature, the degree to which it allows direct and disperse forms of association and involvement.

While the bulk of such processes may be situated in third sector organizations, they can be found in local state-based and municipal organizations as well. If one takes, for example, not-for-profit cultural institutions on the local level, whether municipal or third sector-based, such as libraries, museums and theatres, one becomes aware of the fact that in most European countries these institutions survive to a considerable degree not only on public subsidies and sales but also on donations, the contributions of foundations, sponsorships and individual voluntary commitment; and these voluntary contributions from the civil society no longer have the exceptional and clearly upper class-based character of foundations or charities, or the character of (working) class solidarity that became prominent more than a hundred years ago. These are contributions that seem to be linked primarily with active citizenship. Summing up, one can say that there is a revival of the second dimension of civil society: the socioeconomic dimension of various forms of direct material participation, voluntary work or service development by association building.

SOCIAL SERVICE ORGANIZATIONS AS HYBRIDS: SUGGESTING AN ANALYTICAL CONCEPT

In the context of analysing such developments, the concept of 'hybrids' has been further expanded and differentiated. The impact of the respective components of the state, markets and of the social capital of civil society may vary a lot. But the value of thinking about service organizations according to their possible hybrid character lies in the fact that this approach is sensitive to the role of the less visible components (for example the civil society/social capital components that help a public school to survive). The focus is on the tensions and the side-effects of an intertwining of the different components and rationales, but also on the question of how best to bring out the potential of such a hybrid character and how to lessen its risks. Organizations that manage this to some degree have been labelled 'social enterprises' (Borzaga and Defourny, 2001; Evers, 2001; Laville and Nyssens, 2001). Four different dimensions of hybridization can be distinguished (for a more detailed presentation, see Evers *et al.*, 2002; for the concept of hybridization, see also Laville and Sainsaulieu, 1998).

The Analytical Concept of Hybrid Organizations: Four Dimensions

The first dimension concerns *resources*. Taking schools again as an example, it becomes clear that market components can be shaped by a differentiation of roles within a wider state financing (Gardin and Laville, 1998), for example the acquisition of additional financing in the course of a public subscription to take part in a model project. The supportive elements of civil society that have material effect vary greatly. Following the concept of Evers (2001), they can be best assembled under the label of 'social capital'. Usually, in the debate on the third sector, only two such 'social capital' resources are mentioned, volunteering and donations. Obviously there are many more forms of such resources to be taken into account: the links with foundations, various kinds of (public–private) partnerships and the impact of special support associations.

Two other dimensions that are constitutive of the hybrid character of an organization are *goals* and *steering mechanisms*. In the school system, for example, steering takes place through market mechanisms. The parents can choose between different public schools that compete for pupils. At the same time, there is a hierarchical steering mechanism at work by curricula and quality standards; finally, the local civil society also has a say, through the school board or the influence exerted by a parent support association. These different steering mechanisms that operate simultaneously have to be seen in conjunction with goals. The fact that neither a state public nor a third sector service provider is directed by the overarching goal of profit constitutes both a chance and a challenge. There is the chance to constitute a complex agenda, made up of various goals, but the challenge is to balance it and to keep the diversity of goals compatible. Taking once again the example of a school, one can see that state-based quality criteria should be fulfilled, while attempting to put the accent on a special provision and service that helps in the rivalry with other local schools. Finally, the linkages with partners in the neighbourhood may influence the agenda as well.

Processes of hybridization with regard to resources, goals and steering mechanisms can finally lead to the establishment of a new and different *corporate identity* that reflects the multiple roles and purposes of the organization. In interviews with leaders of organizations (Evers *et al.*, 2002, pp.72f) there were recurrent remarks such as the following: 'We aren't any more a public institution but rather a social enterprise' (a school director); 'We want to be a well managed enterprise and simultaneously an institution that expresses the core values of "Diakonie" – giving extra time for social and personal care' (the leader of a home care service run by the 'Diakonie', a protestant welfare agency); 'We have to learn to respect the commercial dimension of what we are doing, cope with state regulations and at the same time get better rooted locally by more "fund and friend raising"' (the director of a museum). These quotations have been chosen to illustrate an unfinished and perhaps to a certain degree open process of search for an identity – beyond the traditional offers of being a clear-cut public service, private enterprise or third sector organization.

THE COSTS AND ADVANTAGES OF THE PRESENT PROCESSES OF HYBRIDIZATION

Organizations that are undergoing the kind of shifts described above expose both problems and potential. It has to be taken into account that, usually, hybridization processes cannot be seen as a part of an overarching strategy but must rather be understood as coping strategies. Without support from a social and political movement or a government policy, such processes have limited room for manoeuvre. Yet they differ from mere practices of adaptation (for example to a general trend of managerialism and privatization) to the degree that these coping strategies imply goals and aspirations such as defending professional standards, defending the public character of an institution or the attempt to respond to the commitment of other citizens and organizations.

Structural Risks and Potentials

Services and organizations that cultivate several dimensions may have an advantage when it comes to answering a variety of different expectations, or at least in balancing expectations and goals that otherwise seem only to be realized to each other's cost. In practice this could mean that, instead of having only the juxtaposition of private commercial schools, a 100 per cent public school system and a sector of 'faith-based' and pedagogically different schools, with each sectorial solution having its respective costs and limits, an opening up of the public sector might provide new possibilities. Schools could then be managed more autonomously, while the framework of state regulations would help maintain uniform standards, without the imposition of barriers to enriching the basic qualities of the school according to the degree of success in 'networking' with various supporting social organizations.

However, one may imagine at the same time the costs of such heterogeneity. To what degree will it be possible to maintain the integrative tasks of a public school system, once competition begins to force the schools towards selecting as early as possible those pupils that are 'bad risks' and 'bad investments' (pupils whose successful education needs more input while their misbehaving may spoil the school image)? Furthermore, it is well known that matching various and different resources (public and private, financial and non-financial) can greatly increase the time needed for management. In addition, the budgeting logic of public households and the logic of making risky investments, but also the logic of making quick management decisions and the logic of participation, will always be in a state of tension with each other.

Besides such questions concerning the structural risks and potentials, there are questions with regard to the actuality of processes of hybridization, given the present state of the economy and the limits of coping strategies that are usually not backed by a concomitant public strategy for a renewal of welfare and social services. For the most part, then, costs and advantages of hybridization processes are hard to disentangle and it is difficult to measure the net results.

Costs and Advantages Depending on the Policy Context

In practice one can mostly find processes of both *deprivation* and *enrichment*. What enrichment of services may mean can be easily figured out if one thinks of the examples of schools and cultural institutions already mentioned. In the field of elderly care services, there have been various international contributions (see, for example, Laville and Nyssens, 2001) as well as national studies (with respect to Germany, see Evers *et al.*, 2002) showing that the dynamics of local initiatives can make it possible to reach out to resources to which an elderly home as a closed institution will not have access (for example, visiting services, partnerships and so on). However, at the same time such advantages have to be set against processes of deprivation that result from the retreat of political authorities, the downgrading of services and a narrowing of their ambitions. Furthermore, the danger of a creeping commercialization of public cultural institutions in the context of shrinking public support and the need to operate in more businesslike ways is well known. Usually, no plan for volunteer support can simply counterbalance the massive effects of a retreat of public authorities from political and financial commitment, both in state public and third sector-based organizations providing services.

Alongside the effects of decentralization and of handing over autonomy, making small units fully responsible for risky undertakings that are sometimes out of their control, another challenge arises. Once again it can be expressed in contrary ways, by the terms '*diversity*' and '*inequality*'. Perhaps the best example of these issues can be found in the two coexisting child care systems in Germany: the patchy system that has grown with municipal support and responsibility in Western Germany and the all-covering system as it was inherited in the new *Länder* from the former German Democratic Republic (GDR). The charm of more cultural diversity in the West is clearly linked with its patchy character. In the present debate about schools, a recurrent argument against more autonomy of the single school unit is that more dependence on local resources and support will then lead to a stronger mirroring of the social and cultural inequalities in a more localized school system. Furthermore, while schools or theatres need to be in touch with their local surroundings, too close a relationship with those who are most powerful within the area may disturb the autonomy needed for both pedagogics and the arts. Professional autonomy perhaps ought to be guaranteed by the support of a distant authority. Possibly every reader can quite easily develop conceptual answers that help to balance the need for guaranteeing more choice and diversity on the one hand and equality of access and standards on the other. However, the real question, for example for local politicians and managers, is how to cope with changes that are clearly unbalanced in this respect.

Another pair of intertwined chances and risks is represented by *participation* and *clientelism*. The usual discourse about the goods of strengthening the civil society, giving citizens more say in matters that have a direct impact on their daily lives, and about rolling back the influence of bureaucracies that are far away from the places and settings they control, is rather simplistic. In fact it is a difficult question to what degree elements of participative democracy and of a kind of 'contracting out' should take over some of the space held so far by representative and professional politics. The assumption that decisions on service systems run by a multi-stakeholder board are by nature superior to the ones made in the sub-committee of a local parliament is doubtful. There is perhaps as much clientelism to be found in self-administered social bodies and in participative processes as there is clientelism resulting from the interaction of representative institutions and bureaucracies.

From Processes to Concepts of Hybridization: Making Use of Hybrids as Social Enterprises

The chances and difficulties that have been sketched point to the key role of politics and, more precisely, to the need for concepts of social services that strengthen the potential while limiting the costs of such processes of hybridization (Vaillancourt and Tremblay, 2001). However, before raising questions of 'good governance' of a mixed welfare system (Klijn and Koppenjan, 2000) one should look at the real state of the debate in welfare politics in Europe. The time of unmixed market orientation seems to be over and a kind of new consensus has been established on the fact that governance should matter and therefore needs to be modernized. But there are few signs that changing forms of governance will also imply the readiness to include those inputs from the civil society that have been described before. The reader may check against the reality of her or his own country in what policy sector and to what degree issues like strengthening user involvement in service provision, partnerships, multi-stakeholder arrangements and other related items have won ground.

Given such a background, the operational working title of *social enterprises*, as has been suggested for example in the UK debate (see Chapter 6), taken up by cooperatives or networks of scientists like the EMES group (see the contributions in Borzaga and Defourny, 2001), and as defined by the authors, simultaneously represents two things. It describes realities and it points at a future wherein, it is hoped, the crucial element of social enterprises – the presence of civil society and its social capital – can have more impact and win more acceptance. The definition of a social enterprise as a special form of social service provision that takes shape by hybridization would then be as follows:

- it has a considerable degree of autonomy;
- it is using this autonomy in order to develop an entrepreneurial style of action;
- it is ready to balance social goals and steering inputs, as they come simultaneously from state-related and local civil society-based stakeholders, against its market relations;
- it is purposefully safeguarding positive social effects not only for the individual users but also for the larger community.

THE THIRD SECTOR, CIVIL SOCIETY AND THE RECASTING OF SOCIAL SERVICES: THREE CONCLUSIONS

It has been argued that changes in the development of social services and welfare states have led to hybridization processes in many organizations that provide social services. Public services may take characteristics that were traditionally a hallmark of third sector organizations only, such as the strong impact of social capital resources and links to local or group-specific settings, and third sector organizations have increasingly been influenced by state public funding, purposes and regulations. At the same time managerialism and a competitive environment have gained importance throughout. In three concluding remarks what can be seen as the most important implications of the approach as it has been sketched here are underlined, both for the orientation of academic research and for a debate on social services, welfare and the third sector.

One Should Underline the Communalities Rather than Only the Differences Between Many Social Services Provided in the Public and the Third Sector

Given the fact that many third sector organizations build strongly on public rules, programmes and money and that state public organizations often allow for a considerable degree of direct local and group-related participation, it is often hard to say where the third sector ends and the public sector begins. The more public services involve not only representative democracy and hierarchical administration but also local autonomy and various forms of social and civic participation, the more the difference between them and third sector organizations is diminishing. Drawing a line between hybrids in the public and the third sector would then be more a political task. The challenge would, for instance, consist in defining the 'critical' level of impact of public authorities dominating other co-structuring principles where one should say that an organization is no longer to be seen as third sector-based (for a discussion of this point, see Anheier and Kendall, 2001, p.243).

Civil Society Concerns Social Services and Welfare Institutions in the Whole Public Realm, Not Just Those in the Third Sector

The second conclusion concerns the fact that the perspective here is crucially different from the usual one of strengthening a far-reaching third sector as the only possible antidote to a development that is marked by an ever-increasing intimate mix of big business and big administration. The perspective suggested here is instead concerned with reinvigorating the public sphere at large by strengthening fundamental principles of a civil society as, for example, participative forms of governance and direct forms of self-organization and user involvement, even though such an impact of 'civic' principles is valid to different degrees for services that serve the public good in either way, whether state/municipality-based or preponderantly civil society-based.

There is then no such thing as a 'civil society sector'(Salamon and Anheier, 1997). It would be misleading simply to identify the benign effects of building a more civic society with the growth of a third sector. Once the notion of a sector is seen as secondary to the need for analysing the impact of different co-structuring 'principles' (for example competition, state control, user involvement) in a given field of welfare services, one comes to the point where, in a mixed welfare system, it will not be the sector that matters but the balance of competing principles that structure a policy field and the organizations to be found there. 'It might be better . . . to generalize original nonprofit aims so they can apply to other organizations as well. Strategies to civilize service-delivering institutions and make them more democratic . . . should no longer be restricted to nonprofits' (Dekker, 2001, p.67; a similar argument that insists on the central role of voluntary *action* rather than of a voluntary *sector* has been given by Perri 6 and Diana Leat, 1997).

A Concept of Civil Society Should Entail and Acknowledge the Social and Economic Everyday Participation of Citizens

It has already been underlined in the first section of this contribution that there are many notions of the civil society that view the socioeconomic dimensions of participation as casual and rather marginal features. One aspect of that is the neglecting of the distinct 'local' and 'reform' economies of service organizations which are tied to a specific community, or which took shape as a part of the cooperative or mutualist legacy. Another aspect of that is to neglect components of a civil society such as voluntary work, various forms of community involvement, local self-help or user involvement in social services.

Concepts of civil society as a mere space for deliberation and for the defence of interests do in fact only know two (service-) producing agencies, the state and the market. Consumer lobbies, public debates and new forms of governance, together with state regulation and financing, are trusted to ensure that more private businesses in social service provision work for the citizens, enabling them to act as informed and protected consumers. The trust in the civilizing impact of the public space and of the critical reasoning of a civil society can then well be used to justify more market provision in matters of welfare. From such a perspective it can be seen to be consistent when the European Union, on the one hand, plans to abolish special state support that 'privileges' third sector or public service providers competing with commercial providers on a European market (Commission of the European Community, 2000a) while, on the other, building a stronger partnership with NGOs (Commission of the European Community, 2000b), giving by means of European Social Forums more voice and greater visibility to organizations that defend the interest of the citizen as a consumer of private and public services. However, against such a concept of civil society, it has been argued that, in face of services and 'politics at a distance' (Putnam, 2000, p.341), the interest in and competence for a qualified public reasoning might get lost. Critical reasoning does (not in each and every individual case, but in general) presuppose real experiences of people being involved as cooperators or stakeholders of service organizations. If one agrees that a stronger civil society is needed, to what extent does this entail an agreement on the need to strengthen everyday forms of commitment and involvement that contribute to different forms of 'economy' in service provision? Should such things as voluntary commitment or social cooperatives only be exceptional features, in service niches or emergency cases? Or should a degree of active involvement be a part of the design of the everyday 'mainstream' services of the future welfare state? Only by debating this question will the flourishing civil society rhetoric get a more precise meaning with respect to the future of social services, the third sector and the welfare state.

REFERENCES

6, Perri and Diana Leat (1997), 'Inventing the British voluntary sector by committee – from Wolfenden to Deakin', *Nonprofit Studies*, 18 (2), 33–45.

Abzug, R. (1999), 'The nonprofit and the informal sector: A theoretical perspective', *Voluntas*, 10 (2), 131–49.

Anheier, H.K. and J. Kendall (2001), 'Conclusion. The third sector at the crossroads? Social, political and economic dynamics', in H.K. Anheier and J. Kendall (eds), *Third sector policy at the crossroads. An international nonprofit analysis*, London and New York: Routledge, pp.228–50.

Anheier, H.K., L. Carlson and J. Kendall (2001), 'Third sector policy at the crossroads. Continuity and change in the world of nonprofit organizations', in H.K. Anheier and J. Kendall (eds), *Third sector policy at the crossroads. An international nonprofit analysis*, London and New York: Routledge, pp.1–16.

Badelt, C. (1997), 'Entrepreneurship theories of the non-profit sector', *Voluntas*, 8 (2), 162–78.

Baethge, M. and I. Wilkens (eds) (2001), *Die große Hoffnung für das 21. Jahrhundert? Perspektiven und Strategien für die Entwicklung der Dienstleistungsbeschäftigung*, Opladen: Leske & Budrich.

Ben-Ner, A. (2000), 'On the boundaries of the mixed economy: The nonprofit sector between the private and public domains', paper presented at the ICTR, University of the Negev, March; and Centre for Civil Society, London School of Economics, June.

Billis, D. (1984), *Welfare bureaucracies*, London: Heinemann.

Borghi, V. and M. Magatti (eds) (2002), *Mercato e societa. Introduzione alla sociologia economica*, Rome: Carocci Editore.

Borzaga, C. and J. Defourny (eds) (2001), *The emergence of social enterprise*, London and New York: Routledge.

Calhoun, C. (1998), 'The public good as a social and cultural project', in W.W. Powell and E.S. Clemens (eds), *Private action and the public good*, New Haven and London: Yale University Press, pp.31–9.

Cohen, J.L. and A. Arato (1995), *Civil society and political theory*, Cambridge, Massachusetts: MIT Press.

Commission of the European Community (1996), *First report on local development and employment initiatives*, SEK (96) 2061, Brussels.

Commission of the European Community (2000a), *Communication from the Commission: Services of general interest in Europe*, COM (2000) 580 final, Brussels.

Commission of the European Community (2000b), *The Commission and non-governmental organisations: Building a stronger partnership*, discussion paper, Brussels: European Commission.

Deakin, N. (2001), 'Putting narrow-mindedness out of countenance. The UK voluntary sector in the new millennium', in H.K. Anheier and J. Kendall (eds), *Third sector policy at the crossroads. An international nonprofit analysis*, London and New York: Routledge.

Dees, J.G. (1998), 'Enterprising nonprofits', *Harvard Business Review*, 76 (1), 55–68.

Dekker, P. (2001), 'What crises, what challenges? When nonprofitness makes no difference', in H.K. Anheier and J. Kendall (eds), *Third sector policy at the crossroads. An international nonprofit analysis*, London and New York: Routledge.

Dekker, P. and A. van den Broek (1998), 'Civil society in comparative perspective: Involvement in voluntary associations in North America and Western Europe', *Voluntas*, 9 (1), 11–38.

Dubiel, H. (2001), 'Unzivile Gesellschaften', *Soziale Welt*, 52 (2), 133–50.

Eme, B. and J.L. Laville (1988), *Les petits boulots en question*, Paris: Syros.

Eme, B. and J.L. Laville (1994), *Cohésion sociale et emploi*, Paris: Desclée de Brouwer.

Esping-Andersen, G. (2002), 'The sustainability of welfare states: Reshaping social protection', in B. Harris-White (ed.), *Globalization and insecurity. Political, economic and physical challenges*, London: Palgrave, pp.218–32.

Etzioni, A. (1995), *The spirit of community: Rights, responsibilities, and the communitarian agenda*, London: Fontana Press.

Evers, A. (1990), 'Shifts in the welfare mix: Introducing a new approach for the study of transformations in welfare and social policy', in A. Evers and H. Wintersberger (eds), *Shifts in the welfare mix. Their impact on work, social services and welfare policies*, Frankfurt a. M. and Boulder, Colorado: Campus Verlag and Westview Press, pp.7–30.

Evers, A. (2001), 'The significance of social capital in the multiple goal and resource structure of social enterprises', in C. Borzaga and J. Defourny (eds), *The emergence of social enterprise*, London and New York: Routledge, pp.296–311.

Evers, A. and C. Sachße (2003), 'Social care services for children and older people in Germany: Distinct and separate histories', in A. Anttonen, J. Baldock and J. Sipilä (eds), *The young, the old and the state: social care in five industrial nations*, Cheltenham, UK and Northampton, MA, USA: Edward Elgar, pp.55–80.

Evers, A. and I. Svetlik (eds) (1993), *Balancing pluralism. New welfare mixes in care for the elderly*, Aldershot: Avebury.

Evers, A., U. Rauch and U. Stitz (2002), *Von öffentlichen Einrichtungen zu sozialen Unternehmen. Hybride Organisationsformen im Bereich sozialer Dienstleistungen*, Berlin: edition sigma.

Gardin, L. and J.L. Laville (1998), *Local initiatives in Europe. Economic and social review*, Paris and Brussels: LSCI, CNRS, European Commission.

Gartner, A. and F. Riessmann (1974), *The service society and the consumer vanguard*, New York: Harper & Row.

Granovetter, M.S. (1992), 'Economic action and social structure: The problem of embeddedness', *American Journal of Sociology*, 91 (3), 481–510.

Habermas, J. (1962), *Strukturwandel der Öffentlichkeit. Untersuchungen zu einer Kategorie der bürgerlichen Gesellschaft*, Neuwied: Luchterhand, reprinted 1990, Frankfurt a. M.: Suhrkamp.

Johnson, N. (1998), *Mixed economies of welfare: A comparative perspective*, London: Prentice-Hall Europe.

Klijn, E.H. and J.F.M. Koppenjan (2000), 'Public management and policy networks. Foundations of a network approach to governance', *Public Management*, 2 (2), 135–8.

Laville, J.L. (ed.) (1992), *Les services de proximité en Europe*, Paris: Desclée de Brouwer.

Laville, J.L. and M. Nyssens (2000), 'Solidarity-based third sector organizations in the "proximity services" field: A European Francophone perspective', *Voluntas*, 11 (1), 67–84.

Laville, J.L. and M. Nyssens (eds) (2001), *Les services sociaux entre associations, état et marché*, Paris: La Découverte.

Laville, J.L. and R. Sainsaulieu (1998), *Sociologie de l'association*, Paris: Desclée de Brouwer.

Perret, B. and G. Roustang (1993), *L'économie contre la société*, Paris: Seuil.

Pollitt, C. (2000), 'Is the emperor in his underwear? An analysis of the impacts of public management reform', *Public Management*, 2 (2), 181–99.

Putnam, R.D. (2000), *Bowling alone. The collapse and revival of American community*, New York: Simon & Schuster.

Salamon, L.M. and Helmut K. Anheier (1997), 'The civil society sector: A new global force', *Society*, 34 (2), 60–65.

Streeck, W. and P.C. Schmitter (eds) (1985), *Private interest government: Beyond market and state*, London: Sage.

Vaillancourt, Y. and L. Tremblay (eds) (2001), *L'économie sociale dans le domaine de la santé et du bien-être au Canada*, Laboratoire de recherche sur les pratiques et les politiques sociales, Montreal: Université du Québec à Montréal.

Zimmer, A. (1999), 'Corporatism revisited – The legacy of history and the German nonprofit sector', *Voluntas*, 10 (1), 37–50.

Index